Also by McKay Jenkins

The Peter Matthiessen Reader (editor)

The South in Black and White:
Race, Sex, and Literature in the 1940s

THE
WHITE
DEATH

THE
WHITE
DEATH

Tragedy and Heroism in an
Avalanche Zone

McKay Jenkins

RANDOM HOUSE

NEW YORK

Grateful acknowledgment is made to the following for permission
to reprint previously published material:

FULCRUM PUBLISHING: Excerpt from *The Avalanche Book*. Copyright © 1992
by Betsy R. Armstrong and Knox Williams. All rights reserved. Reprinted
courtesy of Fulcrum Publishing, Inc., Golden, Colorado.

KIVAKI PRESS, INC.: Excerpts form *Deep Powder Snow* by Dolores LaChapelle.
Copyright © 1993 by Dolores LaChapelle. Reprinted by permission
of Kivaki Press, Inc., 828-684-1988 telephone, 828-684-7372 (fax).

Random House and colophon are registered trademarks of Random House, Inc.

Library of Congress Cataloging-in-Publication Data
Jenkins, McKay
The white death: tragedy and heroism in an avalanche zone / McKay Jenkins.
p.   cm.
Includes index.
ISBN 0-375-50303-X
1. Avalanches.   2. Avalanches—Montana—Glacier National Park.   I. Title.
QC929.A8 J46 2000   363.34'9 21—dc21   99-043307

Random House website address: www.atrandom.com

Printed in the United States of America on acid-free paper

2 4 6 8 9 7 5 3

First Edition

Book design by Mercedes Everett

For
Katherine

For
Walter Cumming and Wes Davis

And in memory of
Jerry Kanzler, Clare Pogreba, Ray Martin,
Mark Levitan, and James Anderson

Probably most catastrophes end this way
without an ending, the dead
not even knowing how they died
but "still alertly erect in fear and wonder,"
those who loved them forever questioning
"this unnecessary death," and the rest of us
tiring of this inconsolable catastrophe
and turning to the next one.

— Norman Maclean,
Young Men and Fire

Acknowledgments

❄

For their patience and selfless willingness to share difficult memories, I bow to Jean Kanzler, Jim Kanzler, Dr. Morton Levitan, Bud Anderson, Don Anderson, Ruby Martin, Bonnie Schellinger, Esther Gruell, Peter Lev, and Pat Callis.

In and around Glacier National Park, I am indebted to Bob and Ann Frauson, Willie Colony, Jerry DeSanto, Jim Kruger, Charlie Logan, Butch Farabee, and George Ostrom; also Deirdre Shaw, George McFarland, and Ray Cunan at the Glacier Park Museum, Brian Kennedy, former editor of the *Hungry Horse News,* and the folks at the Izaak Walton Inn, especially Mark Ambre.

In Jackson, thanks to Deb Frauson, Rod Newcomb, and Freddie Botur. Elsewhere, thanks to John Montagne, Terry Kennedy, Robert Madsen, Knox Williams, and the staff of the International Snow Science Workshop. Thanks to Brian Sali for sharing his burial experience, which he courageously first presented at the ISSW conference in Bend, Oregon.

The written work of a number of professional avalanche hunters has proven invaluable, and invigorating. Anyone interested in digging deeper into snow science, mountain history, or avalanche safety is encouraged to look at the work of Monty Atwater, Colin Fraser, Edwin Bernbaum, Ed LaChapelle, Tony Daffern, Bruce Jamieson, Gerald Seligman, Bernard Mergen, and Knox Williams and Betsy Armstrong. A fuller list of suggested reading can be found at the end of this book.

My dear friends Wes Davis, Peter Landesman, Jim Yardley, Walter Cumming, Carla Jenkins, Brian Jenkins, and Monica Frei Jenkins all read early versions of the manuscript and helped immeasurably, as did my agent, Neil Olson, a man of intelligence and grace. Courtney Hodell, my editor at Random House, is a model of vision and clarity; her skills as an editor improved the book enormously. Jennifer Prior copyedited the manuscript and cleaned it up nicely. Thanks also to Tim Farrell and Dennis Ambrose at Random House, and to my research assistant, Chris Bohlman, a fine writer in his own right, and the talented staff of the interlibrary loan office at the University of Delaware. Also, thanks to Tim Burdick and Mark Jeong for their early assistance and expertise; and to Don Jenkins, Denny Jenkins, Ben Yagoda, Chris Sheldrick,

Howard and Jill Savin, and Ingrid Hinckley for their enthusiasm and friendship. And to John McPhee and Peter Matthiessen, mentors.

Finally, thanks to my wonderful wife, Katherine, who convinced me after a day of backcountry skiing in Glacier National Park to go sit in on a slide show about avalanches by someone named Bob Frauson. As always, she opened my eyes.

Contents

❄

Prologue

✳

Wellington, 1910

*For unless human nature has changed
considerably through the ages, what is
considered news, and therefore may be
remembered when the normal events of daily
life are long forgotten, is the unusual,
particularly the violently unusual. And what is
more violently unusual than a natural
catastrophe?*

— Dorothy Vitaliano,
Legends of the Earth

One of the stories we have come to tell about wilderness is that disasters are only disasters when people are killed. If a hurricane hits a Caribbean beachhead that has never been developed—no homes destroyed, no cars overturned, no electricity knocked out—there won't be any footage of a reporter in foul weather gear, standing out in the rain, describing the terrible scene. If a tidal wave rolls across the Atlantic and fails to flip a single boat, the human community will never hear about it. If a fifty-thousand-ton mud slide obliterates an unpopulated slope somewhere in the middle of the Andes, we'll never know. Yet the simple point is that these terrific forces exist, and always have; they are as much a part of the interplay between weather systems and geography as sweet sunshine and summer rains. Natural forces become natural disasters only when they get in the way of human endeavor; danger is only danger when it is filtered through the human imagination. This is as true for inanimate forces as it is for so-called dangerous animals—wolves, grizzly bears, great white sharks—which have been systematically sought out and destroyed to eliminate human fear. The trouble with hurricanes, and tidal waves, and mud slides is that they can't be hunted down and shot.

There are few more "dangerous" places on earth—few places where it is easier for people to die—than the high mountains. Pilgrims looking for God, miners looking for gold, mountaineers looking for both: all have found mountains unmoved, indifferent to their noble intentions as well as their base ones. Throughout recorded history, legends abound detailing the dangers that come to those foolish enough to test the world's high places. Russian, Czech, and Slovak folklore tells of mountain creatures with the face of a woman, the body of a sow, and the legs of a horse. When storms raged in Germany, villagers believed that the ghostly Wild Huntsman was abroad with his pack of baying hounds, riding furiously and slaughtering everything in his path. In the fifteenth century, mountain travelers were often led through the high places blindfolded, since the Alps were thought to contain visions that might drive them mad. Residents of the Swiss mountains believed that atop the Matterhorn was a ruined city inhabited by the souls of the dead. The East African Mountains of the Moon, given their name by Ptolemy, were thought to be so enticing that whoever looked upon their snowy peaks would be drawn to them as if by a magnetic pull, and could only be released by death. Echoes were the voices of ghosts, storms the carnal revels of Satan and his witches.

For centuries, Europeans avoided climbing mountains, for fear of upsetting the dragons they knew to inhabit them. Some of these beasts were thought to look like serpents with the heads of cats, others had bat wings and long, hairy tails; an eighteenth-century scholar gathered "depositions," given under oath, about these beasts. "There are dragons with and without wings," it was reported, "with and without legs, with and without crests; dragons with cat faces, with human faces, and with nondescript faces; dragons that breathe fire and that do not breathe fire." An Alpine traveler named Johann Scheuchzer wrote in his 1723 book *Itinera Alpina* that although surely "some dragons were fables . . . from the accounts of Swiss dragons, and their comparison with those of other lands, such animals do exist." Early Europeans were content to leave the mountains be, to live by the rivers, travel the valleys, and, only when necessity compelled, to cross high passes. When wars or pilgrimages or the search for new horizons demanded that they cross these passes in winter, travelers often found their greatest fears realized. The old myths were right. Dragons did exist. Not as fire-breathing beasts, but as avalanches.

Able to bury entire armies and lonely wanderers alike, avalanches were particularly terrifying because they seemed to come crashing and foaming out of the mountains with no predictability, and no warning. Worse, in most cases they erased all traces of their victims, causing even the levelheaded to think they had been brought on by some sort of black magic. The record of a 1652 Swiss witch trial states plainly that "witches are the causes of avalanches." In the Swiss canton of Uri, an old woman dressed in black already under suspicion for witchcraft met a dire fate when villagers reported seeing her riding down a hillside on the wave of an avalanche, quietly turning her spinning wheel. Just as she began praying in thanks for her deliverance from the slide, townspeople grabbed her, threw her on a pile of wood, and burned her alive.

If their contemporaries living in the lowlands told stories about ogres and trolls living in forests or under bridges, children in European mountain villages learned to dread the waves of snow that broke over their towns every winter. The mountain historian Colin Fraser quotes a folk expression intended to teach about the strange and deadly ways of the Alps in winter: *"Was fliegt ohne Flügel, schlägt ohne Hand, und sieht ohne Augen—das Lauitier!"* (What flies without wings, strikes without hand, and sees without eyes—the avalanche-beast!)

From at least medieval times, clairvoyants, magicians, and soothsayers have been summoned to locate avalanche victims, who, unlike those drowned at sea, could at once be right under their feet and irretrievably lost. Modern search parties, with satellite mapping, radio technology, magnetometers, and rescue helicopters, fare little better; just like their forebears, they frequently know that bodies are somewhere in the resting cascade of snow, they just don't know exactly *where*. By the time they figure it out, their mission has often become not search and rescue but body recovery.

If the avalanche beasts could not be convinced to give up their victims, perhaps they could be stalked and destroyed with heavy artillery. Because avalanches, given the right conditions, are the only cataclysmic natural events that man can trigger whenever he chooses, snow rangers have, since World War II, planted or launched hundreds of thousands of artillery shells into the mountains in an effort to make them safe as ski slopes or roadways. Patrollers talk about the "war" on avalanches, about making "preemptive strikes on the enemy." They tell of heroic efforts at "taming the mountain" by dropping explosive charges from "helicopter sorties." A former Utah snow ranger recalls diving into a shack near the top of a lift line to avoid being hit by a howitzer shell launched from below; once inside, he heard shrapnel "tinkling on the walls."

Snow and avalanches have acquired sinister intent, it seems, and should be given no quarter. Yet despite this violent effort to steer an inexorable natural process, massive highway slides and tiny backcountry killers alike remain both mystifying and deadlier today than they have ever been. There is something unnerving about this, as there is about anything that mocks the notion that our minds, our technology, and our bravery will somehow prevail even in the face of the most awesome natural events. Despite the evidence—despite the hundreds of people who die in avalanches every year—the forces of nature, we try to tell ourselves, are under our control. Our getaway homes, our highways and railroads, our ski resorts; all creep deeper and deeper into the hills of the backcountry. In the mountains, we have decided, the dragons have been tamed. We have grown comfortable whistling in their lair.

In late February, 1910, Train No. 25, en route along the Great Northern Railway from Spokane to Seattle, was passing through the Cascade Mountains when a multiday winter storm, dropping as much as a foot of snow an hour, closed the tracks. The train, with five passenger cars, came to a stop in the town of Leavenworth, on the eastern slope of a range of peaks reaching as high as 8,000 feet, and was soon joined by the smaller Train No. 27, carrying mail. After several hours of digging, workmen cleared the tracks and the trains continued, but only for a short distance, when strong winds forced them to stop again. A few miles down the track, the storm also disrupted electrical service in the Cascade Tunnel snowshed, a sloping structure built over the tracks meant to allow trains safe passage beneath sliding snow. It wasn't until the evening of the next day that the trains were dug out of 30-foot drifts and able to pass through the snowshed. The trains chugged along as far as Wellington, a tiny hamlet a quarter mile down the track that served as headquarters for tunnel work and engine repair. The town consisted of little more than the Hotel Bailets, a collection of small buildings used as boarding house, general store, post office, dining room, and tavern. A half dozen sleep shacks lay to the east of the hotel.

The snowstorm soon developed into one of the heaviest ever recorded so late in the Cascades' winter season, and railroad officials closed the main line and ordered the trains to pull off the track and onto parallel sidings, short sections of track where trains could pass one another, just beyond the town. With snow falling 11 feet in a single day, the pack got deep fast, covering 900 feet of track to a depth of 25 feet. In some places only the tops of the telegraph poles could be seen.

The slopes above the tracks were in unusually precarious shape. The natural tree cover that once served to anchor heavy winter snowfall had recently been converted into a mass of stumps and snags, the victim of extensive clear-cutting and burning. What was left was not only a scarred hillside, one that would take decades to repair itself, but a fatal absence that might not have been so obvious to men whose work is conducted under sunny summer skies. The slope above the tracks was now dramatically less stable without its tree cover—particularly in winter, long after the lumberjacks had packed away their crosscut saws.

The juxtaposition of the two emblems of progress—the railroad, a major transportation corridor, and the forest, a source of raw building material—might not have seemed so dramatic had the humble collection of buildings, shorn of its protective forest, not become ripe for a major avalanche disaster. Sure enough, late on the night of the twenty-fourth, with the weight of the snow now surpassing the capacity of the slope to contain it, a small, 50-foot-wide avalanche rumbled down, crossed the tracks where the trains had been parked earlier in the day, and destroyed a cookshack where the train's passengers had finished the last of their three meals just hours before. Two men who had served the passengers and remained in the shack were killed. This was just the beginning.

From Friday through Tuesday, the trains, now blocked in both directions, sat idle, and the storm continued to dump snow on Wellington. Working with plows, the rail crew tried to keep up with the snow as it came down the hillside above, each new avalanche mocking the crew's cleanup efforts. With the cookshack destroyed, passengers' only relief from their berths was a slog through the snow to the hotel to eat and send telegrams to their families, but by Saturday afternoon the telegraph lines went dead, ending all communication between the passengers and crew and the outside world. The snow kept falling.

A rotary plow with a 12-foot-high "bite" trying to return to Wellington after clearing the tracks was stopped dead by an avalanche 800 feet long and 35 feet deep—and so full of tree stumps and debris that plowing the tracks became impossible. By Sunday, the rail crews had been working for five days to clear the tracks, and, with the tracks no clearer than before, were nearing the point of collapse. Passengers on the train were growing increasingly restless and disgruntled. One man observed that the slope above the train—the once fully forested slope that was now a denuded sheet—had changed its appearance since the storm began; the once-visible stumps of the fallen trees had been so deeply covered that the slope looked like "an immense quilt of pure white snow." Soon afterward, while on his way to buy tobacco at the hotel, the same passenger turned around and saw "part of a hill simply fold up and start sliding with a roar," snapping the few remaining trees in its path. Although this slide did little damage to the town itself, it seemed an ominous sign of what was to come.

During the day on Sunday, the snow turned to sleet, and by the time warm rains began Monday, the passengers were distraught; the trains had not moved for six days, and the snow in some places had drifted to depths of 20 feet. At 1:20 Tuesday morning, in the midst of a wild electrical storm that dumped rain on the deep snowpack, a mass of snow a quarter mile wide, half a mile long, and 20 feet deep sheared off the mountain and came roaring down. An electrical engineer named Charlie Andrews watched as the slide that many had feared for days swept the entire train into the Tye River Canyon, 150 feet below. An account of the tragedy, *Northwest Disaster* by Ruby El Hult, would later report Andrews's memory: "Just as he reached the bunkhouse, a new sound sprang into being behind him. He wheeled, and in another vivid lightning flash saw White Death moving down the mountain above the trains. Relentlessly it advanced, exploding, roaring, rumbling, grinding, snapping—a crescendo of sound that might have been the crashing of ten thousand freight trains. Colossal it was—in the manner the world might end. Onward it rolled in a majestic wave, crumbling the whole canyon wall before it. It descended to the ledge where the side tracks lay, picked up cars and equipment as though they were so many snow-draped toys, and swallowing them up, disappeared like a white, broad monster into the ravine below. . . . Silent and as though moving in nightmare, he and the other men began to light railroad lanterns and button on coats for the descent into that valley of hell."

In Wellington, the hotel was out of reach of the slide, but the rescuers pouring out of it found that everything else had been swept into the canyon below the track. Of two trains, seven locomotives, a rotary snowplow, several boxcars, the water tower, and the engine house, they found on the surface only shattered bits of wood and steel. In a driving rain, rescuers searched the debris, fearing further avalanches at every moment. After six hours, 14 people were found alive, but many others had been broken by or drowned in the snow. Seven hours after the avalanche, a shovel crew heard faint tapping noises and dug out the end of a mail car that had broken open. Four railroad employees, packed into a corner of the car that had not been crushed, emerged, only slightly injured. One can only guess at the horror of those buried as they listened helplessly to the search crews digging above them, who were unable to hear their cries. One of the most haunting facts of avalanche burial is that victims, conscious but unable to move inside their tomb of snow, can often hear their rescuers but can't make themselves heard. Why shouts and screams can move through snow in one direction but not the other, the legendary avalanche researcher Monty Atwater has written, is a mystery that has yet to be explained.

Dug out from the wreckage at the bottom of the canyon, one passenger marveled at having survived. "The coach lifted and went hurtling through the air. It kept falling, falling with many grinding noises. I was catapulted forward and found myself lying in my pajamas in the snow." Said another, "The car was tossed up as though it were a juggler's ball, turning over and over. We were thrown from the top to the bottom and from the bottom to the top. The coach seemed to strike something and burst open like an eggshell." A third, a woman, was dug out after eleven hours lying crushed beneath both heavy snow and a fractured tree trunk, the last of the 22 survivors. "I had no sense of time—only that eternities of agony had passed," she reported. "Then, with dazed disbelief, I heard voices and the clink of shovels above me. Summoning all my courage, I called a weak and feeble 'help.' "

A larger rescue party finally arrived from Scenic around one in the afternoon; recovery efforts continued for more than a week. On March 13 another avalanche fell upon the track at Windy Point, sending a rotary train into a canyon below and killing one man. When spring finally came to the North Cascades, the last body in Wellington was found, bringing the final count to 96, still the highest number of people killed by an avalanche in the United States.

The Cascade Tunnel has long since been closed, and the town of Wellington, later renamed Tye, no longer exists, abandoned after the route finally proved too dangerous. The summer after the tragedy, the railroad spent $1.5 million building an additional mile of snowsheds, in hopes of preventing further avalanche disasters. In 1929, however, the Great Northern gave up on the route, bored a $25 million, eight-mile tunnel lower in the mountain, and relocated 40 miles of track. The only sure way to avoid avalanches in that stretch of the Cascades, it seemed, was to stay out of their way entirely.

It would be another fifty years before avalanches would again capture the country's attention, when skiers and mountaineers would begin moving into the backcountry in unprecedented numbers. Some of these people would be skilled, some of them incompetent. Some would be lucky, others would not.

Part 1

Fracture Zone

Chapter 1

❄

Snow mountains, more than sea or sky,
serve as a mirror to one's own true being,
utterly still, utterly clear, a void,
an Emptiness without life or sound that
carries in Itself all life, all sound.

— Peter Matthiessen,
The Snow Leopard

Many years ago, on a cold afternoon high in the mountains of north-western Montana, a quiet little boy named Jerry Kanzler lit a tree on fire to call his father back. The elder Kanzler, Hal, his rugged gait quickening as it always did when he got into the backcountry, had disappeared more than a mile up the trail, and the sun was going down. For Hal Kanzler, the mountains of Glacier National Park were sanctified, transporting. The freshness, the clarity, the rigor that he found among the peaks thrilled him in ways that life in the low-lands, with its attendant ambivalences and domestic responsibilities, could not. His sons, he vowed, would learn their lessons high in the hills, and he didn't think that ten was too young an age to begin.

Hal's musing was cut short by the burning tree. Looking back, it dawned on him that mountains could be hard on those still too innocent to ponder chal-lenges to the soul. Ten-year-olds like to romp around the hills like goats. They like to throw stones off ledges and listen as their voices disappear into the canyons. The burning tree, like an oracle, told Hal that his son was worn out, and wanted to go home. Reluctantly, Hal gathered up his young charge, and started down.

A marine captain who had seen action at Okinawa in World War II, Hal was what local climbers called a "pusher": when everyone else in the group was falling-down tired, Hal Kanzler would press on, hiking through the pain of blisters or cold, and he expected his sons to do the same. During another hike, this time with his thirteen-year-old son, Jimmy, Hal stood on the edge of a giant snowfield that, like many frozen expanses in the northern Rockies, was shot through with a lacework of bottomless trenches—some open to the sky, some masked by unreliable crusts of snow—that could swallow a small boy and never spit him out. The way to cross the snowfield, Hal decided, was carefully, and with ropes; if Jimmy fell into a crevasse, Hal told a companion, "we'll just pull him out." Travel in the backcountry, like all matters of the spirit, was fraught with peril and worth the risk.

An electrical engineer who had worked on the Hungry Horse Dam just south of Glacier National Park, Hal Kanzler had marked time with several companies in Montana and Texas before settling into a job with the Anaconda company as a manager of a reduction plant that turned bauxite into aluminum. He rose to become chief of mechanical and electrical operations for Anaconda's western division by the age of forty-three. A hardworking and widely admired businessman, Hal, like many rural Montanans then and now, had an intense love of the freedom that comes from living in close proximity to great expanses of wilderness. "As a working man in this world," he would tell his sons growing up in Columbia Falls, "one of the freedoms you have is the ability to get away into the wilderness and hike and fish."

As a mentor to his sons, Hal was as good as his word. As soon as his two boys were big enough to carry packs, Hal loaded them up with gear and led them into the mountains. An avid hunter and fisherman, whose wildlife photographs and magazine articles had been published locally and in national magazines, Hal frequently wrote first-person adventure stories in which he expressed his love of wilderness through the eyes and deeds of his sons. "It's a funny thing about youngsters," he would write in an article for *Field & Stream.* "They complain about getting tired, but they can rest for only five minutes at a time. Then they have to throw rocks, chase something, climb trees, or outrun the dog." In 1963, he took his boys up Mount St. Nicholas, a sharp-topped pyramid that is considered one of the more difficult climbs in the park. Jim was fifteen, Jerry twelve. Along with their water bottles and lunches, they carried a mirror. The boys' mother, Jean, waited at the foot of the mountain with a mirror of her own; when her men made it to the top, mother and sons signaled to each other that everything was okay. On the way down, Jerry laughed and laughed.

Northwestern Montana was a very small, very conservative place in the 1960s. Stuck in the middle of a cluster of tourist towns, Columbia Falls had a population of about 3,000, many of whom worked in the aluminum plant or timbered the boundless forests of the Flathead Valley. People knew each other. "We had it all, I'm telling you," Jean Kanzler says. "On ladies' day at the ski resorts, I got lunch, a lesson, and a lift ticket for five bucks." When Anaconda threw company Christmas parties, bowling tournaments, or fishing derbies, employees who had worked together for years would bring their families together for gatherings surpassed in community spirit only by high school basketball games. In good years, the Columbia Falls team would end their season parading through town on the city fire truck. Fillers in the local newspapers ran to homespun advice: "What has become of the old-fashioned man who thought he should pay his debts in full?" Display advertisements pushed farm equipment that could "put up to ¾ ton of hay into one bale." It was a place where people relied on neighbors when harsh winters isolated the community from the outside world. People knew each other's business. The exploits of neighborhood children turned up regularly in the news pages. In January 1963, the *Hungry Horse News,* the local newspaper, carried a photograph of a sweet-faced, twelve-year-old Jerry Kanzler and three young friends pointing pop-guns over the walls of their snow forts; staring forlornly at the camera is a dog named Brownie.

As Jerry and Jimmy Kanzler grew, their adventures around northern Montana became well known. Thanks to the influence of their father, they were turning into two of the region's most enthusiastic mountain climbers, at a time when mountaineering in the United States—and Montana particularly—was still in its infancy. For young boys, Glacier National Park was a good place to grow up. Mountains were everywhere. The Flathead River, famous for its trout fishing, was only a bicycle ride away. People, especially people who climbed mountains, knew the Kanzlers, and respected them. "Everyone in town was infatuated with those boys," says Terry Kennedy, whose father worked as a foreman at Anaconda and who became an accomplished climber in his own right. "In those days nobody knew too much about this stuff. Hal was not a Yosemite climber. He was self-taught. He was a driving force. He'd scramble up peaks with his buddies and then get them to scramble up two more. He was so far above his partners that he probably couldn't find anyone to keep up with him."

"In social life Hal was everywhere, from small song fests at the Big Mountain to the hoity-toity cocktail circuit," George Ostrom, a local journalist, would later write of his friend. A gadfly whose gregarious demeanor led some to think of him as a kind of local P. T. Barnum, Ostrom seemed to be known personally by most people in northwestern Montana. His sharp opinions on everything from national politics to small-town gossip had been broadcast in northern Montana for years, and his writing had appeared in local newspapers just as long. To Ostrom, Hal Kanzler was both a hiking companion and an emblem of the finest that Montana had to offer. "He was gregarious, extroverted, and gung ho. He was also introverted and self-reliant to the point that he once insisted that he be left alone to ride out the ravages of a recurrent malaria attack on a high mountain ledge, while the rest of the party went on without him."

The exploits of Hal and the boys were most frequently pursued outside the watch of the boys' mother, Jean, who early on had come to terms with her husband's and sons' outdoor ambitions. Although not a climber herself, she had accompanied the family on a weeklong backpacking trip into the Bob Marshall Wilderness; in an article he wrote for *Field & Stream* entitled "Big Game Hunting with Camera," Hal included a photograph Jean had taken of a "hasty retreat" he made when confronted by a sow grizzly and her two cubs.

For such a rugged man, Kanzler had a photographic eye frequently drawn to the tender: a tiny fawn, curled up in a grass nest; a teetering, newborn mountain goat; a baby fox. For his backcountry photographic work, Kanzler had modified his gear by screwing a camera and telephoto lens to an old rifle stock; one of his favorite photographs was of a golden mantle chipmunk that had climbed up on the stock and was peering through it, as if lining up a shot of its own. Kanzler liked the picture so much he had it put on his personal stationary. To help lure his subject, his son Jim later revealed, Hal had smeared his scope with peanut butter.

After years of close observing, Kanzler had developed a striking capacity for wonder. For another article in *Field & Stream,* he described one of the most unusual things he had ever seen in the wilds of Montana: a pair of ram horns "locked together like a Chinese ring puzzle" that had been found at the bottom of a ravine. The horns, which had been discovered by a cowboy employed by the National Bison Range, told a strange story: two male rams, in the midst of an annual November head-butting ritual, had somehow managed to lock their horns together so inextricably that they died without settling their differences. "Their story is an example of the ironic ways of nature," Kanzler wrote. "The two great rams had lived together, played together, and fought and died together."

As had many in his generation, Hal Kanzler initially came to know the wilderness through sport. He had been a national collegiate champion marksman, and as an adult had climbed enough mountains and killed enough large animals to rank as something of a local hero. But as he got older, he began heading into the woods without his gun, and began to take a deeper interest in conservation. He was a charter member of the Montana Wilderness Association, a group founded by Dr. John Montagne, a geology professor at Montana State University in Bozeman, who would later become a mountaineering mentor to both Jerry and Jim.

"Hal Kanzler could hold his own in the boardroom of a large corporation, in a canoe on white water, or on a landing with the U.S. Marines, but he seemed the happiest to me when climbing some windswept peak," Ostrom once wrote. "He came on like thunder over the peaks when he wanted to, or his presence could be like the calm on a deep mountain lake when the storm had passed . . . Hal Kanzler, like all doers, made friends fast. He had to. He was in a hurry. We all used to wonder, 'How far is that guy going? What makes him go?' "

One day, out in the hills, Hal found that he couldn't get up a particularly difficult rock face, and decided to learn about technical rock climbing. He bought the books, and bought the gear, and pretty soon was counted among the most knowledgeable climbers in the area. His sons, Jim and Jerry, growing up in the shadow of the northern Rockies and in a household full of mountaineering books, soon got hooked on climbing as well, and joined their father on a number of climbs that would have made less hardy souls shudder. Indeed, Jimmy and Jerry had already decided that they would spend their lives in the mountains. Their father had taught them the incalculable value of open space, the soulful lessons one can learn from animals and rivers and cliffs. As they followed their father into the backcountry, first wide-eyed, then gradually more competent, the Kanzler brothers learned of the world through physical experience. They watched their father, and tried to emulate his movements. They admired his strength, his fitness, his freedom in the hills. Where Jimmy was strong, Jerry was graceful, a natural, gifted gymnast on the Montana boulders.

By the time the boys were eleven and eight, Hal had taken them to the top of Mount Jackson, one of Glacier's toughest climbs. Five years later, he joined Ostrom, the two boys, and one of their friends in a climb of the 8,700-foot Great Northern, a peak in the Great Bear Wilderness named for the railroad. Despite their youth, the three boys already had thirteen years of climbing experience among them. After so many trips with Hal, the Kanzler boys were well versed in the use of climbing techniques. They knew how to rig rappels and belays, how to arrange their body weight and balance their movements as the walking turned vertical. They knew about scree fields, and the changeable Montana weather that makes high-altitude hiking unpredictable in any season. "Lesser peaks," Ostrom wrote of the Great Northern climb for *Field & Stream,* with photos by Hal Kanzler, "had taught them the menace of loose rocks, rotten ice, and unexpected storms. They knew the value of proper clothing and equipment. They were ready." The boys climbed the west face of the mountain, including an especially steep ascent of more than 4,000 feet. They followed a ridge about half a mile before traversing an alpine meadow, then crossed a snow patch and swung up through a notch to the south. Once through the notch, they reached the main face of the peak, where the only hazard arose in the form of rocks kicked down onto climbers below. Rather than climb single file, the group walked side by side, at least until they were forced to cross a steep snowfield near the top with the help of belays.

Upon reaching the summit, Ostrom wrote, the boys were smitten by the spectacular view. To the south, million-acre Bob Marshall Wilderness; to the west, the 40-mile-long Hungry Horse Reservoir, and the peaks of the Swan and Mission Ranges. Glacier National Park and the Continental Divide lay to the north. After signing the climbing register, the boys frolicked, boot skiing down a snowfield. Aware that descending mountains can be more dangerous than climbing them, the boys "took no foolish chances" on their way down. "It is a common weakness of climbers—the young especially—to seek shortcuts, but the boys resolutely avoided this temptation," Ostrom wrote. "Just before entering timber, Jim, Lee, and Jerry looked back. Their happy smiles reflected their deep satisfaction at having conquered a formidable mountain—and gratitude to the mountain for just being there."

In August 1959, four years before the Great Northern expedition, Hal had taken his young boys on another backpacking trip, this time to Boulder Pass. The pass lies in the northern section of the Livingstone Range, considered the most rugged terrain in all of Glacier. A photograph of the journey shows the boys, with Trapper Nelson wooden framepacks strapped to their backs, walking alongside their beaming father. Jimmy wears a red shirt, Jerry a blue flannel; their dad has a brown leather camera case slung around his neck. In the background of the photograph, ten raven miles to the east, stands the tallest mountain in Glacier National Park, Mount Cleveland.

Ten years later, at the age of eighteen, Jerry Kanzler would die on Mount Cleveland, along with four other boys his age, in one of the worst avalanche disasters in United States mountaineering history. Jimmy Kanzler would risk his life trying to save him. Hal Kanzler would be dead as well. Their story hangs over the mountains of northern Montana like a winter mist.

Chapter 2

✳

*There is no sight in nature quite so peaceful
as the white blanket of newly fallen snow
which covers fields, woods and mountains
alike. All living sounds are hushed and even
human footfalls become muffled. Yet beneath
this canopy of almost death-like calm, in
reality there is no rest.*

— Gerald Seligman, *Snow
Structure and Ski Fields*

From the earliest reaches of history, avalanches have had a way of
humbling even the most heroic human endeavors. In 218 B.C., the Carthagin-
ian general Hannibal left southern Spain with some 90,000 soldiers, 12,000
horsemen, and three dozen elephants, crossed France, and climbed into the
Alps on his way to attack Rome during the Second Punic War. In the mountains, the elephants were placed at the front of the column; the belligerent
Celts and Gauls who lived in the mountains reportedly "beheld these beasts
with superstitious awe." After defeating its foes in a number of terrible skir-
mishes, Hannibal's army reached a pass—perhaps the Little St. Bernard Pass,
perhaps the Col de la Traversette, perhaps the Col du Clapier—on October 26;
to cheer his depleted, exhausted troops, Hannibal exclaimed that they had
"climbed the ramparts of Italy, nay, of Rome. What lies still for us to accomplish is not difficult." The trouble was that the Alps on the way down toward
Italy proved far steeper than on the way up from France. Worse, November

storms had covered the glaciers with snow, concealing deadly crevasses and loading the steeper slopes with heavy blankets of snow. Although they encountered no enemies during their descent, thousands of soldiers and horses were lost to avalanches.

By the time the army reached the plains on the eastern slope of the mountains, some 18,000 men, 2,000 horses, and several elephants were lost, as many as half of them to cold and avalanches. An epic poem about the journey by Silius Italicus (A.D. 25–101) reports that "There where the path is intercepted by glistening slope, [Hannibal] pierces the resistant ice with his lance. Detached snow drags the men into the abyss and snow falling rapidly from the high summits engulfs the living squadrons."

In 1499, Kaiser Maximilian ordered 10,000 soldiers to invade the Engadine Valley; as the army crossed a high mountain pass, 400 men were carried away by an avalanche. "The panic created by this occurrence soon changed to laughter, however," a Swiss account reported, "when the men buried under the snow emerged from it one by one as if they rose from the grave, and although many of them were injured, none were lost." The survival of so many men caught in a slide is, historically speaking, miraculous; it is rare, once caught, for even single victims of large slides to survive. The same year, 100 mercenaries were killed as they crossed Great St. Bernard Pass.

As people settled in Europe's mountain regions, death tolls began to rise proportionally. In 1569 an avalanche smashed through the ice of a lake near Davos, Switzerland, with such force that it killed a large number of fish by concussion and threw them out onto the land. In 1808 in Trun, Switzerland, it snowed more than 15 feet in three days. The sun finally emerged, precipitating a large avalanche. It came down in a westward direction, destroying a number of houses, then careened up the opposite side of the valley and destroyed a large forest. It then recoiled down, destroying more forest. Like a scythe slashing back and forth through the valley, the avalanche swooped again to the west, and returned again to the east, flattening a dozen cowsheds. Then it was back to the west again, this time burying a barn full of cattle. One more time it recoiled to the east, flowing over some hills with enough force to mass again; heading west, it buried houses to their rooftops.

Wide-eyed historical accounts of avalanches abound. An 1843 book entitled *Travels in the Alps of the Savoy* called avalanches the "greatest and most resistless of catastrophes which can overtake the Alpine pedestrian." A document known as the "Montafon Letter" reported that, after an avalanche buried 300 people in 1689 in the Montafon Valley, a priest carrying the sacrament to the dying was buried by one avalanche and then unburied by another. The lucky priest was hardly the first man of the cloth to find himself endangered by snow. In the tenth century, on the eve of his marriage, the wealthy Bernard of Menthon renounced all worldly temptations and devoted his life to saving others. After joining the Augustine order, and determined to help pilgrims crossing the mountains, he founded a monastery in A.D. 962 at an altitude of 8,000 feet on what was then known as Mount Jove. Every morning, monks would set out from the hospice in both directions, looking for pilgrims to guide back to the monastery. Between 1436 and 1885 (the year telephones allowed pilgrims to notify the hospice in advance), not a winter's morning passed that men did not leave the comfort of St. Bernard's Hospice to assist lost travelers, or to rescue those who had run afoul of the weather, Colin Fraser writes. The monks were kept busy; by the eighteenth century some 15,000 people per year crossed St. Gotthard Pass, and the St. Bernard Hospice found itself serving some 400 meals a day. The monks, of course, were also at risk; between 1810 and 1845 alone, a dozen were killed in high mountain avalanches.

Given the loveliness of the snow crystals that create them, it can be said that even monstrous avalanches are born serene. Snow begins simply enough, forming somewhere between the troposphere and the stratosphere, between 30,000 and 40,000 feet above the earth, where atmospheric temperatures dip down to 75 degrees below zero. Floating above the clouds are thousands of species of bacteria, fungi, and protozoa, along with the pollen of some 10,000 species of flowering plants and untold quantities of atmospheric dust—each a possible nucleus around which water molecules may freeze. These nuclei are exceedingly small: it takes as many as ten million of them to form a single raindrop, and perhaps a million frozen ice crystals to make one snowflake. The flakes they form are legion: a million billion may fall on a single acre of land during a ten-inch accumulation.

As these clusters float downward, they grow from invisible particles to fragile collections of crystals, depending on the amount of water vapor and the temperature of the air. For reasons peculiar to the bonds of hydrogen and oxygen—as true for ice cubes as it is for snow—snow crystals initially take the form of flat hexagons, but then gradually change as if an invisible hand were turning a kaleidoscope. Winds can sweep them thousands of feet up or down, and with each change in temperature the crystals change form. As they evolve, the six points of the hexagonal plates gradually grow or lose their spindly arms, or dendrites; high winds can break these arms, sending smaller fragments forth to begin evolving in their own right.

Like children, individual snowflakes are, during their growth period, as varied as the forces that touch them. The shape of a new snow crystal depends in part on the temperature of the air around it. Although scientists have over the years developed a number of different systems for categorizing basic snow crystals, the International Commission on Snow and Ice has come up with ten: plates, stellars, needles, columns, capped columns, spatial dendrites, graupel, sleet, hail, and a catch-all category called "irregulars." As even the music of their names suggests, there is a great aesthetic difference in the way these crystals look. Capped columns are structurally simple, at least compared to ornate stars. They look like empty bobbins of thread, but their peculiar shape extends their reach: while still floating in the atmosphere, they can act as countless millions of prisms, refracting light in such a way that halos are perceived surrounding the sun or moon on a winter day. Graupel, the homeliest crystal, is formed when water droplets float through regions of fog or cloud and become bonded to hardened pellets; by the time it reaches the ground, graupel looks like frozen blobs of brain tissue. Stellars, with their ornate lattice of six delicate arms, are of such variety that their number borders on the infinite, and there is some poetry in this. It would be a shame if there were three kinds of stars and thousands of varieties of miniature floating brains.

Flakes descend at an average rate of a foot per second, although needles, more aerodynamic, fall faster than stars. In most cases, flakes that fall the greatest distances attain the most beautiful and ornate patterns; flakes that land atop high mountains, deprived of their chance to evolve, are generally simpler than the ornate structures that fall all the way to sea level. With so much evolution, it is often said that no two snowflakes are alike. Whether or not this is true, a Russian meteorologist claimed in 1910 to have observed 246 different kinds of snow in a single year near St. Petersburg. Wilson Alwyn Bentley, a Vermont farmer, published a photographic portfolio with 2,453 microphotographs of individual flakes taken between 1884 and 1931. He also knew that he had barely begun his list. Indeed, since a single cubic foot of snow may contain as many as ten million individual flakes, and since over time enough snow has fallen on the earth to cover it to a depth of 50 miles, the claim of eternal snowflake idiosyncracy seems mathematically unfathomable.

It should also be remembered that snow isn't white. Snowstorms are made up of billions of tiny, clear prisms, each of which breaks up all light that strikes it into the entire spectrum; snowflakes are, like the water that forms them, actually clear. Refracting all the light that passes through them, snowflakes flood the visual field not with one color but with *all* colors. The confused eye, unable to handle such a burst of sensory overload, turns the flood of colors back into whiteness, often with serious physical side effects. Blinded by so much whiteness—a so-called whiteout—a skier or hiker can quickly become completely disoriented and nauseated, much as he would feel on an utterly gray day spent rolling on a tumultuous sea. Losing any sense of a horizon, those caught in a whiteout can become overwhelmed by vertigo, a state in which the connection between the eye and the inner ear becomes so confused that one's very sense of footing becomes unreliable. In a whiteout, a skier may be so caught in the thrall of a storm that he is unable to see the gloved hand in front of his face, let alone the slope passing beneath his feet. Assuming he is standing still on a flat surface, he may discover that the slope is in fact nearing vertical, and that he is in fact flying down a hill at 30 miles per hour; tragically, he may discover this only after he has crashed into a tree, or gone sailing off a cliff.

As ephemeral as snow is in the air, it becomes even more mysterious once on the ground, and has long been a source of rhetorical rumination for poets and scientists alike. A swirl of ethereal, airborne snow flowing over a high mountain ridge mirrors in both its aspect and physics a plume of sand blowing over a dune. Snow "falls in soft crystals of infinite variety yet lies in a heavy sameness on the land," writes Bernard Mergen, in his book *Snow in America*. "It obscures the familiar yet reveals new shapes, it comes in the season of darkness yet makes both day and night more brilliant with reflected light, it arrives with the killing frost and the disappearance of many plants and animals yet preserves seedlings and tiny creatures under its warming blanket, it is pure and beautiful yet volatile and transitory, it confines the body yet releases the imagination." Twentieth-century snow science has confirmed what superstitions used to suspect: snow, particularly as it masses and moves, turns into one of the strangest, most intriguing, and most potentially destructive substances on earth. Throughout the history of snow research, pioneering American avalanche researcher Monty Atwater has written, ski rangers and scientists alike have agreed on one thing: snow is the most "recalcitrant" substance on earth. "Snow seems averse to being studied. When it is poked or disturbed or manhandled in any way, it changes quicker than a chameleon, from one kind of snow to another, leaving the observer baffled."

A very dry snowpack may in fact comprise 95 percent air and only 5 percent water; very wet snow might hold as much as 50 percent water. An easy way to visualize this is to think of the amount of melted snow required to make an inch of water: 20 inches of snow at 5 percent water density, or just two inches of snow at 50 percent density. The weight of any pile of snow is thus the product of its depth multiplied by its water density. Since the average ten-inch snowpack can weigh as much as 100 tons per acre, it is easy to see why shoveling snow has become such a regular cause of suburban heart attacks. If the average water density of snow is about 10 percent, in places like California's Sierra Nevada snow can contain 40 percent water and weigh 200 pounds per square foot; since it snows up to 400 inches a year there, it is also easy to understand what Californians mean by "Sierra Cement."

External factors, such as a strong wind, can also have an effect on the density and weight of a snowpack. A strong wind can jam crystals together and so fill empty spaces with ambient moisture that the pack reaches a density five to ten times that of the original snowfall. Once a windblown layer is buried under new snow, of course, things get more complicated. Cohesion is suddenly a matter not just between crystals, but between layers of snow as well. As the snowpack gets deeper, each layer is compressed by those above it, gradually becoming thinner and thus more dense. Denser layers below can be stronger than fluffier layers above, and become increasingly so as the weight above increases. Snow is also "visco-plastic"; it can flow like a liquid, and stretch or compress without losing its structure, like some solids. A snowpack on a slope can stretch or "creep" downhill for some time before it finally breaks along a fracture line. Analogies for this are hard to come by, since snow has such unique physical properties. It is as if bread dough, spread over a tilted cutting board and adhering to the wood, began to stretch downward until the gluten bonds snapped and sent the released half crashing to the floor. The variations in cohesive strength between one particle of snow and another, between one layer and another, or between snow and the ground are, according to Ed LaChapelle, another early American avalanche researcher, "among the widest found in nature."

This is particularly true given the wide variety in the shapes and sizes of individual snow crystals. Any given layer of snow can be 85 to 95 percent air, with the interlocking arms of individual crystals forming a kind of web around it, but the hardness of a wind-packed layer of old snow may be 50,000 times that of light, fluffy snow. Cohesion between layers depends primarily upon two factors: "interlocking" between the arms or necks of the different snow crystals and "sintering," or cementing, between layers. Snow crystals can last an instant and melt. At other times, they can pack so tightly that they almost achieve the consistency of stone; snow compressed over hundreds of years into glacier ice is hard enough to carve valleys through mountains and turn boulders into powder. Snow cover varies with virtually everything that influences its fall, from the temperature, moisture, and wind speed of the air to the geography, latitude, and altitude of the ground on which it falls. And since snow falls on roughly half of the North American continent, its characteristics and personality are as varied as the people it falls upon.

The places where snow falls most heavily are the world's mountain ranges, which make up about 20 percent of the earth's continental land mass, and which, by holding weather systems in place, become some of the wettest places on earth. Snow will also vary depending on what layer it occupies; snow deposited on the ground in December will have characteristics decidedly different from snow layered above it in February. Individual layers can be thick or thin, frozen solid or soft and damp. As a rule, thick layers of snow represent consistent snowfall within a single storm; thinner layers can be formed by wind or snowmelt between storms, or by "surface hoar," the wintertime equivalent of dew. Usually formed by nighttime moisture precipitating onto a cold snowpack, surface hoar is beautifully constructed of feathery crystals, makes for great ski conditions, and is one of winter's most delicate features. Under a microscope, surface hoar crystals are often revealed to take the shape of hexagons, each with sharp angles formed by two opposite sides longer than the other four. This geometry means that surface hoar is also a significant factor in avalanche formation, since hexagons, their angular sides scraping up against each other rather than locking together, have trouble bonding, especially on the horizontal plane. If a layer of surface hoar becomes covered by subsequent layers of snow, it may be able to withstand compression from above but will slide instantly once set in motion. One beautiful, utterly common layer of feathers, laid down in a single night, can mean a month of danger.

Chapter 3

❄

*What's down there if you're not a social
person and you don't go to parties and you
really think differently from other people?
There was nothing there except traffic and
noise and smog and a general flurry of people
who were not particularly looking for
something better. People in the mountains are
searching for something better. It doesn't even
matter if it's there or not, it's the search that
counts.*

— Royal Robbins, quoted in
Nicholas O'Connell,
*Beyond Risk: Conversations
with Climbers*

From the beginning, Jimmy Kanzler had shown a skill and maturity in the backcountry that outstripped many of his elders. His father was very proud, and boasted frequently of his son's prowess in his writing. "Jim propped his elbow on his knee and angled the muzzle up toward the rock point," Hal wrote in a *Field & Stream* article about a hunting trip he took with his young son. "I gritted my teeth, for I knew how hard the .30-06 was going to boot the boy when he triggered it from that awkward position. But there was no time for sideline advice; the young billy had seen us, and his curiosity wouldn't hold him much longer." The three-year-old, though not large, would still make a fine trophy for a thirteen-year-old boy on his first big-game hunt.

Father and son had been planning this trip for four years, ever since Jim had gotten his first lessons in mountain climbing at the age of nine. In 1960, when Jim was twelve, Hal had taken him on an extended hunting trip in the Kootenai River area in the extreme northwestern corner of Montana, still one of the state's most remote regions. Father and son spent two weeks hunting bighorn sheep; during the trip Hal dropped a full-curl ram that got his name in the record books. Hal had given Jim a Springfield A3 rifle that year for Christmas; the following summer, Jim did well enough at a shooting match, his father wrote, "to expand my chest a little." One morning the two woke before dawn to hike to the rough country near a peak called Daughter of the Sun, where Hal and some climbing buddies had seen goats before. A little before three that afternoon, Hal pointed out a goat standing 350 yards away on the other side of a saddle in the mountain, and woke his napping son. Shouldering his rifle, Jim fired, and missed, and missed again. Hal fired, and also missed. When the goat bolted, father and son ran in pursuit along the ridge, finally spotting it above and 200 yards ahead of them. Hal told his son to aim for the "boiler room" behind the front leg, and Jim shot.

Jim didn't miss this time, Hal wrote, but "folded him up quick and dumped him off the ledge." The goat tumbled down the slope and "end-overed" behind the next ridge. Jim's shot had gone straight through the goat, severing its spine. Hal's eldest son was thrilled. " 'That makes two big-game hunters in the family,' Jim said with a grin. 'Let's start training Jerry next spring. In only two years there'll be three of us. Man, we'll have it made!' "

As Jimmy filled out, he grew into a body blessed with a number of physical talents that allowed him to gracefully maneuver his way up the face of steep rock walls. Of medium build, with broad shoulders and a somewhat stooped gait, he had a muscular upper body and—even more important—very strong hands. Once, in a barroom doorway, he was observed performing dozens of pull-ups using nothing but his fingertips.

Jimmy seemed to have inherited his passion for the mountains from the family's Swiss, German, and French ancestors, his father would write later. Jimmy spent summers in the mid-1960s working in Glacier National Park on the "blister rust" crew, named for a fungus they were trying to keep from destroying the park's white pine trees. His off days were spent climbing some of the park's most impressive peaks, including Mount Merritt, which, at just over 10,000 feet, is among the tallest mountains in the park. But Merritt was just the beginning. During the summer of 1966, Jimmy wrote to his father to ask for a box of pitons, small oval or D-shaped pieces of aluminum hardware with snap-gates, used, among other things, to clip climbing ropes into anchors hammered into sheer rock walls. A box arrived in the mail with a sternly worded note warning Jimmy not to climb two of Glacier's most treacherous peaks: "These pitons will *not* be used on the North Face of Mount Cleveland or the North Face of Siyeh."

The note did not say anything about Mount St. Nicholas, another of the park's major challenges, so Jimmy promptly led a party of four to the top. Mount St. Nick, as it is known, is no walk in the park; one guide reports that "most climbers will not fully enjoy the time spent on top, because they will be preoccupied with thoughts of the poor rock, the sheer cliffs, and the tremendous exposure awaiting them during the descent." But to Jimmy Kanzler, Mount St. Nick was just a warm-up. His father's warning in the box of pitons had perhaps been more astute than he realized: the route Jimmy and his friends were really plotting to tackle was indeed the north face of Mount Cleveland, at four thousand vertical feet the most precipitous big wall in the continental United States. All they needed was a team.

During Jimmy Kanzler's senior year in high school, Hal had taken a new position with Anaconda and moved the family 120 miles southeast to Butte, a copper mining town that was considerably tougher than pastoral Columbia Falls. Paralleling the explosion in the use of electrical and telephone lines, Butte had become a major source of the world's copper supply in the 1890s, and boomed again during the high copper demands of the First and Second World Wars. But the town had also gone through a number of busts, including during the 1960s, as tougher environmental laws raised production costs, and cheap copper from South America began to flood the world market.

For the Kanzler family, the move from the Flathead Valley, a paradise of trout streams and wild backcountry, to a boom-and-bust mining town was difficult, but big patches of good country—Yellowstone, the Bitterroot Range, the Humbugs—suddenly became closer. The family enjoyed Butte a great deal, Hal maintained in a letter to a friend. The Beartooth and the Teton ranges were suddenly a lot closer, he wrote, and offered new territory to explore after seventeen years of living in the Flathead Valley. Clearly, both Hal and the boys would have plenty of ground on which to tramp around, new peaks to climb, and lots of wildlife to photograph.

For high school kids, however, life in Butte was harder than it was in the bucolic Flathead. In Butte, the sons of miners would often establish themselves with their fists rather than their hiking boots. Soon after their arrival, which because of Hal's position at Anaconda was announced in the local paper, the Kanzlers' home was robbed. Not long afterward, while Jerry was walking home from school carrying Hal's old trumpet, which he was learning to play, he got jumped by a group of local toughs. The gang came up from behind him and battered both the boy and the horn.

"There was a lot of fighting in those days. I saw people getting their heads smashed in on the streets," Jimmy Kanzler remembers. With so many young men looking for a fight, recruiters for the Vietnam War effort had no trouble finding volunteers. When Jim grudgingly tramped in to show his draft card, he was turned away—the town had long since filled its quota with willing volunteers.

As shy, newly transplanted mountain climbers, Jimmy and Jerry considered themselves lucky to find friends in Butte like Clare Pogreba and Ray Martin. As students at Butte's Montana College of Mineral Science and Technology, Martin and Pogreba were known as Mutt and Jeff to their family, friends, and professors alike; Ray was a gangly six foot six with a grin as broad as his face, Clare a stocky five foot two, with the sloping, fleshy nose of his eastern European forebears. Standing next to Martin, Pogreba's head came to just under his friend's armpit. Avid rock climbers, they had founded the university's climbing club, quickly became central figures in the local climbing community, and, with the Kanzler boys, started exploring the granite towers outside of town known as the Humbugs. Far more predictable than the crumbly mountains of Glacier, the Humbugs offered considerably more opportunity for the boys to work on their technical rock-climbing skills.

Along with the Kanzler boys, Martin and Pogreba had climbed in and around Butte and Glacier National Park for years by the time they reached their twenties, but it was through the energy of Hal Kanzler and his sons that Ray's interest in backcountry exploration deepened. "Mr. Kanzler was a mountain climbing enthusiast, and I'm sure it was through him and his boys that the interest was passed on to all of the others," recalled Ray's mother, Ruby, a modest woman who spent much of her life as a cook in local restaurants. "Then having a mountaineering club at the Tech—the sport really took on an added interest."

Like the Kanzlers, Pogreba and Martin were rugged kids, the sons of men who spent their lives working with rock. Clare's father, Russell Pogreba, who came from German-Polish stock, had worked for cement companies in Butte and in Texas, and by the mid-1940s had moved to a Butte chemical company that made phosphorous and baking powder. Born in 1947, Clare got his name because "there were so many Daves and Johns. We just wanted something different," said his mother, Esther, a hairdresser in Butte. As a boy, Clare developed a keen eye for two things: rocks and photography. He and his father would spend hours out looking for rocks and taking pictures of Montana's mountains. A geological engineering major at Montana Tech, Clare also worked as a staff photographer for the student newspaper. When he joined his father on elk hunting trips, Clare would take only pictures; his mother considered him "too tenderhearted to shoot them."

In 1965, the same year that his uncle was shot down and lost over Laos, Clare got a call from his mother at the service station where he worked—she had gone into labor, and needed a ride to the hospital. "I'd called my husband at work, but he said, 'I have chemicals all over me,' so Clare picked me up," Esther said. "Clare carried my suitcase in, and they thought he was the father, which was pretty funny since he looked so young. He loved that little girl. He took pictures and pictures and pictures of that baby. Looking out of barrels. Looking out of wastebaskets. He would carry her around on his shoulders. She was always the first thing he would see when he came home."

As he got older, Clare's fascination with mountains continued to grow. He didn't date much, his mother said, because dances were on weekends and that was the only time Clare and his friends had to go up into the hills. Clare met Ray Martin in junior high school, and the two immediately began exploring the local mountains together. When the Kanzlers moved to Butte, the hiking group not only grew in number but in collective talent, and together the foursome began polishing their skills as technical climbers, using ropes and intricate hardware imported from Europe to scale rock faces that to the casual observer would seem utterly devoid of handholds. Clare became so taken with climbing that he took to flooding sections of ramp inside the college football stadium during cold snaps to construct a long sheet of ice at a 45-degree angle—perfect for practicing his new love of ice climbing. At the end of the day—after classes and work—he would walk three miles from his home to the ice sheet to practice, inching his way up the imitation frozen waterfall using crampons and ice axes to keep from sliding down to the 50 yard line. He would come home banged up and scratched, his mother said, but happy.

By the time he was eighteen, Clare had a green belt in karate, but had also developed troubles with his feet that kept him out of the service; he had to wear special lifts under his heels to correct his gait. With the army out of the question, he decided that he would join the Peace Corps—he would go to Nepal, he declared, and be that much closer to the Himalayas. All he had to do was graduate in February 1970. Before that, however, he wanted to climb Mount Cleveland. Determined to further develop his winter skills, Clare drove to Jackson, Wyoming, one winter for a two-week course in avalanche training. As always, Ray Martin was by his side. By the end of the course, the two young climbers figured they knew all there was to know about avalanches.

While Pogreba was intense, focused, even obsessive about his climbing, his best friend was a smiling, cheerful boy, a balancing force to Pogreba's drive. "I guess a mother is always prejudiced, but he seemed to get along well with everyone," Ruby Martin said. Ray was known as a "rock hound" for his avid collecting and trading of specimens he found in the mountains. He had cards printed up, with spaces to glue rocks and their names underneath. Affixed to the top of the cards were postcards showing the mines or the mountain where Martin had made the find. On the back were details of each specimen— the mineral contents, the rock's geologic history. Ray placed these cards in shops around Butte, where tourists or mineral collectors would see them and call him up for a sale or trade. "He did very well with this endeavor," Ruby Martin said. "He had quite a business built up." While he was at Montana Tech, Ray also worked in the assaying department for the same company that employed his father, Arthur, a deep-pit contract miner who spent long years drilling and blasting for gold, silver, and copper. Like many miners, he ended up with emphysema, a disease that would eventually kill him.

Perhaps because his father had spent so much of his life in the bowels of the earth, Ray decided to spend his time high above it. As he entered his late teens, Ray began spending summers in Alaska, working as a firefighter. During the summer of 1969 he was back in Alaska installing and inspecting Cold War communications equipment for the Federal Electric Corporation. The job entailed climbing up huge radio towers, an exhilarating enterprise that only made the work more attractive to Ray. An adventurous spirit, he had told his mother that technical mountain climbing wasn't enough, that he wanted to take up skydiving. "Raymond, can't you pick something that's not so dangerous?" Ruby Martin asked her son. "He said, 'Mom, if you had your way I would never get off the couch. I would just sit at home and never get outside. But while I'm alive I'm going to live and enjoy myself, doing things I like. When my time comes to go, it could be walking across the street or whatever, so don't worry all the time. You can't control destiny, 'cause I'm going to live my life to the fullest.' "

By all accounts, Jerry Kanzler, given his gymnastic training in school, was the most accomplished acrobatic climber of the group. In addition to his early climbs with his father, Jerry had made a trip with Jim to Oregon and Washington to climb some of the highest mountains in the region: Mount Rainier,

Mount Hood, Mount St. Helens, and Mount Adams—all in a week. Jerry at the time was fourteen. Three years later, Jerry climbed the north ridge of the Grand Teton—a difficult ascent that had become a rite of passage for a number of early American climbers—and considered it "easy," Jim said. "Climbing the north ridge was no big deal to him." Back home in Butte, whenever Jerry made a nice move on a rock in the Humbugs, he would let loose with "outbursts of delight." Peter Lev, a skiing and climbing instructor at Montana State who went on to become a co-owner of the world-renowned Glenn Exum climbing school in Jackson, Wyoming, considered Jerry the best student he'd had in his mountaineering class.

Beyond his technical skills, Jerry had developed a personal style that was at once jaunty and sweet; a shy boy taken with wearing eccentric hats, his demeanor had none of the aggressiveness of his father. "Jerry stood out in a crowd. He had a flamboyant personality that was unusual in that he also seemed the epitome of kindness, a saint almost," said Terry Kennedy, who had met Jerry through the Boy Scouts. "He had the kind of authority that kids looked to. He always stood up for the underdog, for some kid who wasn't as strong as the rest. That really impressed me. He seemed like such a kind person without being meek. A most unusual individual."

A photograph that Hal Kanzler took of his youngest son shows Jerry, age ten, laying flat on the rocky summit of Glacier's Mount Jackson. He is lying on his stomach, mouth agape, head cradled by an elbow. One leg is bent at the knee, and rests against a sharp chunk of rock. With a different bed, he would look serene. Flopped on the bare rock, he looks broken. "That picture always looked like a place close to heaven, where Jerry was," Jean Kanzler would say.

As had a number of fine young Montana climbers, Jerry as a teenager fell under the tutelage of Dr. John Montagne, a professor of geology at Montana State whose interest in the outdoors had led to the creation of the country's first snow science course in the early 1960s. Montagne had worked as a naturalist for the Park Service in the Tetons, then, after receiving a Ph.D. in geology at the University of Wyoming, became a kind of dean for the small group of Montana State mountaineers, both as a professor and as a political activist. An ardent and effective defender of wild lands who helped found the Montana Wilderness Association, Montagne fought powerboaters who were damaging rookeries on Yellowstone Lake and worked to defeat a proposed dam on the Sun River that would have destroyed winter elk habitat; Montagne still refers to motorboats and snowmobiles as "predators." It was through the

Wilderness Association that Montagne met Hal Kanzler; Montagne's son Matt later became one of Jerry Kanzler's close friends. By the time of the 1969 Mount Cleveland expedition, the elder Montagne had also become one of Montana's leading and most sought-after avalanche experts, and when Jerry Kanzler or any other local climber wanted to learn about winter mountaineering, it was to Dr. Montagne that they turned.

Montagne's training as an avalanche expert had begun long before his academic career. In the Second World War, Montagne, whose French Huguenot family name had been de la Montagne ("of the Mountain"), had run a climbing school for one of the fittest and most highly trained groups of soldiers America has ever produced, the 10th Mountain Division. Veterans of the mountain troops were scattered all over the northern Rockies in the late 1960s, so it is perhaps not surprising that, in different capacities, a number of them became the last men to see Jerry Kanzler and his friends alive.

Chapter 4

❄

*I can say with little hesitation
that I have just emerged
from the worst physical ordeal
of my entire life.*

— Robert Ellis,
See Naples and Die

During World War I, as the Austrians and Italians fought it out in the Tyrol Mountains, soldiers discovered the effectiveness of launching explosives onto the slopes above each other, bringing down avalanches that killed far more effectively than their weapons. Colin Fraser has estimated the loss of life from avalanches in the war to have been between forty thousand and eighty thousand. In one account of the Tyrolean campaign, entitled *Kampf über die Gletschern* ("Battle over the Glaciers"), and reported by Fraser, a soldier breathlessly exclaimed that "the White Death" had claimed countless victims in the mountains. "The snowy torrents are like the deep sea; they seldom return their victims alive. The bravest of the brave are covered by the heavy winding sheet of the avalanche. It is no glorious death at the hands of the enemy; I have seen the corpses. It is a pitiful way to die, a comfortless suffocation in an evil element."

Avalanches had proven so effective a weapon in previous mountain conflicts that an American named Frank Harper decided to outline their use for troops in World War II. "The practice of loosening snow avalanches from their hollows and hurling them down upon the enemy cost not only hundreds but thousands of lives," he wrote in his 1943 book, *Military Ski Manual.* "Patrols worked their way up the steepest mountain walls and started the avalanches by throwing a rock, or sometimes by a well-aimed shot from a howitzer that could be fired from a distant position." One Great War veteran told Harper that there was "nothing simpler" than causing deadly avalanches to drop on the Alpini, the Italian mountain troops. "We waited seven hours for the Alpini. We laid the rope around the snow-crest; each of us held a rope-end in his fist. When the enemy came, there was nothing left to do but saw the rope into the crest; we waited until the column was below us. There was nothing but smoking snow to be seen, and nothing but a terrible thundering to be heard. We followed the avalanche, on trouser-seats and boot-soles, and rescued seventy-five men from the snow." Clearly, if the United States was going to fight effectively on a European continent split down the middle by mountains and—who could say?—in the mountains of east Asia, American troops would need specialized training.

During the early stages of the Second World War, millions of Americans had seen newsreels of Finnish soldiers in hooded all-white bodysuits, looking like armed scientists working in outdoor "clean rooms," attacking the Soviets on skis and then slipping away before their ill-trained enemies knew what hit them. Because so much of the European theater was defined and protected by mountain ranges, penetrating these impossible lines of defense became one of the war's most intriguing challenges. Heavy artillery and troop transport were impossible luxuries; what was needed were quick-moving, flexible ski troops. Harper drew clear distinctions between "soldiers on skis" and "alpine ski troops," the latter a highly specialized group of winter mountaineers who knew as much about thriving in the world's most inhospitable climates and terrains as they did about firing rifles or throwing grenades. The trained alpine force would be "a ski troop on the steep slope of a mountain, every man equipped with a submachine gun strapped to his side, equipped with dagger and hand-grenades; each in a white hood and white cape," Harper wrote. "They race downhill with enormous speed, almost invisible in the white eternity of the mountains, and almost noiseless; a ghostly regiment. Behind them come machine guns and field pieces on sledges, every piece hooded in white. Armed with speed, the troop penetrates the forest region of the mountain, overruns the enemy's outposts scattered in the wood, and pushes irresistibly down into the hostile village."

One way to penetrate the German front would be a surprise attack in the mountains of Italy, but high altitude fighting required a level of training never before undertaken by the United States Army. In November 1941, after a year and a half of lobbying Washington, Charles Minot Dole, the head of the National Ski Patrol System, was finally encouraged to recruit the country's best skiers and mountaineers to begin training. Early recruits received technical rock climbing instruction in the Seneca Rocks of West Virginia, where they drove some 75,000 pitons into the mountain walls; a military climbing guide used at the time, entitled *Manual of American Mountaineering*, became a civilian climbing bible after the war was over. But the mountain troops began to garner their first real notoriety during their training on Washington's Mount Rainier, where their effect on the national media was pronounced. "They are getting in trim by leaps and bounds—leaps from paratroop transport planes into ten-foot snow banks and bounds up the rocky facades of some of our best western mountains," exclaimed *Popular Mechanics* in December 1942, one year after Pearl Harbor. "To these lean, hard, bronzed mountaineers, a polar expedition would be little more than a weekend holiday. They'll scout miles through forests and across treacherous ice fields, often with thousand-foot cliffs falling away at one side of the trail, and then turn in at night to slumber snug in a two-pound sleeping bag at 50 degrees below zero."

Later the division relocated to Camp Hale, near the town of Pando, about 20 miles outside of Leadville, 9,500 feet above sea level in the Colorado Rockies. One eager candidate submitted a letter of recommendation to Dole that said, "This nominee will not become lost if there is no sun to go by. He will not starve if he has no rifle with which to shoot game. He will not freeze if he has no cover and snow is on the ground. I know because I teached him myself. Signed, His Big Brother Hiram." The candidate was accepted.

Among others who accepted the challenge were some of the most rugged and experienced outdoorsmen from both Europe and the United States, including Walter Prager, twice a winner of Europe's Gold Kandahar ski race and a former coach at Dartmouth College; Torger Tokle, a Norwegian who held most American ski jump records; and Paul Petzoldt, an American mountaineer and later the founder of the National Outdoor Leadership School, who, during a 1938 attempt on K2, the second-highest mountain in the world, had climbed to 26,000 feet, the highest point ever reached at the time. Also signing up were David Brower, who would later become the head of the Sierra Club, the founder of Friends of the Earth, and one of the country's most influential environmental activists, and Friedl Pfeiffer, who later became coach of the U.S. Ski Team. Those who agreed to help train the men included Arctic explorers from Sweden, Antarctic explorers from England, meteorologists, dog-team drivers, and mountain rescue experts, notably Ome Daiber, the Seattle-based mountaineer who was a cofounder of the national Mountain Rescue Council. In all, it was the finest collection of wilderness experts ever assembled, a group that over the next five decades would change the way North America thought about its mountains.

The mountain troops trained for three full years, waiting for a call to fight. The conditions in Colorado were particularly severe—winter temperatures were often well below zero—and the training brutal. When it opened in December 1942, Camp Hale had barracks for 14,000 men, corrals for 5,000 mules, and kennels for 200 dogs. Although the surrounding mountains gave the camp a dramatic backdrop, they also created serious health problems for the troops, locking in the coal exhaust from passing trains and causing countless cases of "Pando Hack." A visiting *Denver Post* reporter wrote that "its streets are rivers of mud. Its parade ground is a sea of the same. . . . It is not a pretty sight to see these spring days. But its men are. For in no place in this war-torn globe will you find better specimens of physical manhood."

These were also the troops who pinned pictures of mountains above their bunks rather than starlets. Francis Sargent, a former governor of Massachusetts and a 10th Mountain veteran, remembered his peers, while on leave, climbing up the sides of Denver hotels. "My God, half of the sonuvaguns in the outfit would rather go climb some rock than go down to town and look for booze and broads. I remember thinking it was the damnedest thing to act like that. But, of course, when the 10th got a few drinks under their belts they'd go into their hotel climbing act, which no other outfit could top. And there never was anything wrong with the 10th when it came to girls, come to think of it— not once they came down the mountains and got their skis off, anyway."

While in training, however, the men were constantly sick from the unprecedented physical duress and exposure to cold and altitude. Another newspaper report noted that the troops, "after 40 days, have to be able to carry a 75-pound pack 20 miles in 8 hours at 12,000 feet above sea level—this while on snowshoes." In a memoir of his experiences in the 10th Mountain Division, Robert Ellis reprinted a letter he wrote home in April 1943 describing the legendary "D-Series" training maneuvers, which an official army report called "the most grueling training test ever given to any U.S. Army Division." During a storm that would dump eight feet of new snow in the high mountains and drop temperatures to 30 below zero, some 12,000 troops left their barracks on skis and snowshoes for six weeks of training maneuvers. Soldiers carried some 90 pounds of gear on their backs, and practiced war games at 13,000 feet. One day, more than 100 cases of frostbite had to be evacuated.

Easter weekend 1943 was the worst. Saturday night, Ellis and his regiment started on snowshoes and skis through snow up to their waists. They hiked until 1:30 A.M., then laid out their sleeping bags and fell asleep in the snow. They were awakened two and a half hours later, packed up their gear in a snowstorm, and began climbing again to outflank another regiment. With no sleep, empty stomachs, and suffering from extreme cold, they hiked through a blizzard for four hours, when Ellis and another soldier fell out to rescue a companion who had fainted in the snow. After building a shelter and snatching some rest, Ellis and his mate, by now without food or water other than handfuls of snow for thirty-six hours, had to hike 15 miles to the next nontactical "problem area," where they stayed for a day and two nights. "My feet were covered with blood from where the snowshoe laces and shoepacs had cut my feet and toes. The medics bandaged me up, and when Wednesday rolled around I was ready again. Everything went all right until Friday when I got dysentery somehow, and was up all Thursday night as well as Friday morning. Feeling terribly weak and nauseated I again left the forced march and was given medical attention at the battalion aid station. I rested for a couple of hours, and then set off to find the company.

"I caught up with them about noon, and we hiked on in regimental offensive until 10:00 P.M. We slept until 4:30 A.M. and continued the attack until around noon when the problem ended. They decided the men could no longer stand two more weeks of maneuvers, so the ordeal ended after three weeks. We made the 20-mile trip back to camp and arrived really tired. Along with other discomforts my back and shoulders broke out with sores, my fingers cracked at the ends, my ears were frozen once, etc. I've been tired many times but never so completely washed out in every way. The never-ending snow and standing for hours in an icy fox hole was almost unbearable."

By the time the "D-Series" was over, the army reported the "proud record" of no fatalities and only 195 cases of frostbite, 340 injuries, and nearly 1,400 cases of sickness, including more than a total 1,100 evacuations. One account of military training noted that the 10th Mountain Division, "the most elite U.S.

Division in the twentieth century in terms of intelligence scores, fitness and training," suffered five times more illnesses and injuries preparing for combat than any other American division in the Second World War.

The ski troops became one of the most glorified branches of the military, with press and newsreel coverage of their high mountain training a point of great national pride. But the troops were itching to put their training to work. Finally, in December 1944, army brass decided that knocking the Nazis off their perch high atop a mountain ridge in the Italian Apennines would allow Allied forces to take control of Highway 64, a major supply route to Bologna 35 miles north of Florence. But the ridge was well protected; some 80 guns covered the approach, and all the roads and bridges were heavily mined. Nicknamed Operation Encore, the unprecedented plan was to have climbers trained by the 10th Mountain Division scale a 2,000-foot vertical wall the Germans thought impregnable and take the enemy by surprise. When the Americans arrived in Italy, they were greeted by air-dropped German leaflets that read: "You have seen Naples, now you will die. This is not Camp Hale, where you had 15,000 men skiing at the foot of Tennessee Pass."

The audacious plan to capture the German stronghold on Mount Belvedere called for advance troops first to knock out a heavily armed perch atop a ridge called Serrasiccia-Campiano in Italian, but known to the Americans as Riva Ridge. At 7:30 P.M. on February 18, soldiers trained in technical rock climbing began fixing ropes to the wall leading up the ridge. One by one, climbing all night, the mountain troops followed the course up the face. A dusting of new snow covered the rock face and upper slopes of the mountains. Searchlights behind the combat area scanned the low-hanging wall of clouds and reflected a scattered, shadowy light over the slopes below. But the valley itself and the ridges were dark. Climbing in the dead of night, lead climbers hammered steel pitons into the rock, attached carabiners and ropes, and offered fixed lines to those who followed. When the advance teams reached the top around midnight, they signaled to the battalion units below that they could begin their ascent in force. These units each took a different route up the face of the cliff, hidden by the haze that hung over the mountains. "With a biting and wet wind whipping them about, the climbers clamored cautiously up the wet rocks with the aid of the preset ropes, fearful that any dislodged rock that clattered down the cliff face would be followed by bursts of enemy machine guns and grenades," veteran Robert Ellis recalled. "Inevitably some rocks did fall, causing the climbers to halt in dread anticipation of the hail of death to follow. 'Perfect fear casteth out love,' joked the Briton Cyril Connolly in his travesty of I John 4:18, and members of the 10th came to fully appreciate the remark in this introduction to combat."

The climb took all night. By 4:00 A.M. the next day, the 10th Mountain Division battalions had climbed over the top and completely surprised the Germans. For two days the two sides exchanged gunfire, until other American units were able to make the climb and overtake the German stronghold. While the mission was a complete success, allowing the Allies to capture not just Riva Ridge but Mount Belvedere and the entire ridgeline, five days of intense fighting left the mountain troops with heavy casualties, and more would die as the troops advanced through Italy's Po Valley. Private First Class Richard Ryan wrote home of the horror his 85th Regiment encountered. "Roads choked with dust when the tanks went by. My feet blistered. Now and then a dead Yank sprawled on the road; or a German with the top of his head sliced nearly off. Went through a village completely bombed out—leveled. The smell of death hung over that little village like a cloud."

By the time the war ended, 992 of the 14,000 10th Division had been killed, and 4,000 more wounded. Remarkably, only one American officer was taken as a prisoner of war, a Jewish battalion surgeon from Montana by the name of Morton Levitan.

On top of Mount Belvedere, Levitan left his aid station in the early afternoon of February 22, 1945, to treat a badly wounded soldier up on the ridge. "After I checked the first seriously injured soldier up there, I persisted and did not return as I had intended with the litter bearers," Levitan reported. "I should have suspected I was going the wrong way when the sniper started firing rapidly and I could hear bullets ricocheting from the rocks to my right. But I didn't think this was quite the moment to stop and think things over, and kept running. Suddenly, a German soldier stood up a little to the left of the path. I stopped. We looked at each other a few moments. As I was running, not carrying a gun or anything in my hands, he didn't point his rifle at me. He took me down a short path to a dugout just below the trail. The dugout was well constructed, even had polka-dot red curtains on the windows. One German was snoring away on a top bunk, never woke up while I was there. There was another soldier and the one I had run into hung around curious to hear my story, and a young officer who couldn't have been much over twenty. I hadn't even caught my breath when he asked me if I knew who was responsible for the war. I answered, 'No, who?' He said, 'The Jews.' I said, 'I'm a Jew.' He smiled benignly at me, assuming I had misunderstood, and corrected me.

'No, I didn't mean that you were a Jew. I meant that the Jews are responsible for the war.' To which I rejoined, 'I understood what you said. I'm a Jew.' Well, that stopped the conversation."

Over the next two months, Dr. Levitan was tramped through the Italian countryside along with a number of other prisoners of war, and by mid-April was loaded onto a train bound for Germany. Soon afterward, the train was bombed by Allied planes on the Brenner Pass, and forced to retreat to a camp in the town of Brennero. When it moved out again a few days later, a German sergeant made sure, with a single word, that the prisoners took note of a landmark outside the passing train. Dachau.

The camp northeast of Munich where Levitan and other Allied officers were imprisoned was under the supervision of the Luftwaffe, which in an odd twist turned out to be fortunate for the prisoners. As the Allies advanced, the SS decided to make the officers march to a mountain camp for a final stand, but the Luftwaffe officials wouldn't allow it. Three weeks later, tanks driven by the American 4th Army rolled into town, and Dr. Levitan was free to return to Montana, unharmed.

By 1959, Dr. Levitan had set up a practice with the Veterans Administration Hospital in Helena, Montana, where Arthur Martin, Ray's father, became one of his patients. Dr. Levitan passed on his love for the mountains to his son Mark; Mark's enthusiasm for the mountains paralleled that of the young Kanzler boys, whose path he would fatefully cross years later. Dr. Levitan and Mark had scaled the Grand Teton in Wyoming through the National Outdoor Leadership School, founded by fellow 10th Mountain Division veteran Paul Petzoldt. Like a lot of other young climbers, Mark was unusually intelligent, and seemed drawn to technical climbing by the mechanical challenges it offered. Even today, when studying an approach to a rock face, climbers—sounding like the professional physicists that many of the best in fact are—will refer to a wall's "problems" that merely need solving. Walls in which nonclimbers would see only glasslike smoothness, or impassable overhanging cliffs, or unfathomable traverses, are merely rich with "problems" that an experienced climber will solve with little difficulty. Indeed, climbers, also like physicists, grant their highest admiration to those who can solve the most difficult problems with the most elegance, grace, and economy.

When it came time to pick a college, Mark, whose thick glasses gave him an air more scholarly than rugged, decided to head east to Columbia, entering the fall before one of the university's most tumultuous years, 1968. In April, Mark's first spring in New York, Columbia students protesting the Vietnam War occupied five buildings; soon afterward, the administration and police cracked down and arrested some 700 people. As a navy ROTC student and the son of a Jewish military doctor who had been taken prisoner of war, Mark did not share the raw antimilitary sentiments of his peers. "He got disgusted with the way the school gave in," Dr. Levitan recalled. "He despised them for kowtowing to the students." After his freshman year, Mark transferred back to Montana State University in Bozeman, about 90 miles east of Butte. Since Montana State did not have an ROTC program, Mark had signed up for further navy training in San Francisco, to begin preparing for Vietnam.

If he struggled with the political upheaval in New York, one thing Mark wasn't doing at Columbia was climbing mountains. Back at Montana State, however, he enrolled in Peter Lev's ski mountaineering class, and soon became friends with another bookish part-time climber named James Anderson, whose interest in the mountains also seemed as intellectual as it was physical. An Eagle Scout, Anderson had graduated from Bigfork High School, where he was a halfback on the football team and a half-miler in track. "There is not a single memory in my mind of Jim that was not of complete happiness and contentment," Anderson's scoutmaster recalled. "The only reprimand I ever gave the boy in five years of scouting was for being too brave. What a wonderful flaw!" He played cornet in his high school band, and sang in the chorus. The Andersons had moved to Montana from Minnesota in 1946 so James's father, Ed, who had nearly died of pneumonia, could find a drier climate. By the late sixties, James had three brothers and three sisters, a tightly knit group that became all the closer after their parents' divorce. A geology major while at Montana State, James had organized the Mission Ski Club, but had also become deeply interested in Eastern philosophy. "He was a great searcher, beyond the run of young men of his age," said Father D. A. Okorn, Anderson's Catholic priest. "He would ask himself, what is the meaning of life? What is a human being?"

James Anderson's contemplative side was mirrored in Jerry Kanzler, another MSU student who considered mountains to be not only challenges to his formidable athletic skills, but as places where he could escape the pressures of family life. Like most teenage boys, Jerry had sometimes chafed under the tension of living at home with his parents, and would head for the hills at the slightest provocation. When Hal and Jean quarreled, Jerry would hit the road. He traveled less and less frequently with his dad, whose demeanor seemed to have darkened considerably in recent years. Hal's trips into the mountains seemed less joyous, more strained, than when his sons were younger, as though he were having trouble working through some of the domestic pressures back in the valley. To his peers, Hal Kanzler seemed not to have fully shed the traits that had served him so well as a Marine Corps captain in Okinawa. He was hard on himself, hard on his friends, and, it seems, especially hard on his sons.

"He wore me out mentally whenever we got together to plan a political action, a research program, or a magazine story," George Ostrom would later write in a newspaper tribute to Hal. "Two times he pushed me physically to the point where I had blood in my shoes and then he said 'Let's try for one more mile.' I can only make suppositions as to what it was like to be the wife or son of such a man, but I know very well what it was like to be the friend of him. In my opinion, Hal had one weakness, and that was his inability to recognize the basic frailties of man. He was highly intolerant of human weakness, and because of this attitude he found it difficult to demonstrate his true feelings toward those he loved and toward those he respected. When a situation arose which called for tenderness or diplomacy, he usually found this the only situation in which he was uncomfortable. I believe he never completely found the answer to this problem . . ."

In fact, there was a brooding side to Kanzler that seemed to arise more frequently as he got older. Hardened as he was—by his experience in the war, his friends imagined—his emotional landscape in his mid-forties came to seem as jagged as the mountains around him. "He had seen his buddies blown up in front of him, saw the big guns on the ships hit his friends and blow them to pieces," his wife, Jean, said. "People just kept dying on him." Back home, Hal's prodigious physical energy was occasionally matched by a repressed ferocity that left those around him chilled; the anger he swallowed still emanated around him like a vapor. Calling Kanzler's demeanor "depressed," although perhaps clinically accurate, would do its complexity a disservice. He had been a leading figure in his community and a mentor to his sons, and if his peers thought of him as a stern man, they forgave his intensity in light of his rectitude. Besides, he kept his troubles to himself. Perhaps, in the end, like many veterans of his time and ours, he was unable to fully balance himself or return contentedly to civilian life. Domestic affairs, even when punctuated by excursions into the Montana wilderness, left him feeling boxed in. "Even as a kid, I knew Hal was driven," says Terry Kennedy, a close friend of Jimmy's. "I remember him saying that he knew too many friends who were killed in the war, that he was going to live his life for his buddies as hard as he could and as long as he could."

As it turned out, Hal's life began to seem harder and harder. There was word of explosive anger, of fights with his wife. It seemed as if his unquiet mind could only reach equanimity when exhausted by the rigors of difficult terrain. In a 1966 letter to a friend, written when he was forty-five, Hal wrote of the considerable physical energy he still enjoyed, and of his passion for the hills. He had lost little of the drive he had as a younger man, he wrote, and looked forward to many more years of backcountry exploration. Nonetheless there was, as there always seemed to be when Hal spoke of his plans, an air of wistfulness to his words, as if he sensed the shortage of time in his life. If he lived fifty more years, he sensed, he still could not take all the photos he wanted, or reach all the Montana summits.

Increasingly, as he aged, Hal's exuberance seemed to be peppered more frequently with anger and reproachfulness. Although they had stood loyally by him in their early adolescence, watching their father's black moods turn clear once he got up in the hills, Jerry and Jimmy, as they got older, looked forward to getting out of the house. It was difficult watching a man they as youngsters had adored, who had taught them so much about the backcountry, becoming so bitter, so intractable. What was driving his anger? His boys had no idea. By the time he was sixteen, Jerry, shy, independent, and sensitive, felt particularly uneasy around his father's sharp edges, and took to the road more and more frequently. This was not the father he wanted to remember. The father he knew was a sportsman, a philosopher, a man devoted to the holy high places.

Late in January, Jimmy Kanzler woke up in the middle of the night with a nightmare that his little brother was falling off a mountain. He didn't ponder the dream until later, but in hindsight it seemed an ominous sign. Just a few days after this, well before dawn on the morning of January 21, 1967, Jerry got up to hitchhike the 90 miles from Butte to Bozeman to ski at Bridger Bowl. His zeal for skiing was not unusual; he had gone to great lengths before to get into the mountains. But his determination to leave the house that morning struck his brother, Jim, as something more, as a reaction to the confines of living at home as a teenage boy. Whatever the reason, Jerry was not at home when, later that morning, his father took out a beautiful, Western-style single-action Smith & Wesson .44 Special revolver, which he himself had fitted with carved elk antler grips, and shot himself in the chest.

Chapter 5

✻

*Only when men become as gods
will they have full knowledge of the
nature of beauty, and meanwhile they may
follow all sorts of paths in their pursuit of it.
It is the pleasantest of all life's quests, and
the climber, as he pursues his pilgrimage, is
reminded at every stage of it that he is in
the right way. From start to finish he has the
pageant of the sky enacted daily and nightly,
and he is in the best place of all to see.*

— R.L.G. Irving, *The Romance
of Mountaineering,* 1938

Hal Kanzler's suicide came as a shock to his entire community. Considered a model of Montana fortitude and dignity by his neighbors and fellow employees, he had apparently so masked his depression that few would understand his final action even decades later. Certainly, in its fierce emotional rigidity and physical discipline, Kanzler's life fit a pattern of terse masculinity made notorious by Ernest Hemingway, who had used a shotgun to end his own life across the border in Idaho just a few years before. Aggressiveness, frustration, and rage had for years been vented in the mountains, alpine winds cooling minds overheated in the low country of domestic life. In the end, perhaps as legs grew weary, the old dark impulses were jammed back down, pushed off on wives and children. And finally, violently, released.

It fell to Jim, the eldest son, to drive to the ski resort and tell his brother the news. "It was like I stabbed him with a large knife," Jim recalled. "He reacted physically." Jean Kanzler, in her terrible grief, asked her elder son to get rid of the pistol Hal had used to end his life, and Jim obliged by giving it to Ray Martin for fifty dollars, on the condition that the two friends would reverse the sale if Jim ever decided he wanted the weapon back. Distraught, Jean and her sons moved to Bozeman, 90 miles southeast, just three weeks later.

George Ostrom heard the news of Hal's death upon his return from a brief vacation, and was terribly shaken. "Hal Kanzler demanded a lot from the mind and body God gave him," Ostrom wrote in a tribute to Hal in the *Hungry Horse News,* and later reprinted in his own *Kalispell's Weekly News.* "Perhaps he demanded too much, but however anyone else may judge him, I am positive of my own judgment. I have proudly shed few tears in my manhood life, but last Saturday night when I came home from Big Mountain and found that Hal Kanzler was dead, I cried, and I knew the world had lost one helluva man, and I explained it that way to my eldest son."

What impact Hal Kanzler's death had on his sons is hard to quantify. One can only wonder at the confusion left by such a man, who had been so highly charged in everything he undertook but who ended his life so suddenly, and so violently. Perhaps his volatile energy had no other place to go. Perhaps, in the end, even the Montana wilderness was not enough to quiet his mind. One thing about the aftermath is certain. His boys continued to climb mountains. "What Hal's death did to those boys was terrible," Ostrom said. "All of a sudden they were out there risking their lives needlessly, trying to prove something to their father. We always felt a little guilt, wondering how much we encouraged these kids to do dangerous things." Six months after Hal's death, the Kanzler brothers—with no father to tell them not to use their carabiners on difficult rock faces—began making plans with Pogreba and Martin to become the first ever to climb Glacier's Citadel Spire, a 7,750-foot peak topped by a 350-foot pinnacle protruding up from Porcupine Ridge. This was no simple climb; a black-and-white photograph Pogreba took of the ridge looks like a crude wall made by wet sand dripped through the fingers of a child. The four boys, accompanied by half a dozen friends who tagged along to watch, caught a boat from Waterton, a tiny Canadian border town, to the Goat Haunt ranger station on the American side of the park, and walked three miles to Kootenai Lake through ice-cold swamps and nearly impenetrable thickets of willows. An hour and a half of bushwhacking—a hardship made exhilarating by the sight of a moose and a grizzly—brought them to the base of the spire, and 300 feet of hard scrambling brought them to the wall.

The boys roped up, and put on their helmets for protection against the cascading rocks, which throughout the climb threatened to knock them senseless.

Their first pitch allowed them to traverse the face to the spire's south side, around an exposed vertical rib of rock. After hammering an angle piton into the crumbly rock to protect against a sudden fall, they climbed up a large crack, driving more pitons 25, 40, and 60 feet above the first one. The final pitch proved difficult, mostly because of the rotten rock that gave way with each step upward; relief from the raining rocks came only as the team was able to walk the last few feet to the summit—the first people ever to arrive. At the top of the peak, the boys took a self-portrait: from left to right, the photo shows Clare Pogreba, Jerry Kanzler, Jim Kanzler, and Ray Martin. Between Pogreba and Jerry, as if posing for the photograph, is the dramatic visage of the north face of Mount Cleveland.

Plainly, the boys had chosen their next challenge, and soon began planning a climb that even they seemed to know would be life-threatening. "After Citadel it was obvious to us that Cleveland would be next," Jim Kanzler said. "Pogreba was the driving force. He said he knew he wouldn't make it to thirty—whether it was going to be in a car or on a mountain, he knew he wasn't going to live a long life." Indeed, there may have been some of the same forces at work in Pogreba as there were in Jim's father; both were single-minded, driven, able to galvanize other climbers with their exuberance for the hills. Pogreba had the added advantage of youth; his body was in its muscular prime, his climbing skills highly refined. He was a nimble climber with an as-suredness that came from having confronted precarious situations in the past and overcome them. He trusted his ability to read a situation, however threat-ening, and react spontaneously. His confidence was infectious.

The boys' pride in their ascent of Citadel Spire was evident to all who knew them. Pogreba broke from the group's tradition of keeping their exploits quiet by writing a piece about the climb for *Summit,* one of the leading climbing magazines of the day. On July 18, 1967, a handwritten letter arrived at the home of Arthur and Ruby Martin from their son Ray at Montana Technical College. "Dear Art," the letter began. "This is a little something to let you know we appreciated the way you let us take over your house while we were there. We really had a good time! If we ever get up that way again you can be sure we'll stop in and see you; and I'm sure we'll be up again—after that *Great Face of Cleveland.*"

The letter was signed "From the guys who climbed Citadel Spire, Clare Pogreba, Jim and Jerry Kanzler, Ray Martin. Thanks, Ray."

Climbing Citadel, impressive in itself, had plainly fanned the boys' desire to climb a far more daunting peak, Cleveland's great north face. At 4,000 feet, the north face is one of the highest vertical walls in the United States, and in 1969, it had yet to be climbed. The boys' determination to attempt such a difficult ascent was in keeping with any serious climber's desire to stretch the boundaries of the sport. Since there were few pockets of the park that the boys hadn't explored on foot, the only challenges left were vertical. And since most peaks in the park had already been climbed, the only thing left to do was to scale intimidating faces that lesser climbers—or older climbers—wouldn't even consider. Jim Kanzler, who like many other climbing enthusiasts is an amateur historian of the sport, said that by the late sixties the only way for hotshot climbers to make their bones was to attempt highly technical climbs up increasingly challenging faces. "Historically, what did [the older generation] leave us? As the younger generation, you want to break new terrain, do something new. Kids now call it flashing—they drive by a wall in their cars, look at it, and do it. They don't want foreknowledge. Just figuring it out, making their own decisions, as opposed to reading about it in a guidebook and going up the dog route."

The young climbers' reverence for the peaks of Glacier continues to be shared by anyone who visits the park. Unlike the southern Rockies of Colorado, which boast 53 peaks over 14,000 feet, Montana's mountains are, in height at least, comparatively modest. Colorado's Rocky Mountain National Park alone has more than 100 peaks over 10,000 feet; only six mountains in Glacier are that high, a fact that makes hulking peaks like Mount Cleveland, at 10,448 feet, seem all the more daunting. Unlike other mountain ranges, there are no discernible foothills here. You come up the Flathead Valley from the south, or from the plains to the east, and there it is: a mighty fortress of mountains, rising without preamble from the flatland, beckoning and forbidding your approach. The mountains are visible from many miles off, and dominate the landscape much as the ocean dominates coastal New England. Even if one is looking the other way, the mountains are always there, filling both the geographical and the imaginative space.

The million acres of Glacier National Park are in fact shot through by parallel mountain chains, the Lewis and Livingstone ranges, and the park straddles both sides of the Continental Divide. In winter, because they grab and hold rain clouds moving in either direction, the mountains of Glacier are blanketed by incredible amounts of snow; along the divide, the average snowfall can reach 1,000 inches—more than 80 feet—per year. After the brutal winter of 1996–97, one member of the road crew plowing the Going-to-the-Sun

Road that bisects the park reported measuring 25 feet of snow beneath his bulldozer even as he pushed another 25 feet ahead of him.

Dubbed the Crown of the Continent by George Bird Grinnell, and the Backbone of the World by the Blackfeet Indians, the mountains of Glacier have become something of a mecca for geologists, who find in the park's rock, among other things, some of the oldest multicellular plant fossils in the world. Unlike the solid granite formations of Yosemite, or the volcanic peaks of the Cascades, the mountains in Glacier are sedimentary, made largely of a calcium-rich rock called dolomite. About a billion and a half years ago, what is now mountain was the bed of an ancient sea. For hundreds of millions of years, thousands of feet of mud settled to the bottom of this body of water. As the mud deepened, it became compressed by the weight of the soil and water above it, and eventually formed into rock—argillite, quartzite, limestone, and dolomite. Over time, the sea gradually filled, and, for a billion years, the rock sat solid and undisturbed, the topmost layer of a continental plate that was drifting west toward a collision with a Pacific plate bearing islands the size of California and Alaska. During the collision between these plates, which occurred between sixty million and seventy million years ago, the Pacific plate dived beneath the North American plate, and heaved the floor of the dry sea vertically, folding and faulting it into a chain of mountains 300 miles long, 50 miles across, and 20,000 feet thick: Glacier National Park.

Besides the formation of the sedimentary rock, of course, the defining event in the lives of the northern Rockies was the activity of glaciers, which gouged out the tremendous valleys and steep rock walls that lend the park its singular majesty—a "geologic opera," as David Rockwell, a Glacier natural historian, has called it. Glaciers the size of Antarctica arrived in the area two million years ago and retreated only ten thousand years ago, grinding, scooping, and sculpting the rock into the shape it assumes today. The glacier-gorged Lake McDonald, which greets visitors driving along the Going-to-the-Sun Road, is 472 feet deep.

Where the glaciers receded, valleys are now filled with lush forests and meadows. Living within the park are several hundred mountain goats and bighorns, which so captured Hal Kanzler's imagination; some 3,000 elk create trails that hikers often find more hospitable than whacking their way through the fierce underbrush. The North Fork Valley and the Belly River Valley, which define the western and eastern edges of the park, are among the only places in the continental United States in which the entire top of the food chain is intact: black bears and grizzly bears, mountain lions and wolverines and coyotes; even timber wolves are starting to make a return after decades of relentless hunting, trapping, and poisoning. It is, in effect, a backpacker's paradise, in large part because it has been saved from man's overuse.

The several forks of the Flathead River run remarkably high in spring, carrying snowmelt from the mountains and turning a gray-green from glacial debris. The rivers are famous for cutthroat trout, and bullhead and kokanee salmon are abundant as well, providing great quantities of food for the local birds of prey. In one year, 352 bald eagles were spotted along a one-mile stretch of McDonald Creek. Because they straddle the Continental Divide, the mountains of Glacier provide spring snowmelt to a number of different watersheds. From one mountain, Triple Divide Peak, water drains west, pouring eventually into the Columbia River and thus the Pacific Ocean; north, winding its way to Hudson Bay; and southeast, finally pouring into the Gulf of Mexico.

With its high mountains acting as a kind of catch basin for winds from both east and west, the park is graced with more than 1,000 plant species and 100 different wildflowers, many of whose seeds have blown in from out of state. Depending on the elevation, a hiker will find a rainbow of wildflowers: yellow glacier lilies, burnt orange Indian paintbrush, purple asters, blue lupines. Individual plants, like individual peaks, carry their own stories: bear grass, a three-foot-high stalk topped with what looks like a scoop of lemon sherbet, is eaten not by bears but by elk. Bladderwort and sundew are carnivorous, preferring a diet of insects and crustaceans; white globeflower grows on glaciers; locoweed induces insanity; mountain death camas poisons; sarsaparilla heals.

Because the climate is both northern and elevated, there are only about 18 kinds of trees in the park, including larch (conifers that nonetheless lose their leaves in the fall) and 30 shrubs and bushes, notably the huckleberry, which grizzly bears love above all other food. Once, at the height of the huckleberry season, Jim Kruger, a helicopter pilot who has flown over the park for more than thirty years, saw 50 foraging grizzlies inside ninety minutes.

Established as a park in 1910, Glacier in its early years saw just 4,000 visitors a year, many of them horsepackers who rarely ventured up into the high peaks. By the 1960s, with interest in the outdoors in full swing, more than a million people were coming every year—many of them to scramble up slopes that, although not exceedingly tall, were nonetheless physically challenging. Indeed, it wasn't until the 1950s that the park's rangers even considered high mountain work to be part of their job description. With so many people hiking—and finding trouble—in the backcountry, rangers needed to become expert climbers as well as naturalists and tour guides.

This was not an easy task. The mountains of Glacier comprise huge fractured cliffs and scree-covered slopes, similar in structure to rock faces of the Swiss Alps and the Italian Dolomites. The rock is so porous and friable that in several places, most famously on the Weeping Wall, along the Going-to-the-Sun Road, one can see water dripping straight out of the rock. The mealy rock, degraded by millions of years of rain and wind and snow, makes technical rock climbing significantly more dangerous than in places like Yosemite or the Tetons. Because the rock was formed underwater, rather than in the molten core of the earth, its individual layers tend to break off or slide under stress, particularly the argillite, a friable metasedimentary rock like shale, and the limestone and dolomite, which are also sedimentary and too soft to hold a piton. In other words, the leperous rock doesn't hold, it sloughs. "Most places, if the rock has good holds, you climb it," says a former park ranger named Willie Colony. "Here, holds come off in your hands—you take 'em out and look at 'em, put 'em back." Robert Madsen, another talented local climber and friend of Mark Levitan, who would go on to climb all over North America, has said he's been "more frightened climbing that crap in Glacier than [looking down from] 3,200 feet of granite in Yosemite."

Looming over all the other mountains in the north-central section of the park is Mount Cleveland, named for President Grover Cleveland in honor of the establishment of the Lewis and Clark Forest Preserve in 1898. Although the mountain is only a touch higher than several other peaks in the park, the summit affords unmatched views; in addition to the Glacier peaks stretching out to the south, one can look deep into Alberta and British Columbia to the north, into Idaho to the west, and, to the east, perhaps a hundred miles across the prairie. But it is not just the views that make Mount Cleveland so appealing to climbers, it is the mountain's remoteness, its remove. Because it is comparatively inaccessible, sitting miles and mountains away from any road, Cleveland cannot be driven to and climbed in a day, like other peaks in the park; there is no danger here of bumping into chubby tourists in black cotton socks. Better still, the peak looks over superior habitat for many of Glacier's largest mammals. The Kootenai Lakes region, for example, just a couple miles south of Waterton Lake, provides habitat for countless moose, and one of the continent's highest concentrations of grizzly bears. Cleveland's neighborhood is also exceedingly quiet, far from the hubbub of the park's centers of tourist activity. There is only the wind, blowing over the ridges.

The mountain itself is, in parts, utterly steep and bare. The grinding of glaciers and the ceaseless polishing effects of snow and rain have left the mountain looking severe, sharp-edged, barren. There are no pockets of trees, no places for climbers to hide, especially on the north face, which at its upper reaches is essentially a striated vertical wall. Even the most experienced climbers who had attempted the north face left shaking their heads. Marshall Gingery, a former Glacier employee and author of the trail map used during the 1960s, along with a physician named Tom Nichols, had started to climb the north face in September 1956, but had made it only to one of the high ridges, about three fourths of the way up. The summer before Pogreba and his boys would begin their ascent, the climbing-guidebook author J. Gordon Edwards had made it to the base of the north face with an eye toward climbing it in winter, but decided it wasn't possible. Coping with cascades of snow in addition to the warm weather troubles of falling rocks seemed foolish. "It's a big mountain broken up into spires, ridges, but not a winter climb. That's certain. I wouldn't try it."

The circumspection of members of the older generation offered a counterpoint to the determination of the young Montana climbers to scale peaks no matter how intimidating. Age—and too many close calls—have a way of bleeding off some of the bravado on which young climbers subsist. Ranger Willie Colony, who had pulled broken climbers off the floors of more than one national park said, when asked about the north face, "There's no way we can judge it climbable."

To those who knew Mount Cleveland, the broader west face was a more tenable, if less heroic, means to the summit. Topped by a vast amphitheater, or "cirque," formed by millennia of snowmelt and erosion, the west face offered a far easier route up. James Anderson had climbed the west face twice before with his brother Bud; the boys had overnighted near the summit. Bud remembers feeling thrust up among the stars, and peering out over the dark valley at "one of the most beautiful nights I ever saw." The Andersons' ascents, however, had been accomplished in summer; half a mile across, Mount Cleveland's bowl-shaped western face changed character dramatically in winter, its geometry making it exceedingly dangerous avalanche terrain with even the slightest snowfall. A climber caught in a bowl is at far greater risk than one on a flat slope, since a fracture line, running across the top of a bowl, can release the bowl's entire contents in one great rush. Climbing a bowl is like climbing half a funnel, the wider end above catching and compiling snow until it can no longer hold it all. Once the strain becomes too great, the snow dumps down the bowl from all sides, like sand pouring through an hourglass, and picks up momentum as it flows downhill. By the time the funnel narrows, toward the bottom, the snow is running fast, and very deep.

Plans for a winter ascent of the Great Face of Cleveland, as Ray Martin described it to his parents, began to come together in earnest in the summer of 1969, two and a half years after Hal Kanzler's suicide. As his summer job working the DEW Line in Alaska came to an end, Martin returned to catch up with his family and get back into the Montana mountains with Clare Pogreba. At twenty-two years old, Martin and Pogreba were the oldest in their group of climbers, and considered themselves the leaders in spirit, if not necessarily in ability; even they considered the Kanzler brothers to be superior mountaineers. To sharpen their skills before mounting an assault on Cleveland, and to sort out who would make up the team, they put out the word for a warm-up, Thanksgiving-break climb of Mount Wilbur, one of the most challenging mountains in the park. Jim Kanzler agreed to go, and convinced Jim Anderson and Mark Levitan, whom he had met at Montana State, to come along as well.

Although at the last minute Martin and Jerry Kanzler were unable to make it, the team was joined by a Swiss climber named Jurg Hofer, and Pat Callis, a chemistry professor at Montana State who had become a mentor to his younger climbing friends. Callis's presence alone had multiplied the mountaineering prowess of the fledgling Montana climbing community. While in college at Oregon State, Callis had climbed with the legendary Willi Unsoeld, a theology professor at the university and one of the first Americans atop Everest. Later, Callis enrolled in a doctoral program in chemistry at the University of Washington—where Unsoeld had also received his Ph.D.—in part because the school was near good climbing in the northern Cascades. During the 1960s, Callis had become one of the country's hottest young climbers. In 1963 he and his partner, Dan Davis, climbed the north face of Mount Robson, one of the prizes of the Canadian Rockies. Just the year before the Cleveland trip, he and the notorious Warren Harding had made a historic first ascent of Lost Arrow Direct in Yosemite. Closer to home, Callis had pioneered routes in the Humbugs outside of Butte, and, not long before the Cleveland trip, had found a new way up the north face of Lone Mountain, southwest of Bozeman. His partners were Jerry, Ray, Clare, and Peter Lev. Callis was so well regarded by fellow climbers that one protégé calls him "the Gandalf of Montana mountaineering."

For the most part, the Wilbur trip went according to plan, although the team was forced to spend a night up high in what turned out to be unexpectedly cold weather, with 80-mile-per-hour winds at the summit. Like the climb two years before of Citadel Spire, however, the ascent of Mount Wilbur from the outset was merely a prelude to Mount Cleveland. The timing seemed fortuitous: the weather in northern Montana had been unseasonably warm through November, and so far there had been little snow. "It was a really unusual fall," Pat Callis recalled. "There were hardly any storms. That was why we were out climbing. Most winter ascents get done during times like this—during lots of high pressure and no snow. Those guys were in love with the north face in a way that's hard to understand, but I understood it perfectly."

Jim and Jerry Kanzler's mother, Jean, was also well aware of their plans. "They designed some of their own equipment," she said. "They worked on ice. They climbed Mount Wilbur over the Thanksgiving holiday as a prelude to what they really wanted to do. Some people might have thought they were rinky-dinking around, but these boys were dead serious. They studied Mount Cleveland from every angle. They did the practice climbing for it. They were near professionals and rock climbing was their way of life."

Just a couple of weeks before the Cleveland trip, Jerry Kanzler, Pat Callis, and Peter Lev, the fine twenty-nine-year-old climber who had taught mountaineering skills to Jerry at Montana State, decided to make one more warm-up climb, this time in the Tetons. Lev and a team that included the respected winter climbing specialist George Lowe hoped to climb the east ridge of the Grand Teton; Callis and Kanzler and a couple of others were going to climb the Chouinard Chimney of Mount Owen, which had never been climbed in winter. Named for the pioneering climber Yvon Chouinard, the Chimney is a series of vertical stacks, gullies, and ledges that lead from a glacier straight to the summit of Mount Owen. Callis considered the Chimney "a dank nasty place in summer, but I thought a potential great ice gully in winter." With ice axes and crampons still in a relatively primitive state of development, the stretches of sheer ice climbing would be particularly trying; even the experienced Callis called the idea "audacious." Just as the teams were beginning their climbs, one of the first big storms of the season blew in and began dumping snow. Still down at the base of the mountain, Callis and Kanzler decided to wait out the storm inside a hastily built snow cave. Higher up, Lev's group, which had gotten a head start, began retreating quickly in the face of the blizzard. Perhaps because of their collective weight, or simply because of the instability of the slope, the Lev group kicked loose an avalanche that descended within spitting distance of Callis and Kanzler's cave while they were still inside. "The wind blast and ice cloud were incredible," Callis said. "We knew something wild was happening. I crawled out of the hole and couldn't see a thing, just a horizontal wind blast. That tempered my attitude." Both teams abandoned their climb and drove home. Jerry Kanzler in particular didn't want to do anything foolish so close to the attempt on the real prize, the Great Face of Mount Cleveland.

Chapter 6

✳

*It is difficult to protect oneself against ice
sheets sliding down from above which are
capable of hurling entire caravans into the
gaping abysses.*

— Strabo,
Geographica IV 6, 6, A.D. 16

About the time that Jerry Kanzler and Pat Callis were coming back
from the Tetons, Jim Kanzler, back in Montana, was busy getting married and
having a son. He had also just landed a job as a ski patroller at the Bridger
Bowl; suddenly, the young mountaineer had a family to support. If the job
meant less time for rock climbing, at least Jim was still getting paid to work in
the mountains. Better yet, Jim was able to rub shoulders with some of the most
experienced avalanche men in the country, many of whom were 10th Mountain Division veterans who, on returning home, had sought places to apply
their unprecedented experience. In the decades following their return from
Riva Ridge, some 2,000 10th Mountain veterans became ski instructors; more
than 60 American ski resorts—including Aspen, Vail, Steamboat Springs, Sun
Valley, and Squaw Valley—were founded, managed, or had their ski schools
directed by former mountain troops.

One of the most pressing concerns for the veterans in charge of ski resorts in the West was—and remains—the control of avalanches, and part of Kanzler's responsibilities at the Bridger Bowl would be to learn the use of explosives. Perhaps because they were skiers first and soldiers second, 10th Mountain Division veterans in charge of avalanche control quickly turned to something they knew well—military artillery—to bring down snow slides before they fell on unsuspecting skiers. Military-issue howitzers had been in use by Forest Service personnel since the end of the Second World War, but a new weapon had recently been developed, jury-rigged for the mountains and tagged with a name that sticks to this day: the "avalauncher." A kind of mortar with a long barrel at one end attached to a compressed air cylinder, the avalauncher was initially known as a "soup gun" because it had been tested in the early 1960s by firing cans of soup, which resembled in size if not potency the charges that would later be used to trigger avalanches.

When it came to the use of heavy artillery in the mountains, there was only one man for Jim Kanzler to see: Monty Atwater. Atwater, another veteran of the 10th Mountain Division, had returned from the war and was immediately hired to research and control avalanches at Alta, a ski resort in the middle of one of the most notoriously dangerous mountain chains in North America, Utah's Wasatch, just east of Salt Lake City. With peaks rising sharply to 12,000 feet, the Wasatch are battered by weather from three directions: west from the Pacific; northwest from the Gulf of Alaska; and north from Canada. Winter snowfalls of 35 to 40 feet are not uncommon, and on such precipitous slopes, the snow does not grip the mountainside long before it cascades downward. Once a gaudy silver mining camp, Alta was so susceptible to avalanches that, in a vestige of Victorian concern for feminity, women were not allowed to stay in the mining camps in winter. The town had been nearly obliterated in the winter of 1863 by avalanches and forest fires that broke out when coal and woodstoves were overturned. With all the anchoring trees either knocked down, burned up, or cut for lumber or firewood, avalanches were worse than ever. In the winter of 1873–74, a slide destroyed half the town and killed 60 people. Ten years later, another avalanche in the same town killed 12 more, and in February of the following year 16 people were killed and the town almost completely destroyed. An unpublished masters thesis by Utah State University's Anthony Bowman has estimated that between 1865 and 1915 up to 250 people were killed by avalanches in Alta's Little Cottonwood Canyon alone.

Atwater's knowledge of mountains, combined with a bemused fearlessness in the face of routine danger, made him an ideal avalanche researcher; his own father had been one of the few survivors of a 1903 avalanche in Telluride, Colorado. Atwater's memoir, *The Avalanche Hunters,* is full of dramatic moments told with a wry detachment befitting a man whose job required not just that he work in the presence of killers but that he actively seek them out. His book includes the list of gear he picked up from Arnold's Army Supplies in New York City, which included nine 105-mm howitzers; one diving suit with drop seat; 2,750 fatigue hats; five cannon balls; and one knapsack full of frankfurters.

Taking a tip from the Swiss, who had been using explosives to defuse avalanches for years, Atwater began experimenting with charges in 1948, when he took an entire box of dynamite to a spot near the highway next to Alta's Mount Superior. "The echoes bounced energetically from mountainside to mountainside. Nothing else happened." Controlling avalanches, it seemed, required something more than blowing a big hole in the snow. Fortunately, Wasatch National Forest kept a supply of wartime demolition explosives called tetrytol, designed specifically for its shock power; tetrytol generates shock waves at 25,000 feet per second, nearly three times the rate of dynamite. Atwater decided to try out his new weapon on the snowpack built up on Rustler Face, a precipitous, avalanche-prone slope he referred to as "an unbroken mustang." Knowing little about the nature and effect of tetrytol, Atwater tossed the whole 20-pound haversack onto the Face. He got more than he bargained for. When the shock wave hit, Atwater felt like the top of his head had been sheared off. Sure enough, he recalled, "like a buck startled out of cover, a slab avalanche sprang into the air and went bounding down the slope."

What Atwater and his peers needed was a way to blow up snow without coming so close to blowing up themselves. In the early years, with so little history to go on, the Forest Service required that blasts in the mountains be fired electrically, which meant setting up an elaborate system of circuits and detonating equipment high on a mountain ridge. Forced to unroll wire from their detonating position all the way out to the avalanche slope, patrollers would have to tiptoe out onto faces they knew to be unstable, simply to place an explosive.

In 1956 avalanche experts began swapping electric ignition explosives for ignition caps and fuses, which allowed avalanche experts to make up a whole bagful of bombs before heading out onto the slopes. Once there—skiing by or even riding the chairlift up the mountain—they could simply light a fuse, toss the bomb, and move on, Atwater wrote, "like a newsboy delivering papers."

Also by the mid-1950s, they began using a recoilless rifle to deliver charges. Developed in the late stages of World War II, it is essentially a steel tube, open at both ends and powered by compressed gas; when fired, a window-shattering blast of gas out the rear launches the projectile from the front.

Perhaps typical for a branch of the Defense Department, the Utah National Guard figured that if a little artillery worked to control avalanches, perhaps a lot of firepower would work even better. Atwater was asked if he'd like to try out a 155-mm howitzer, with shells over six inches in diameter. "The muzzle blast alone would blow out every window at Alta," Atwater said, and requested 75-mm French surplus guns from World War I instead. These guns, standing atop a truck-mounted swivel, could turn 180 degrees and cover almost an entire mountain face from one position. With downhill skiing still in its infancy in the United States, the avalanche blasters did not have to concern themselves with hordes of weekend skiers interfering with their exploits. "Those were the halcyon years," Atwater wrote. "No one ever had so much fun hunting avalanches as we did, or ever will again. We learned something new every trip out. It was a time when a gunner could jump up and down in the parking lot, screaming, 'Look at that s.o.b. go!' The avalanche hunter of today is a serious man. Skiing is Big Business."

Needless to say, working with avalanches is also dangerous business, and Atwater did not manage to retire unscathed. In January 1951, after a two-day blizzard that dropped 38 inches of snow, Atwater was out with his partner, Hans Jungster, checking the slopes before turning skiers loose. In those days, he figured the only way to test the stability of slopes was to ski them. If they didn't slide under the feet of the snow rangers, presumably they wouldn't slide under anyone else. As the two experts crossed a series of fields, one would watch from a safe position while the other advanced; at one point, however, the new and inexperienced Jungster came onto a steep, concave chute called Lone Pine Gully, before Atwater was off it, and triggered an avalanche that released the entire slope at once. Atwater fell through the cascading snow until his skis hit the hard base of old snow underneath.

"I was knee deep in boiling snow, then waist deep, then neck deep," he wrote. "Through ankles and knees I felt my skis drift onto the fall line. But I was still erect, still on top of them. The books tell you, *If you're caught in an avalanche, try to ski out of it.* With mine trapped under six feet of snow I wasn't skiing out of anything.

"Very fast and very suddenly I made two forward somersaults, like a pair of pants in a dryer. At the end of each revolution the avalanche smashed me hard against the base. It was like a man swinging a sack full of ice against a rock to break it into smaller pieces."

Years of training and countless hours spent observing avalanches meant that Atwater knew exactly what he was in for. Tumbled violently beneath the snow and in utter darkness, he suddenly popped to the surface again, spat out a chunk of snow stuck in his mouth, and sucked in a breath of air. "I thought, 'So that's why avalanche victims are always found with their mouths full of snow. You're fighting like a demon, mouth wide open to get more air, and the avalanche stuffs it with snow." The next time he surfaced, Atwater took two lungfuls of air, and the cycle continued. "On top, take a breath, swim for the shore; underneath, cover up, curl into a ball. This seemed to go on for a long time, and I was beginning to black out again. Then I felt the snow cataract begin to slow down and squeeze. The squeezing was the result of the slow-down, with snow still pressing from behind. Whether from instinct or a last flicker of reason, I gave a tremendous heave, and the avalanche spat me onto the surface like a seed out of a grapefruit."

This narrow escape was just one of many in Atwater's career. During research at Berthoud Pass in Colorado with Dick Stillman, another avalanche hunter, the two began jumping on a slab to try to cut it loose with their skis. Suddenly, they heard a "Crrrrrump!" and the slab broke. Stillman made it to the safety of the trees, but Atwater got caught. Tumbled end over end, he was dragged over a sharp rock, got a sharp knock on the head, and ended up wrapped around a tree; he remembers only losing his temper and hitting the avalanche with his fists on the way down. The air temperature was ten below zero, and since Atwater was buried in snow, he figured that it must have been the cold that kept his legs from working. They looked straight, and he could wiggle his toes, so he wasn't paralyzed. It was only later that he realized that one third of the way from his hip to his knee, his leg had been 70 percent severed, probably as he was dragged over the rock. Once he had come to rest, the snow had acted as both a good coagulant and an anesthetic; later, Atwater was told by his doctor that there was no other place on the human body where he could have sustained a cut that big and lived to tell about it.

In the early 1950s, Atwater was joined at Alta by a man who over the years would become another of the deans of American avalanche research, Ed LaChapelle. LaChapelle had met his wife, Dolores, during a climb with the Alpine Club of Canada in the late 1940s; soon afterward, when he was offered a position with the Federal Institute of Avalanche Research in Davos, Switzerland, he proposed by mail, and Dolores accepted. Arriving in Alta in 1952, the couple moved with their two-week-old infant into a cabin accessible only by rope tow. Ed didn't have to look far for his research; during the winter of 1953, an avalanche came down behind their cabin, but was split by a rock and caused no damage.

Where the burly Atwater spent most of his time in the field, the slight, brainy LaChapelle was a full-time glaciologist, and soon became an expert on the formation of snow crystals and their effect on the development of avalanches. By the time the team was joined in 1966 by another leading snow researcher named Ron Perla, the Alta group's combined expertise had turned their avalanche study center into a world-class base of research. LaChapelle would go on to become a professor of atmospheric science and geophysics at the University of Washington; his 1961 book, *The ABC of Avalanche Safety,* remains one of the classics in the field.

As influential a scientist as Ed LaChapelle has been, there are few pioneers of winter sports who have so colorfully chronicled their experiences as Dolores. As a teenager in the mid-1940s, she bought her first pair of seven-foot hickory skis in her hometown of North Denver, and became so enamored of the sport that she took a teaching job in Aspen in 1947 just to be close to the slopes. "Aspen was full of men who had been in the mountain troops during the war, and they were taking a few years off to do what they wanted before they had to 'go to work,' " she writes in her 1993 memoir, *Deep Powder: 40 Years of Ecstatic Skiing, Avalanches, and Earth Wisdom.* "Skiing was what we were there for, and that was our life. All else came second in those first years—work, the daily hassles of getting along, sex, and material possessions except for skis."

Dolores may be the only person ever to thank an avalanche for helping her improve her sex life and change religions. During a rocky period in her marriage, she writes, she allowed a casual flirtation with another man to progress too far. While she contemplated her situation during a 1963 ski run in Alta powder, she got caught—and not by her husband.

"I tried the usual ploy. When an avalanche begins, if you can slam your skis down hard, often you can ski out of it; but this slope proved too steep for that. I slammed my skis down, but no hill was under them. I was in the air! Turning over and over. I thought, 'You don't live through this—flying through the air, but it's good I'm dying. I'm tired of this ongoing sexual battle.' Then I landed and I wasn't dead! What a shock. I had to think about getting some part of me out so they wouldn't have to probe for me; because if my husband, who would be called out on the rescue, had to probe I'd never be allowed to ski powder again. So I got one hand out before the snow quit moving. The moment it stopped, it settled into solid concrete; however, I could move my hand, so I knew it was out of the snow, and then I passed out. Since three of the other men were ski patrol, they dug me out quickly and I went on down the hill on a toboggan to the sheriff's car and to the hospital."

LaChapelle woke the next day to find herself in a body cast, but still able to move her toes, which meant she had not been paralyzed. Better yet, she decided, was the fact that since she hadn't died a martyr's death during the ordeal—which she had been willing to do to avoid having extramarital sex— she could now strip off her Catholicism. "Friends could not believe it was that easy for me," she wrote. "But it was that easy because the avalanche had made the decision for me." In a satire of the accident, which she wrote while in the hospital, LaChapelle created a conceit comparing avalanches to love affairs. "The comparison is quite apt since love of powder snow leads to these violent encounters. Always a new slope to conquer, always a new man—much the same thing until there comes the day when the slope does not yield to you but instead picks you up and hurls you through the air over cliffs, smashing you against trees and almost having its final way—of destroying you, the would-be conqueror."

If avalanches are mysteries even to those who spend their lives studying and skiing and climbing among them, they can go almost utterly unnoticed by those who show up at ski resorts expecting to find perfectly safe, groomed slopes. After leaving Alta, Monty Atwater moved to California's Squaw Valley, which despite being a one-lift, one-lodge area at the end of a dirt road had managed to win a bid to host the 1960 Winter Olympics. Laced with steep drops, Squaw would be holding ski races on a number of slopes like KT-22, which lay in avalanche paths. Before and during the Games, Atwater and his assistants used four 75-mm guns, two 105-mm recoilless rifles, and six blasting teams to keep the slopes safe. "Since it proved to be impossible to keep track of every Olympic group, each intent on its own job and unconscious of anything else, we had to scrap such refinements as hazard forecasting and ski testing. We simply blew and skied up everything, every day." During the games, the avalanche hunters invented three new control techniques: dropping bombs from lifts, cutting cornices with bangalore torpedoes, and using delayed-fuse projectiles to bring down hard slab avalanches. Spectators knew only that no one was hurt or killed by an avalanche, and at the end of the

Olympics, someone approached Atwater to kid him that perhaps all that artillery hadn't been needed after all, since there had been no deadly slides. Atwater told him that, in fact, there had been a few avalanches—137 to be exact—but they had been released safely under Atwater's oversight.

Explosives continue to be the most common form of avalanche control. The avalanche researchers Knox Williams and Betsy Armstrong report that some 100,000 hand charges—typically 80 percent gelatin dynamite or cylindrical canisters of TNT, specially made for avalanche use—are thrown onto American slopes every year. Because the vibrations released by the charges travel more efficiently through the air than through the snow, which, especially when wet, can absorb much of the spreading shock waves, charges are frequently strung out along a wire above a slope rather than dropped into the snowcover itself. Two-minute fuses give the bomb tossers enough time to retreat. Accidents are rare. Nonetheless, the millions of bombs that have been thrown since Monty Atwater first used them in the 1940s have killed or seriously injured at least three patrollers in California alone. And there are other hazards. As many as 5 percent of all explosives fired into the backcountry fail to explode, which might not seem so troubling—except that 10 percent of these duds may explode spontaneously later on. Some experts estimate that 3,000 unexploded rounds could exist in American mountains, which, if not exactly a minefield, is still reason to worry for unsuspecting backpackers and mountain goats alike.

Troublingly, the halcyon days of American avalanche research have lagged because of significant funding cutbacks; avalanche experts in this country currently rely on research imported from Switzerland, Japan, and Canada. Alaska's forecasting center, for example, has been closed down completely for lack of funding. In 1985, the U.S. Forest Service eliminated its snow and avalanche research center in Fort Collins, Colorado. The Fort Collins center, renamed the Colorado Avalanche Information Center and relocated to Boulder, is now largely funded by the ski industries and the state department of transportation, which relies on accurate forecasts to help keep its roads open. Together with a loose-knit and overworked group of ski patrollers and backcountry guides at a handful of forecasting centers in the Pacific Northwest and Canada, the Colorado center compiles weather, snowpack, and accident information, conducts computer modeling of avalanche areas, and compares what they find with other forecasters.

How much good avalanche research can do to save lives remains something of a debate. In the 1980s alone, some 1,200 Europeans were killed by avalanches, despite national funding and education on the subject and avalanche experience among the general populace that far exceeds anything found in the United States. In this country, according to Knox Williams, who directs the Colorado avalanche center, "it will take a major disaster to bring the funding back."

Chapter 7

✳

Brooding over some vast mountain landscape,
or among the countenances of mountain
flowers, our bodies disappear, our mortal
coils come off without any shuffling, and we
blend into the rest of Nature, utterly blind to
the boundaries that measure human quantities
into separate individuals.

— John Muir
"Explorations in the
Great Tuolumne Cañon"

Jim Kanzler's job as a ski patroller at the Bridger Bowl meant that he would not be able to make the Cleveland expedition, but his friends Mark Levitan and James Anderson decided to make the trip anyway. Anderson and Levitan were considerably less experienced climbers than the other boys; Levitan, twenty, had gone so far as to tell his more experienced and cautious father that he would only help the boys carry their gear to the foot of the north face of Cleveland, but would remain at the bottom while the more skilled climbers made the dangerous, highly technical ascent. Perhaps to build his own confidence, Levitan called a more experienced climbing friend, Robert Madsen, to see if he wanted to round out the group. Levitan and Madsen had been in the Boy Scouts together, and both had attended Helena High School; Madsen at the time of the Mount Cleveland trip was a freshman at the University of Montana, aspiring to be a doctor.

Like the other boys, Madsen had grown up skiing and climbing. "The big thing when I was eight or nine years old was to hunt elk with my dad," Madsen said. "That's just what we did. When I was a kid I had a .22 for shooting cans, a 12-gauge for ducks, a double-barreled 12-gauge for geese, and a 30.06 for deer. In New York City at that age you learn how to call a cab and how not to get mugged. If your family is into the outdoors, it just becomes a way of life." By his late teens, Madsen had also had some close calls. Once, while cross-country skiing the Going-to-the-Sun Road in Glacier National Park, Madsen and his younger brother Eric got caught on a slope cascading with avalanches. Desperate to find refuge from the snowfall, which was dropping avalanches around them "every five minutes," they hid inside a tunnel on the park's west side and set up camp. Suddenly, an avalanche sealed up one entrance. Terrified that they might be trapped in the tunnel for the remainder of the winter, the boys were forced to spend the night, but managed to dig their way out the following day.

To Madsen, a winter attempt on the north face of Mount Cleveland at first seemed inspired. "We had the opportunity to climb a face that had never been climbed," he said. "In the late sixties people were really competing. There were climbs that could make you famous. Here was a plum—a big wall, and in winter to boot. That's the thing with youth and climbing—if you get an opportunity, you say, 'Let's go!' " But if Madsen relished challenges, the idea of climbing the north face of Mount Cleveland with such a large group seemed too risky. Madsen was an avid technical climber who had become a convert to a philosophy made popular by the world's most daring mountaineer, Reinhold Messner. By the late 1960s, Messner had already made celebrated solo ascents of a number of European peaks before he had reached his twenty-fifth birthday, and would, over the next twenty years, become known as one of the finest mountaineers of all time. He solo-climbed the south face of Argentina's Aconcagua in 1974, and six years later he made a solo ascent of Mount Everest without the use of oxygen. By 1986, Messner had become the first person ever to climb all 14 of the world's 8,000-meter mountains, and in 1989 he and a single teammate skied across Antarctica, pulling their gear along on sleds.

During most of his career, Messner has advocated speed over brute force. Following Messner's exploits through the climbing press, Madsen believed that the only way to make tough climbs was to do it in small groups, two or three people at the most, and get up and down the mountain as fast as possible. More team members than that and the group would be slowed down, and thus at much greater risk from the vagaries of winter weather. "My initial impression was that the [Mount Cleveland] group was too large," Madsen says.

"Everything was happening in the alpine style at that time. Messner had altered the idea of 'siege' climbing for good. This whole thing seemed cumbersome and slow. There were just too many guys."

As it turned out, Madsen and Jim Kanzler were not the only ones to drop out of the group. Clare Pogreba had asked Pat Callis to go, but Callis—particularly after his scare in the snow cave in the Tetons just a few weeks before—declined. "I had a family at the time, so I felt I should stay home," Callis said. "I do remember cautioning them about avalanches. I always wondered if I shouldn't have cautioned them more strongly."

That left the group at five: Jerry Kanzler, Clare Pogreba, Ray Martin, James Anderson, and Mark Levitan. It was a good group, all told; Kanzler, Pogreba, and Martin were very accomplished climbers, especially given their age, and Levitan and Anderson, if less technically experienced, had considerable backcountry training. In his *A Climber's Guide to Glacier National Park,* J. Gordon Edwards refers to the boys as "outstanding mountaineers." Randall Green, the author of *The Rock Climber's Guide to Montana,* refers to the Cleveland group as "some of the most adventurous and bold Montana climbers of the time." In what must have been statistically unlikely, especially given the relative homogeneity of western Montana, each of the boys came from a different religious background. Levitan was Jewish; Martin was Mormon; Anderson was Catholic; Clare Pogreba was Presbyterian; Kanzler was Episcopalian.

Despite the boys' enthusiasm—their plans had circulated through the grapevine of the region's several small towns—veteran climbers remained dubious. Jerry DeSanto, a park ranger who knew Glacier National Park as well as any man alive, considered the idea of climbing the north face foolhardy. "I can't understand what those boys were thinking. I never thought you could rely on people that young—they just didn't have that much experience. The young tend to be rash. They must have been crazy to think they could climb the north face in winter. The snow up there is just cascading down all winter."

In fact, the boys were making the climb on Cleveland not only against the advice of professional rangers, but against the wishes of some of their family members as well. In Butte, Jerry Kanzler and Clare Pogreba laid out their gear on the floor of Esther Pogreba's home-based beauty shop. Coils of climbing rope, angle pitons, bugaboos, carabiners, slings, stout leather boots, a piton hammer. "The cute part was that they had written out a recipe for a Crock-Pot full of stew for a night on the mountain, but all they had was dried food," Esther recalled. "They were so excited to do [the climb]. We said, 'Why would you do this in 30-below weather?' They said [winter] was the only time to do it."

Across town, Ruby Martin, who was used to her son spending so much time climbing radio towers in Alaska, was also worried. On Christmas night, she and Arthur had been invited to a neighbor's house for fruitcake and coffee, but Ray stayed home to get his gear together for the Cleveland trip. He planned to leave early the next morning, he said. As the Martins were leaving, Ray stood in the doorway to say good night, and Ruby Martin kissed her son. "I suddenly got this weird feeling, that I wondered if I would ever kiss him again," she said. "I'm sure it was a premonition. I pleaded with my husband to tell him he couldn't go. Arthur said, 'You can't tell him that. He's twenty-two years old. He'll never forgive you. He could have gone to Vietnam.' What are you going to do with a twenty-two-year-old boy? You can't stop him, but it hurts me that I didn't have the gumption to tell him no. When young people make their minds up to do something, there really isn't much you can do."

At the Anderson home in Big Fork, Jim's sister, Sandy, had tried talking the boys out of the idea, but if Jim had any reservations about his relative lack of technical climbing experience, he didn't let on. "He didn't want to let the other guys down," Jim's younger brother Don said. "Sandy said, 'What happens if you don't come back?' I don't remember his answer. . . ." Anderson's former scoutmaster would later consider the team's aspiration itself to be worthy of admiration. "It is not for me to conjecture what drives young men to conquer mountains. The obvious thing on the other hand is that without this burning desire to conquer we would as a nation long since be reduced to a covey of slaves. This has to be what our greatest leaders, explorers, scientists, journalists, doctors are made of. Each in his own way, of course, but all boiled down, they try harder."

The day after Christmas, the five young Montana climbers arrived at Bob Frauson's ranger station at St. Mary, on the eastern side of the park, to ask his opinion about the north face of Mount Cleveland. They could not have hoped for a more competent adviser, or someone more familiar with the mysteries of snow. Of Swedish and Danish stock, Frauson had grown up the son of a railroad man in Mahwah, New Jersey, just a decade before another Mahwah man named Robert A. Smith acquired the first patent for a plastic snow shovel. As a Depression-era kid exploring the icy hills of northern New Jersey, Frauson would tie an old elastic tire tube around his heels so his feet would stay attached to his hickory skis. He and his friends would build makeshift moguls and ski jumps on the hills near Bear Mountain, New York; the older kids would make Bob test out the slopes first. When he got good at cross-country skiing, Frauson would take over winter paper routes from less adventurous bicycle riders. "I always said it was deep snow," he says, "but I guess I was just short."

By the time he was eighteen, with the Nazis moving into the Alps, Frauson fairly ran to enlist in the 10th Mountain Division. His confidence, perhaps appropriate for such a fit young man, brimmed over. "There were a lot of hotshot skiers back then, but put a 90-pound pack on their backs and then see what they can do," he recalled. Once, while he was umpiring a routine war game in Camp Hale's 50-below weather, Frauson's feet turned "white and hard as coffee cups." It took seven hours and the medical expertise of the man who had been the chief surgeon for Admiral Richard Byrd's expedition to the South Pole to turn his feet pink again.

Frauson celebrated his twenty-first birthday during a reconnaissance mission to the base of Riva Ridge. Several weeks later, he and his A Company climbed the ridge under the cover of stormy night skies and took their position on a high part of the ridge, out of the direct line of German fire. When another company took a series of hard hits, Frauson was ordered to drop his weapon and join the medical evacuation team. With air force planes strafing the ridgeline, a group of engineers rigged up a cable system to transport the dead and wounded from the top of the cliff all the way to the base of Riva Ridge. Getting the wounded into a medical tent at the bottom suddenly took ten minutes instead of ten hours; litters would be sent down with bodies strapped inside and come back up again filled with ammunition.

After VE-day, Frauson's division was supposed to take a week's leave in San Francisco and then help lead the invasion force in Japan, but while they were in transit atomic bombs ended the Pacific war as well. Frauson was sent instead to Nebraska to guard a German prisoner of war camp. After completing his service, Frauson went on to get a degree in industrial arts—he learned furniture making and silversmithing, which he continues to practice fifty years later—from Colorado A&M, now Colorado State. While in college he was diagnosed with Hodgkin's disease, but this barely slowed him down; one day he "went AWOL" from the hospital in order to catch the last football game between the Aggies and their archrival, the University of Colorado.

Like many in the 10th Mountain Division, Bob Frauson had come home after the war and headed straight for the hills. Among other pursuits, he helped cut ski trails and build lift towers in Arapahoe Basin in Colorado and, later,

Big Mountain in Montana. "There was a surplus of skis after the war," Frauson recalls. "You could completely outfit yourself with skis, boots, poles, parka—the whole bit—for about twelve dollars. There were only two sizes of laminated hickory skis at the time—seven feet and seven and a half feet." Collectively, the returning mountain troops changed the face of American winter sports. They brought back from battle all kinds of new technology—quick-release bindings, crampons, feltlike "bunnyboots" for use at high altitudes, aluminum framepacks, mountain stoves, dehydrated foods, down sleeping bags. More than anything else, though, the invention of laminated skis, which replaced the hickory planks worn previously, and nylon climbing rope, which replaced hemp line, thoroughly revolutionized skiing and climbing. Suddenly trekking and skiing through snowy mountains was possible for the average person. Winter sports began to explode.

Frauson's first stint was at Devils Tower National Monument, a high stump of rock in northeastern Wyoming that had recently become famous for a rescue operation that had made international headlines. Just a few years before Frauson's arrival, Charles George Hopkins, a Royal Air Force transport pilot who held world records for most jumps from a plane (2,348) and the longest freefall (20,800 feet), as well as the U.S. record for the fall from the greatest height (26,400 feet), had decided to leap from a single-engine Aeronca onto the top of the tower. The pilot who threw a climbing rope after Hopkins missed his mark, however, and the daredevil was left stranded at nearly 900 feet with no way down.

The Park Service decided to call in some of the country's best climbers to get Hopkins down. First called was Ernie Field, a ranger in Colorado's Rocky Mountain National Park and coauthor of the country's first rescue manual, who helped train 10th Mountain Division troops. But even for such an expert, the tower turned out to be too tough a climb. About halfway up, Field slipped and fell 15 feet, nearly breaking his ribs, and turned around. Back on the ground, Field summoned a pair of cocky young climbers who would over the next four decades become two of America's most celebrated mountaineers: a Dartmouth medical student named Jack Durrance, and Paul Petzoldt, who would later join the 10th Mountain Division and subsequently found the National Outdoor Leadership School. The two ace climbers led a team of eight up what is now known as the "Durrance route," and made it to the top of the tower. By late afternoon, with the tower flooded with photographers' lights, the entire group rappelled down the face and arrived back on the ground.

After his time at Devils Tower, Frauson spent the latter part of the 1940s and the first half of the 1950s as a ranger at Longs Peak in Rocky Mountain National Park, which after the war became a mecca for big-wall climbers. He assisted all kinds of rescues, including one of a seventeen-year-old visitor named Patrick Dwyer, who, during a rappel, free-fell almost 200 feet, landed on a snowfield, and slid another 200 feet before hitting a tree on a ledge less than three feet wide—the only thing preventing him from falling over a sheer wall all the way to the ground. Arriving three hours after the fall, Frauson and three other rangers, with darkness above and snow underfoot, took four hours and ten separate sequences of ropes and slings to get Dwyer down and to a hospital. Frauson and the other rangers were given gold medallions by the Park Service as well as citations "for demonstrating unusual courage involving a high degree of personal risk in the face of danger."

By the late 1960s, Frauson, a large man whose big ears, jowly face, and kind demeanor give him the look of Kris Kringle, was recognized nationally as an expert in high-mountain navigation, emergency rescue, and winter camping. Now stationed at Glacier National Park, Frauson had spent years exploring the peaks of the northern Rockies, and knew the intricacies and moods of winter weather as well as anyone alive. He also knew the community—Frauson and his wife occasionally ran into the Kanzlers at social events—but that didn't keep the ranger, in the mountains, from his appointed rounds. George Ostrom tells a story about a day he and Hal Kanzler were climbing up to a waterfall near Mount Henkel and Altyn Peak, in the eastern part of Glacier National Park not far from the hotel at Many Glacier, to look at the wintering range for bighorn sheep. They had their cameras with them, not their guns, but with hunting season long since over any ranger worth his boots would want to make sure they weren't up there poaching. "It was so cold—we were freezing our butts off—we had to build a fire to keep warm. Well, we're way up there on the top of this mountain, and when we look down we see a ranger way down below. Kanzler said, 'If we stay here and he starts to come up after us, we'll know who it is,' and up he came. It was Frauson. Most rangers would have stayed down in their nice warm cars and waited for us to come down. Well, we were so cold we met him on the way down. He's the only guy who would have done that."

When he trained new rangers, Frauson made no bones about the dangers of high mountain rescue, or high mountain play. He would take his young charges and show them body bags, and tell them, "This is how you'll come back if you go out climbing where you're not supposed to." Likewise, with the backpackers and climbers streaming through his ranger station, he would urge restraint in the company of the mountains. There are old climbers and there are bold climbers, one expression goes, but there are no old, bold climbers: a long life spent high in the hills requires humility before elements far more daunting and unforgiving than the egos of many "mountain men" permit them to admit.

When the Mount Cleveland team arrived at his ranger station and asked his opinion about their plans for an ascent, Frauson emphasized the severe weather patterns that routinely drop over the mountains, explained in detail the dangers of sliding snow at high altitude, and tried to impress upon them the extreme difficulty of rescue should they run into trouble. Moreover, he said, Mount Cleveland was particularly prone to avalanches. Rocky-faced and rising well above the timberline, the mountain was virtually bare at its upper reaches. No trees meant no anchors for the vast fields of snow.

He checked their climbing and camping gear—skis, crampons, ice axes, sleeping bags, tents—and found it to be satisfactory, but felt the boys lacked proper protection for their hands and feet should the weather turn really nasty. Frauson told them they would have been wise to bring a transistor radio; weather forecasts, even if imprecise, would have provided a day's warning should a winter storm blow in from the Canadian north. The boys had enough food for six days, with enough in reserve for one or two days longer. They gave him names and emergency numbers of their "support team" back home: Jim Kanzler at the Bridger Bowl ski resort; Pat Callis and Peter Lev at Montana State.

Of critical concern to Frauson, especially given his military training, was an issue most weekend climbers never consider: the appointment of a group leader, to make hard and fast decisions should demanding situations arise. Decisions about what to have for dinner can be democratically debated; decisions about whether to forge ahead or turn back, in the face of bad weather or unexpectedly difficult terrain, must ultimately be entrusted to an appointed leader, who decides without debate, and without dissent. The leader is often, but not always, the climber with the most experience; it is almost certainly the one in whom the others have invested the most trust. Just as boats depend on captains for critical, often life-and-death decisions, climbing teams need someone to decide, for example, when to push through threatening situations, and when to turn back. In the backcountry, trust is not inspired simply by the color of one's storied past, or by one's ability to tie a quick bowline, or by the volume of one's voice. Trust has to to do, first and foremost, with judgment.

The trouble for the Mount Cleveland expedition was that their most experienced climber, Jim Kanzler, was not along on the trip, and Frauson could sense the leadership vacuum. "I never tell climbers not to do it at all. I just tell them war stories, tell them they have to be at peace with themselves," Frauson said. "The trouble was, their leader wasn't there. I said, 'Who's the leader? You gotta have a leader.' Pogreba smiled and raised his hand and said, 'I'll be the leader,' but he was and he wasn't. It didn't feel right. The judgment on when to turn back is always at issue. They were young fellows who had all kinds of energy, but a little more head was what they needed."

There was also the issue of the notoriety of their plans. For some time, the boys told Frauson, people around the Flathead Valley had been telling them that they considered the expedition foolhardy. Frauson, however, figured his role was not to scold but to advise. "Saying no to something only drives people forward, and that seems to be what happened," he said. "I never say no. I just paint the picture and get them to realize what the end might be. Some people come back and thank me, and some come back dead."

If he didn't refuse to let the boys continue, Frauson did state unequivocally his feelings about the dangers of climbing such a difficult mountain, and particularly the north face, in winter. With cold temperatures and snow in the forecast, the peaks in the northern part of the park would be considerably more dangerous than during the summer, and even then they were hardly gentle. In summer, if there was any snow at all, it was typically found only in relatively stable glacier fields, or in sporadic spots that received little sun. But in winter, when snow fell heavy and deep, climbers would face perils unknown in warmer months. No longer would climbing the mountain be a matter of overcoming crumbly rocks with ropes and hardware and muscles and balance. Snow presented challenges of an entirely different order. "They wanted to try an attempt on the north face—it had never been climbed in summer or winter—but that's just an escalator of moving snow," Frauson said. "I've seen ten or fifteen avalanches a day up there on Mount Cleveland. It's self-cleaning. It avalanches there all the time."

If it became clear that Frauson would have no luck convincing the boys to reconsider their expedition altogether, he did warn them that the north face, in addition to its usual challenges, had recently been glazed over by an ice storm. Climbing it would be nothing short of foolhardy. He argued that they should try the comparatively easier route up the southwest ridge of the mountain, which would require less technical skill, and, if they chose the proper route, could make for a comparatively safe trip. The ridge, though precipitous on both sides, would allow the boys a point of attack free of the rock- and snowslides so prevalent on the north face. It would also enable them to avoid the west face, which although far less steep than the north face, presented serious dangers of its own. Split down the middle by a watercourse and a series of waterfalls, the west face in summer is a manageable climb; the usual approach is up a series of scree slopes to the left of the waterfall, then gradually straight up, some 3,500 vertical feet, through a massive basin. In summer, the west face does not require technical climbing gear, and offers a fairly easy ascent provided one is sure of foot. Even in the summer, though, the course of countless centuries of avalanches is unmistakable: a path of broken trees, boulders, and scattered debris runs off the west face of Mount Cleveland like a river delta, rushing down and then spreading out at the bottom in a broad fan. In winter, snow accumulating on the west face flows down this course as inexorably as water flows from Baton Rouge to New Orleans.

What Frauson didn't know is that Ray Martin may have brought along something they hadn't asked him to examine: the gun Hal Kanzler had used to kill himself. Inside the tightly knit climbing community, a rumor had circulated for some time that the Mount Cleveland team planned to bury the gun on top of the mountain as a ritual to honor Hal. The climb, no matter what Frauson said, was a go.

Like many things in the natural world, snow crystals on the ground lose their fragile beauty over time, metamorphosing from intricate feathers into round or bulbous blobs. This happens for a number of reasons: changes in the weight or temperature of the snow above, for example, can cause individual crystals to change shape, either increasing or decreasing the strength of the bonds between crystals. One result of this so-called destructive or equilibrium metamorphism is that snow crystals break down into smaller, simpler, and usually rounder shapes that are more densely and firmly packed together. Under certain circumstances, on flat surfaces on warm days, for example, water vapor moves between individual crystals, forming rounded bridges, or "necks," between them. Thus snow becomes cemented, or "sintered," and more and more stable, the longer it lies on the ground.

The trouble is, not all snow gets cemented. Under certain conditions, the water vapor invisibly circulating between individual snow crystals acts entirely differently, and contributes to the formation of a layer that skiers sometimes call "sugar snow." Although the term accurately reflects the crystals' poor bonding properties—try squeezing a handful of sugar in your hand and you will get a sense of this—in the context of avalanche formation it is altogether too sweet. Layers of sugar snow, in professional circles, have come to be known as "temperature gradient," or "TG" layers; traditionally, they have simply been known as "depth hoar." Whatever the nomenclature, these layers of unstable snow—made up of "faceted," or sharp-angled, poorly bonded crystals—can be exceedingly dangerous. One winter, as she climbed a rock near Silverton, Colorado, for a cold-weather session of T'ai Chi, Dolores LaChapelle looked down and saw, beneath the shady sides of nearby rocks, a concentration of glittering crystals. "Pressing as hard as I could they would not stick together; they melted first," she reported. "Depth hoar crystals, which often cause death, were here now, lying in my hand as glittering blue diamonds!"

A typical recipe for the growth of a depth hoar layer is an early snowfall, say in October or November, followed by very cold weather. As weeks go by, and the air temperature begins to drop dramatically lower than the ground temperature, snow crystals on the ground begin to look and act very differently. Because the ground, which had previously experienced months of summer sun, remains warmer than the insulating snow above it, snow at depth—and the air surrounding it—is warmer than snow and air on top. And because the warmer air below contains more water vapor than the colder air above, it begins to evaporate upward toward the colder layers. When the water vapor reaches the colder layers, it tends to crystallize anew, just as moist breath will harden into a kind of thin frost inside ski goggles. As the vapor freezes onto the outside edges of existing snow crystals, it changes their form into coarse grains with sharp angles, known as facets, or into hollow cups that telescope downward as more crystals accumulate at their edges. Lacking the many points of contact typical of six-pointed stars, depth hoar crystals slide against each other without bonding, even under enormous pressure from snow piled up above. Some avalanche experts refer to layers of newly formed depth hoar as resembling ball bearings, since the grains not only won't stick together, but will, at the slightest provocation, roll downhill. Layers of depth hoar are separated from the new snow above by a thin eggshell crust that somehow manages, up to a point, to keep the whole snowpack in place. But once the crusty membrane is broken—by the weight of creeping snow, say, or the shock of a falling cornice, or the weight of a hiking boot—the upper layers will collapse into the sugar snow, and the whole thing will rush off downhill in one cataclysmic roar.

Nowhere are the conditions for depth hoar formation as perfect as they are in the late fall and early winter in the northern Rockies of Glacier National Park. There is very low humidity, and winter nights are clear and cold. Early in the season, even if it doesn't snow much, what snow does accumulate will not melt. Add to this late fall or winter snowstorms, which can pile up vast amounts of snow above the weak layer of sugar snow, and serious problems emerge for anyone venturing into the backcountry. Any disturbance through the upper layer—a falling boulder, a footstep—and the eggshell crust can transmit a fracture line hundreds of feet in a matter of seconds.

Because the entire top half of Mount Cleveland's west face forms a giant bowl that is constantly filling with snow, Bob Frauson has come up with a number of colorful metaphors to describe the shape of the west face—or any large bowl—and the way it releases slabs: "parabolic mirror," "self-bailing boat," "bowling alley"; all are efforts to describe a semicircular bowl that catches sun from several angles and funnels avalanches from all sides into a river of snow running straight down the middle. The west face is angled at something approaching 35 degrees—precisely the worst angle for the formation of the deadliest kind of avalanches. Sheerer faces, while perhaps more challenging to climb, are too steep to allow for any great accumulation of snow. But at 35 degrees, a slope can hold a great deal; snow cover can thicken with each successive storm, gradually adding layer after layer of snow. And because it is high, the bowl serves as a virtual snow depository for the prevailing winds; windblown snow can pack the bowl tight and deep, even when the mountain's lower reaches are completely bare. And as any winter climber knows, windblown snow is, when it comes to avalanche danger, exceedingly dangerous. Snow can accumulate in great swirling drifts from all over the mountain, and pack more densely than it ever could simply by falling from the sky. Wind has a way of compacting the snowpack into white concrete, which is fine provided there is nothing unstable beneath it. But if there happens to be a layer of depth hoar—ball bearings—beneath all that weight, then a wind-loaded slope is just waiting to release. Ascending the middle of the bowl, climbers of the west face would be in serious danger of setting off a slide of massive proportions, one that could conceivably bring down the entire mountainside of snow.

The winter of 1969 had already seen some big avalanches up high; some had snapped trees as they rumbled down to the lower reaches of the slope. "That mountain doesn't give a damn about anyone," Waterton Lakes naturalist Kurt Seel told a local newspaper. "It's not unconquerable. It is treacherous. In the summertime, rocks roll constantly. In the wintertime, it's the wind and snow. That mountain is alive all the time."

Like any ranger in his position, Bob Frauson was never simply concerned about the safety of the hikers and climbers asking his opinion about the mountains. He also had in mind the danger that any mishap could mean for his own staff. Rangers called upon to find lost or injured hikers are often put in grave danger themselves, as evidenced by the dozens of rescue workers who have died in the line of duty. Monty Atwater tells of a time when a couple of Alta skiers asked him if they could ski down a particularly dangerous slope even though he had forbidden them to do so. He told them that if they chose to go, they would relieve him of any responsibility for their safety. If they didn't come out of the canyon, he would not follow them in, and wouldn't allow any other rangers to follow them. "No professional I have ever met has any patience with or respect for daredevils," he wrote. "We go after them because we have to." If backcountry adventurers cannot be denied the opportunity to explore dangerous places, they must be clear that their "monumental selfishness" can put less foolhardy people in great danger as well. Once they find themselves in trouble, reckless climbers or skiers expect to blow a whistle, or send up a flare, or light a signal fire, and convince an avuncular ranger to come remove them from their distress. In most cases, of course, even a single lost or endangered person can endanger half a dozen rescuers. The larger the party, the more rescuers needed. Climbers can split up into separate groups, some getting lost and the others not. They can spread over an area too vast for just a few rangers to adequately search. When the region includes high mountains in winter, of course, rescue missions require teams to search vertical as well as horizontal planes. Risk to everyone involved rises dramatically.

Chapter 8

❄

What in the dark I had taken to be a stump
of a little tree appearing above the snow,
to which I had tied my horse, proved to have
been the weathercock of the church steeple.

— Rudolph Erich Raspe,
The Travels and Surprising
Adventures of Baron
Munchausen

Hiking or skiing in avalanche country is like walking around in a valley you know to be inhabited by grizzly bears. Your senses become more alert. You become aware of tiny sounds—every creak of a tree limb, every snap of a twig. In bear country, you become aware, perhaps for the first time in your life, that you are not at the top of the food chain. For once, nothing is so important as the direction of the wind; there is something out there that, with a mix of your own ignorance and bad luck, could finish you off. The same is true in the winter backcountry. When every footstep, on a steep slope, is potentially your last, you tend to pay attention to where you put your feet. The beauty of this arrangement is that this vibrancy, this forced concentration, makes the whole picture sharper. Time slows down. Your actions matter. "Mountains are turbulent places, full of swift violence, where humans are dwarfed by comparison," warns *Mountaineering: The Freedom of the Hills,* a canonical book of technique first published in 1960. "Climbers who cultivate the dynamic view of the mountain will be amazed at the persistence of the continuous destructive forces but never surprised by the rapidity with which conditions can change. The snow that loosens all day and slides in late afternoon, the little midday cloud that unleashes lightning by 3:00—these are things mountaineers cannot control and therefore must learn to recognize and avoid. They are awed by the part natural forces play—and wisely arrange to be elsewhere while the game is on."

The vast majority of avalanches take place without anyone ever seeing them, crashing down a slope like a herd of mythical stallions. All winter long, in all the mountain ranges of the world, snow cascades as surely as waterfalls cascade in summer. It builds up, it sits a moment or a month or ten years, and it slides. Introduce a skier, however, or a climber, or worst of all a snow-mobiler, and slopes undergirded by depth hoar become instantly more precarious. With depth hoar so tenuously constructed to begin with, the addition of even the slightest amount of weight can be enough to trigger a slab avalanche. Indeed, there is much that can be learned from a slope simply by listening to it. If the scariest sound in a Montana summer is that of a grizzly bear crashing through a huckleberry bush, in winter it is surely the unmistakable "whoompf" of a layer of depth hoar collapsing underfoot. "Your weight on the snowpack replicates, in microcosm, the forces brought to bear on the slope," writes Tim Setnicka in his book *Wilderness Search and Rescue*. "By listening very carefully, like at a chamber music concert in black tie and tux, you can discern sudden changes in the structure of the music your feet make on the snow. A particularly hollow sound can be investigated at once by a quickly belayed jump or three on the snow, in an effort to crack off a slab or start a sluff."

A typical backcountry skier who hears a sudden "whoompf" under his skis is in a bad way indeed; the sound indicates that his weight has broken the membrane between the upper and lower layers, and the ball bearings of a broken layer of depth hoar are about to start rolling. Because all of this takes place invisibly, from the formation of depth hoar itself to the fracture lines running through the snowpack, Monty Atwater considered depth hoar the "eeriest stuff on any mountain.

"In effect, depth hoar rots out the underside of a snow pack and leaves it hanging there, supported only around the edges, like a roof," he writes. The rotting process goes on invisibly for days or weeks, until, as gravity drags at the surface layer, the tiniest accumulation of snow, or the slightest vibration, or the cutting of a pair of skis can trigger it. Not even the most experienced snow ranger can foresee precisely when the slab will release. When the edges give way, a whole field can slide, causing an entire mountain bowl to release all at once.

In fact, there are a number of things that can trigger an avalanche, and since only some of them are caused by humans, their genesis has long been a great source of mythology. "And if you don't wish to waken the sleeping avalanche," the poet Johann Schiller wrote, "then walk quietly along the road of fear." Lord Byron wrote that an avalanche could begin with "a breath"; Immanuel Kant said by "a bird." Contrary to legend, however, it is unlikely that a loud noise can trigger an avalanche on its own. In the late 1940s, Atwater discovered that merely dropping explosives in the snow didn't do the trick; sound volume, it turned out, was not nearly as important as vibration in creating an effective trigger. No matter how loud a Swiss guide might yodel, in other words, it is unlikely his voice alone could cause a slide. "Logically, the human voice cannot be excluded from the noises which might bring this about," writes the avalanche historian Colin Fraser, but he believes that 99 percent of people claiming to have started avalanches with their "stentorian voices" have in fact done so with their "clodhopping boots."

Regardless of how it starts, when a "triggering agent breaks a slab and relieves creep tension, the reaction of the snow may be very rapid," Ed LaChapelle writes. "A whole slope may suddenly shatter into blocks before the slab had a chance to be set in motion. If the snow is very dense and cold, such as in a hard slab, the release of tension may be signaled by a sharp cracking sound like a rifle shot. The propagation of a fracture line in snow which is subject to heavy creep tension is extremely rapid, and such fractures may run for many hundreds of yards across a slope faster than the eye can follow."

The word avalanche comes from the old French avalanste, in turn derived from avaler, meaning to let down, lower, or go downstream. Earlier Latin roots are labi, meaning to slip or glide down, and labinae or lavanchiae, meaning a slippery place; the latter also serves as the root for lave, for flowing mud or lava. The Latin derivatives easily give rise to the German word for avalanche, lawine. Strabo, a Greek geographer, wrote of the horrors "of falling into chasms abysmal" during his travels from 64 to 36 B.C. Kant, whose eighteenth-century philosophy is far more admired than his snow science, wrote in his book Physical Geography that "it sometimes happens that for no other reason the snow, due to the dirt which is always carried in the air and is deposited on it, is sundered and thrown down, whereupon, in less than a minute, whole villages may be buried by it. Several persons so buried have been found after a long time and from their appearance it was thought that they had been embalmed. As this dry snow is often held together by only a thin crust it can, by some small accident, for example a bird sitting upon it, be broken, and the entire mass of snow be set rolling down the mountain slope."

Because avalanche paths can routinely cover miles of ground, run thousands of vertical feet down a slope, and be dozens of feet deep, it is no wonder that awestruck mountain dwellers have spent so much time trying to figure them out. In the Andes, folklore holds that a storm will continue as long as the body of an avalanche victim remains in the mountains. Given the number of deadly avalanches in the Middle Ages, it is no wonder that people contrived images of supernatural forces to explain them, Fraser writes. "People thought avalanches omnipotent and incontestable. At best, therefore, they were believed to be acts of God as He worked His divine, albeit abstruse purpose for the world; but more usually they were thought to be diabolical weapons of the powers of darkness." One popular search technique in the seventeenth century involved placing bowls of water alongside the aftermath of an avalanche. Pieces of bread were thrown into the bowls, and the manner and position of the bread in the water somehow indicated the location of the victim. Elsewhere, eggs with crosses painted on them have been placed at the bottom of slopes to protect from avalanches from above. In the early nineteenth century, a one-hundred-year-old shepherd who claimed to be able to predict avalanches by watching the glaciers from which they originated saved an entire town by convincing a popular young couple to move their wedding—and all their guests—to a neighboring village on the projected date of an avalanche. Sure enough, the wedding was moved, the avalanche fell on the empty village, and no one was killed.

Avalanches, by and large, come in two forms, depending primarily on the cohesion of the snow: loose snow avalanches and slab avalanches. Loose snow avalanches occur on slopes on which the snow lacks internal cohesion, that is, where there are weak bonds between individual grains of snow. These are most often observed in freshly fallen cold snow, or in very wet snow. A loose snow avalanche usually begins at or near the snow surface when a small amount of snow is displaced and begins heading downward. This initial mass sets an increasing amount of snow moving, and a fan- or teardrop-shaped avalanche is usually the result. Loose snow avalanches can occur all through a season, and vary in size. Small ones are called sluffs, and are good telltales about the surface stability of a given slope. Loose snow avalanches pose hazards to inexperienced or unwary skiers because they can easily flow into and through a stand of trees, burying those who considered a small forest a safe place to hide. Typically, loose-snow slides can also cause greater problems at the bottom of a slope than in the middle—skiers standing midslope may witness only the beginning stages of an avalanche that could cause serious problems farther downhill.

Far more ominous and more unpredictable than loose snow avalanches are slab avalanches, which over time have been responsible for some 95 percent of avalanche deaths. If loose snow avalanches cascade consistently down slopes that are too steep to allow much snow to accumulate, slab avalanches most commonly form on slopes that allow snow to pile up, releasing an entire block only when an elastic layer of snow is stretched to its breaking point. This can happen in a number of ways. Snowpack that has been stable for weeks can become overly burdened by a new storm and shear off. Spring rain can add tons of water weight and cause the same thing. In the Cascades of Washington and Oregon, for example, relatively warm, wet winters, or rapid warming trends in spring, can increase the water content and viscosity of upper layers of snow or melt a weak bond in lower layers, thus creating enough running water to undermine even solid upper layers. Overnight storms can also prompt avalanches, particularly if the sun is shining the next day. Once the snow has become warm, it gets denser and heavier, and will begin to creep downhill, straining the bonds between the upper layer and those below it. If enough bonds between the layers are broken, a slab can break free.

The course of a slab avalanche has three stages. Most avalanches release in a "fracture zone" of 30 to 45 degrees, but the texture and shape—concave or convex—of the slope also determine its stability. A concave, bowl-shaped slope, for example, acts as catch basin for accumulating snow, and is a good place to look for thick slabs. Once slabs release, they move down a "track"— often a gully or chute that has seen countless avalanches before—and come to rest in a "runout zone," where the snow resettles on a flatter, more secure surface.

With "soft slab" avalanches, stress comes from new snow deposited with the help of wind, slope angle, temperature, and slope aspect (the direction it faces) in areas of high accumulation. The wetter, denser, and deeper the snow, the more weight is added to the pack, and the greater the danger of a slab release. These release most commonly during and after snowstorms. Hard slab avalanches are still harder to predict, since their prime creator is wind, which makes snow denser and harder-packed. The difference between a safe wind-packed slope and one ready to release may be a single weak layer of depth hoar below the surface. Remarking on the frequency of slides, Monty Atwater once wrote that "to me, the mystery has never been that it avalanches but that it usually stays on the mountain so well."

Once the snow becomes sufficiently unstable, a slab of dense snow can begin to slide downhill with almost unimaginable force. Small avalanches can carry impact pressures of up to 1,000 pounds per square foot, enough to destroy a wood-frame house; larger slides, with 20,000 pounds per square foot, can destroy entire forests or crush a concrete building. One of the largest avalanches ever recorded, on a slope near Portage, Alaska, had a fracture line that ran 24 to 36 feet deep and 1,300 feet across. On Alaska's Mount Sanford, in 1981, an avalanche containing an estimated 1 million cubic yards of ice and snow fell 10,000 feet in elevation, traveled eight miles, went up and over a 3,000-foot mountain on the way, and threw up a powder cloud thousands of feet into the air that was visible for 100 miles. Even this monstrous slide seems small compared to a colossal avalanche that came down off Peru's North Huascaran, the second-tallest mountain in South America, on January 10, 1962. At 6:13 P.M. on that day, a Peruvian telephone operator saw a swirling cloud of white blot out the summit of the mountain and seconds later heard a great sound. A fragment of the mountain's ice cap—estimated at 3 million cubic yards of snow and ice—had broken off and fallen over half a mile onto a glacier. Some 175 feet thick, a mile and a quarter wide, and traveling at 20 miles per hour, the avalanche boosted boulders weighing thousands of tons onto benches more than 200 feet above the canyon floor. The slide gouged out so much earth that it multiplied its own mass to an estimated 13 million cubic yards—enough to fill the Louisiana Superdome three and a half times. It dammed the Santa River, and when the dam broke the flood took out all downstream bridges and carried bodies 100 miles to the sea. No one knows the total death toll, since many bodies remained buried, but the avalanche destroyed six villages completely and three others partially. Something on the order of 4,000 people and 10,000 animals died. (Eight years later, near the same site, an earthquake 12 miles off the Peruvian coast released landslides that buried a number of coastal cities that lay in the shadow of Huascaran, sent dust clouds 18,000 feet into the air, and killed some 30,000 people. Scores of communities, Peruvian Air Force pilots told *The New York Times,* were "no longer on the map.")

One of the most dramatic by-products of a slab avalanche can occur when a sliding slab forces very dry, airborne snow down a steep slope like a blast of aerosol. Particles of snow can get airborne and form a globe-shaped cloud of heavy, frosted air that can reach mind-boggling speeds. Japanese researchers, monitoring snow running through a steep gully pitched at perhaps 60 or 70 degrees, once clocked an avalanche at 230 miles per hour. In 1910, six of seven forestry workers in Glarus, Switzerland, were smashed to death by a powder cloud preceding a slab avalanche; the seventh, Colin Fraser reports, "was seized by the wind and flung through the air at tremendous speed, 'head sometimes upward, head sometimes downward like a leaf driven by a storm.' " Hit from all sides, the man's eyes and mouth were completely blocked by the snow. After passing out, he awakened in deep snow that had broken his fall. When asked later, he said he thought his flight had been very brief. In fact, he been sucked to an altitude of 2,200 feet and carried more than half a mile through the air. He emerged with nothing worse than a few broken bones.

Even run-of-the-mill powder clouds carry enormous energy. Because swirling snow makes the air around it three times as dense as air bearing only sunlight—think of the difference between someone blowing on your cheek and spitting a stream of crushed ice—crystal-filled air kicked up by a standard 60-miles-per-hour avalanche has the destructive force of a 180-miles-per-hour wind, well beyond that of a hurricane. Researchers have estimated that an average powder cloud avalanche of 160,000 tons (about 200,000 cubic meters of snow) sliding 6,500 feet at 22 miles per hour will generate 20 million horsepower, or about 2,857 times that of the average Amtrak locomotive. Bob Frauson likes to illustrate the speed of airborne snow by showing a photograph of a 45 MPH road sign on the Going-to-the-Sun Road. The sign had been bent at a 90-degree angle. By wind. The same avalanche ripped all the branches off a nearby tree, and flipped a road-clearing tractor seven times. Such is the intensity of wind generated by a powder cloud that houses battered by an avalanche in Echo Lake, California, in February 1950 looked not like they'd been crushed but like they'd *exploded*. Apparently the airborne snow had entered through doors or windows, become compressed by the walls, and blown the houses apart from the inside.

If the results of slab avalanches are all too obvious to those caught in their path, the way these slabs are formed remains for most people one of winter's more mystifying phenomena. This is particularly true since this highly volatile snowpack forms invisibly in certain mountain ranges in midwinter, when unsuspecting skiers or climbers consider the terrain to be unshakably stable. One of the most common places to find this kind of snow is the northern Rocky Mountains of Glacier National Park.

Chapter 9

❄

*Even the sages who lay claim to knowing all
and go to the mountains in search of long life
put themselves at risk of violent death. All
the mountains, whether large or small, are
haunted by supernatural beings: great ones
on the great mountains, little ones on the
little. And if one does not take appropriate
precautionary measures, they will afflict one
with sickness, injuries, vexations, terror and
anguish. Sometimes the traveler will see lights
and shadows; sometimes he will hear strange
noises. Great trees will crash down on him
without there being any wind; rocks will fall
without warning and strike him dead. . . . One
does not venture into the mountains lightly.*

— Ko Hung, A.D. 320, quoted in
Edwin Bernbaum, *Sacred
Mountains of the World*

Given the presence of depth hoar and the danger of slab avalanches,
the only way to climb the west face of Mount Cleveland, Bob Frauson told the
boys, would be to stay far enough out of the avalanche zone to avoid getting
caught. Traveling up or down the slope's fall line—the route a snowball would
naturally roll—would minimize the chance of shearing off a slab avalanche;
walking straight across a bowl, especially since the boys would be roped together, would be asking for trouble. If even one of them got caught, he would
drag the others down with him. Standard advice for climbers crossing a winter
slope is to travel, if at all possible, from thick stands of trees to big rock outcroppings, and to cross each suspicious area quickly, one person at a time.
Hikers should stay as high on the face as possible, to avoid concave starting
zones and potential fracture lines.

The best way to stay alive in avalanche country, in other words, is to stay
out of the way; once caught, chances for surviving drop very quickly. Slopes

that were once stable become liquid, flowing underfoot. Those who have experienced earthquakes talk of the sheer psychological terror of city sidewalks liquefying beneath their feet; such is the feeling of a firm snowpack giving way and starting to slide. Where one was standing, one is now slipping, both down the slope and into the snow itself. Getting caught in an avalanche is like trying to stand on a surfing wave; it both violently tumbles you forward and sucks you down below. Indeed, people caught in avalanches are advised to try their best to "swim" to the surface of the snow, to try in whatever desperate way they can to keep their head from being carried under. A strong breast stroke has saved a number of people caught facing down the mountain from being carried under; those caught with their feet pointed downhill have had luck "treading snow," with their arms and legs whirling. "With these motions, you may have some control over your depth and direction of movement in the avalanche," one study reports. "If, however, the avalanche is large and turbulent, you will probably be helpless."

Getting rid of ski poles or swimming away from a tumbling snowmobile increases mobility. Grabbing a tree or a bush—anything to keep from being carried away—is a victim's best chance, for once the snow starts flowing, and flying in the air, the primary risk is drowning. Gulping air only increases the chances of inhaling a mouthful of snow that can be impossible to expel.

There are, in fact, several ways to die in an avalanche. About a third of avalanche deaths are due to trauma to the head and neck sustained during the fall, from smashing bones on rocks buried in the snow to the contortions inflicted on a body by cascading snow. "Trees, rocks, cliffs and the wrenching action of snow in motion can do horrible things to the human body," one study puts it. The remaining two thirds of deaths are caused by suffocation.

During a snowmobiling vacation with a couple of friends in the winter of 1998, Brian Sali, a Washington State apple merchant, got tumbled by an avalanche in Oregon and was buried in five feet of snow. "I knew I was moving, but I didn't realize how fast—I traveled hundreds of feet in seconds," he said. "It was very, very soft at first, like I was floating. The only danger I thought of was hitting the sled, but I never did. Finally, I felt like things were slowing down, and I figured I would just crawl out. I found immediately that I couldn't move. Within one or two seconds you can't move at all. At first it was like a light fog, but now it was a very tight black environment. Then you have nothing but your mind and your eyeballs and your face and stomach. You go from floating to being vacuum-sealed, with no reaction time."

Such was the compression of the snow that Sali could suck in the little air that had settled in the pocket around his helmet, but couldn't expand his chest out. In an incredible stroke of good fortune, he was buried with the face mask of his helmet snapped down, which provided just enough of an airspace for him to breathe. Oxygen, however, did little to calm Sali's terror. "At that point I just felt like I wanted to panic. When your brain says thrash, anything you try to do, you cannot do. You just simply cannot do it. After you go through this period of emotion, your brain shuts you down. Which is probably a good thing. After I went through this period of yelling and jerking, yanking, pulling, anything I could possibly do, I remember trying to move the fingers in my gloves and my toes, and I couldn't. All of a sudden it was very very very cold. I just went to sleep. It was very calm, very, very painless. I realized that I wasn't going to make it. After struggling and going through surrendering, and giving yourself up, your mind or your body takes over, one of the two, and says, 'I'm gonna turn the lights off for you. The last thing I consciously remember is saying, 'Help me God.' "

Back on the slope, Sali's two friends, Art Keys and Mark Perry, mobilized immediately. The avalanche wasn't huge, but it still covered a football-field-sized rectangle some 100 yards long and 50 yards wide. Incredibly, they managed to spot the tip of Sali's snowmobile ski sticking up out of the snow, and soon heard that the engine of the buried sled was still running. Immediately, they dug down enough to turn off the ignition. Keys ripped the windshield off his own snowmobile and started using it as a shovel; Perry ran off to cut a sapling to use as a probe. After jamming the sapling into the snow near the sled half a dozen times, Perry felt it hit something solid—Sali's shoulder. They found him facedown, his head between his knees and his arms spread out in front of him—Sali later would say he had no idea in what position he had landed. Once they got his helmet off, Keys and Perry saw Sali's oxygen-deprived face, and quickly dug all but one ankle out of the snow before trying to lift him out. The snow had compacted into such a tight seal around the foot that they were unable to pull it out, and had to spend precious seconds finishing their digging. It is instances such as these—two men unable to pull out a third man's foot—that indelibly illustrate the changeable nature of snow. What had once been light as air had—after warming and becoming compressed during its descent—hardened into unyielding plaster. Sali had been completely mummified. The prospect of being buried under compacted snow, conscious, breathing, but for all intents and purposes paralyzed, is somehow far more harrowing than the image of broken bones and twisted ankles.

Sali's companions managed to get him back to the lodge, where they put him in a cold shower to stabilize his body's core temperature; a hot shower would have caused blood to rush to his extremities so quickly that he might have suffered a heart attack. Sali was then airlifted to a hospital in nearby Bend. A urine sample the color of root beer again revealed the extent to which Sali had been squeezed by the snow: his muscle fiber had been so compressed that it had released protein into his bloodstream. Doctors were less concerned about Sali's muscles than about his kidneys, which were in danger of clogging with all the matter they were being forced to filter. In the end, miraculously, Sali was released with no permanent physical damage.

Brian Sali's rescuers, if less than perfectly prepared, exhibited remarkably good instincts, and the speed with which they acted doubtless saved his life. Some 86 percent of victims rescued within the first fifteen minutes of being buried survive, but if a victim is not rescued in under thirty minutes, his survival chances drop below 50 percent. Only one in three victims will survive if buried for an hour; one in six after two hours; and one in ten after three hours. Stories of people surviving incredibly long burials are legion in avalanche literature. Colin Fraser quotes from a 1765 book with the impressive title *A True and Particular Account of the Most Surprising Preservation and Happy Deliverance of Three Women Buried 37 Days by a Heavy Fall of Snow from the Mountains at the Village of Bergemoletto in Italy;* the women were buried in a stable full of livestock and survived by drinking the milk of a goat that not only lived through the ordeal but actually gave birth to a kid in the midst of it.

Not surprisingly, the angle at which a victim's head comes to rest after an avalanche has a great deal to do with determining his chances of survival; almost twice as many people survive if they are buried faceup as facedown. Probably this is due to the head of the faceup victim sinking a bit and creating an air space. Falling facedown, a victim's mouth and nose only become more solidly packed with snow. But even faceup, the amount of oxygen available to a burial victim is limited. Unlike fluffy snow at the surface, snow crystals smashed together during an avalanche have most of the ambient air between them squeezed out. Worse yet, the warmth of a victim's breath, provided that it is unimpeded by a mouthful of snow, can seal the snow around his mouth much like perspiration seals the inside of an igloo or a snow cave. Within minutes, the breath can form a virtual mask of ice around the face, cutting off any flow of air.

One of the most terrifying things about being buried in snow, Sali found, is the complete absence of perspective or, for that matter, light; before he was rescued he saw more light with his eyes *closed*. Like being roughly tumbled by a wave at the beach, being scrambled amid tons of snow eliminates any sense of up and down, right and left; once buried, surrounded by an utter tomb of snow, it is impossible to determine which way to dig in order to become free. In a panic, a victim might logically dig as fast as possible straight up, over his head. But what if he had landed upside down? Expending precious energy, he would only have dug himself deeper into the snow. How, then, to figure out which way is up? Unlike the scuba diver, who can always follow his bubbles to the surface, a buried skier has no certain way to find safety. There is only one way, albeit exquisitely unmanageable, to tell up from down. And that is to spit.

Whichever way the saliva falls is down. If the spit falls—or drips—straight past a victim's right ear, digging to the left is up, and out. Convincing himself to dig a tunnel to his left, knowing that any false starts might mean quicker death, means trusting that little drop of spittle. Not unlike the way test pilots confronted with acute vertigo during a high altitude spin must trust their instruments and not their guts, which are telling them to PULL UP! at all costs, avalanche victims have maybe one chance to get it right. And trying to watch a dribble of spit, in the dark, in the cold, with little oxygen, perhaps with a number of broken bones, would require an almost unimaginable presence of mind.

That is, of course, provided the snow hasn't already become so compacted and cemented that digging in any direction hasn't already become unthinkable. The trouble with moving snow, especially with moving wet snow, as Sali found out, is that when it stops it tends to settle and harden very quickly. All the air between the individual crystals is squeezed out, and the newly compacted snow becomes impossibly dense.

With so little oxygen available under snow, then, avalanche survival depends critically on the efforts of survivors to dig out their compatriots. There just isn't time to wait for rescuers. When all five members of an expedition get buried, the chances for survival are very slim.

The trouble with the west face of Mount Cleveland, Frauson told the boys, is that like many faces in the higher elevations in Glacier, it is virtually bare. There are no protective stands of trees, and any piles of rocks cascade to the bottom as soon as they accumulate. The west face is therefore wholly devoid of safe havens.

The best option, Frauson told the boys, would be to ascend the face via one of the two ridges that form the sides of the bowl, which would keep the climbers above—and therefore out of—any avalanche danger. He didn't need to remind them that the only way to walk along a ridge in winter is on the windward side. With so much wind at high altitude—mostly coming from the northwest—blowing so much snow around the top of the mountain, ridgelines become crusted over with exceedingly dangerous formations called cornices. Piles of wind-packed snow that hang over precipices like waves, cornices can look like extensions of the rock but are in fact veneers of snow from inches to a few feet thick; snow overhanging a cliff is among the most volatile on any slope. Walking along a ridgeline, climbers can all too easily step out onto a cornice for a better view and find themselves falling through thin air. Gerald Seligman, in his landmark 1962 book, *Snow Structure and Ski Fields,* wrote of them with awe. "Curling over the crest of a ridge, the shrieking storm whirls the snow grains with it, and deposits them with a gentle care fantastic for so wild an agent, gradually fashioning the most perfectly molded cornice coverings to the ridge, every curve a delight to the eye—surely one of the most extraordinary paradoxes of beauty arising from evil." A number of famous mountaineers—Hermann Buhl in the Karakoram and Bugs McNeith in the Canadian Rockies—have walked off cornices to their deaths.

If the ridgelines bordering the west face have trouble spots of their own, just getting to them in winter is no easy trick. Because the west face is, on close inspection, in fact made up of a series of bowls expanding upward and separated by rocky ledges, rather than one single, smooth, and continuous bowl, detecting the amount of snow high on the face is impossible from below. From the ground beneath Mount Cleveland, Frauson told the boys, they might look up and be convinced that the mountain was entirely free of snow—entire swaths of bare rock can be seen from below, with individual boulders plainly visible sticking up from the slope. The trouble is, this view would be incomplete; from below, the walls that separate the bowls hide the slopes above them, slopes that might indeed be packed with stiff, wind-driven snow blown over from the north face. Such snow cover could support itself even if the layers beneath it were so weak that they masked huge air pockets. Such optical illusions had, in the past, suckered climbers into believing they had found a safe, snow-free path to the top; since the slope appeared clean as far as anyone could see, there didn't seem to be any possible danger of avalanches. The same situation could easily present itself on the west face. Even if snow did in fact gradually begin to appear underfoot as climbers made their way up, it could mistakenly be dismissed as thin and harmless, when in fact it was a major avalanche just waiting to unload.

After some lengthy discussion, the boys decided that they would try the north face after all. They also told Frauson not to worry about them until noon on Friday, January 2. As they left, Frauson wrote in his station logbook: "Five boys checked out to climb Cleveland on six-day expedition."

Another phrase, popular at the time, that Frauson might well have tacked on to his notation had been coined two years earlier after three astronauts were killed aboard the *Apollo 1* spacecraft. It referred to missions that proceed despite the considered warnings of experts in the field.

"Go fever."

Enthusiasm at the beginning of the expedition ran high, as it always does. Domestic responsibilities had been left behind. Life had become simplified to meticulously chosen climbing gear, intimate friends, and the glorious mountains. With so much adrenaline and joy running in their veins, the boys felt physically elated; no matter the terrain, they figured, they would not even notice their fatigue until the third day out. They were fresh, strong, and highly skilled, thrilled over the prospect of the final climb of what had been a gorgeous season in the mountains. They camped the first night at St. Mary, then made their way on Saturday, December 27, across the Canadian border to Waterton Townsite, a humble collection of uniform wooden buildings—white, with red asphalt shingle roofs, a door, and two windows on every facade—that served as the administrative headquarters for Waterton Lakes National Park. In Waterton, they checked in with the Royal Canadian Mounted Police, and hired a local named Alf Baker to ferry them by motorboat back across the border to Glacier's Goat Haunt ranger station. Eight miles away, at the other end of Waterton Lake, Mount Cleveland rose mightily above its neighbors, dominating the southern horizon as the boys made their way across the water. The boat ride offered the five young climbers ample time to think about their expedition; the closer they came to the southern end of the lake, the larger the mountain looked, until, at last, it filled their field of vision. The Goat Haunt station had long been closed for the winter, but it served as a convenient trailhead. The ride across the lake was exhilarating, and freezing. Temperatures were stuck in the high teens during the day, and ice had already begun to form on Waterton Lake. As the boys scanned the gray skies and the snow-dusted slopes jutting up all around the lake, their enthusiasm for the trip would have been tempered by the cold. The autumn had been unusually mild, but winter weather in northwest Montana is never certain, especially up high, and there is no way to tell how things will feel at 8,000 feet when you are standing down below at 4,000. Winds whip faster, ambient moisture turns to snow. Although there were only a few inches of snow on the shore of the lake and in the nearby foothills, how much snow had accumulated at higher altitudes was impossible to know.

Baker dropped the boys off at about 11:00 in the morning. Jerry Kanzler wore a full beard under a blue balaclava, but his thin mustache, under a fleshy nose and dark eyebrows, gave away his age. Jim Anderson was the first ashore. Spinning around, he snapped a photograph of Clare Pogreba, who wore an orange slicker, baggy pants, and a dark knit hat as he pulled the little aluminum boat ashore, with Kanzler in a blue canvas-shelled jacket preparing to hand out a pair of wooden snowshoes. Protruding off the bow were three sets of metal ski poles, their baskets pointing outward like a bunch of flowers. Ray Martin, already ashore in his winter coat with a fur-lined collar, knelt on the nearby dock, arranging backpacks and a long pair of wooden skis.

These first moments of organization were done hastily, the boys stamping the cold from the boat ride out of their feet and rubbing their hands after handing over aluminum ski poles and packs. The distribution of gear at the moment your last contact with home disappears can be poignant; the moment Baker left, they were on their own, stuck with their equipment, their experience, and each other. It's one thing to plan a trip in a warm living room back home, and another thing to feel confident, out in the subfreezing mountains, that the guy bending over his pack on the dock really could, in a moment of crisis, save your life.

The dock on which the boys unloaded their gear was covered in snow. Once they had hauled out their gear, Baker turned his boat around and left the boys behind, an American flag on his bow snapping in the winter breeze as he returned to Waterton Townsite. Anderson took another photo, this one of Mark Levitan on the dock checking his gear with his back to the camera; Kanzler looks back over his shoulder at Anderson, and Ray Martin, wearing a skull-hugging balaclava and towering over the others, smiles from out on the dock's edge. Perhaps Levitan was nervous, knowing that at least sections of the Mount Cleveland climb were beyond his ability. Perhaps Martin was nervous as well; his time spent atop peaks in Montana and radio towers in Alaska notwithstanding, he, too, knew that Cleveland would be the most difficult climb he had ever attempted. And since he and Pogreba had organized the expedition, he may have felt some additional responsibility; indeed, with Baker's departure, Martin and Pogreba, both twenty-two years old, became the senior members of the group.

Perhaps because they were hiking off-season, when there were no rangers to check their progress, the boys did not sign the Goat Haunt registration book, a simple procedure that is considered standard even for day hikers. A signed register gives park rangers their first point of reference when looking for lost climbers. The Mount Cleveland team did not plan to get lost. So far, they had simply retraced the steps they had taken to get to the Citadel Spire the year before, and getting to Cleveland was no great chore; there it was, straight ahead of them, an impossibly dominating landmark.

The trail leading to Mount Cleveland is easier to follow in the winter than in the summer, when thick brush covers much of it. Anderson snapped a picture of a set of cross-country ski tracks leading toward the north face of the mountain; multiple pole marks make it plain that the boys moved along in single file, the leader breaking trail and the others following in his tracks. The mountain, blue-gray in the overcast light, juts up above a passing cloud. Its north face, utterly barren of vegetation, looks like an inverted arrowhead, chipped out of stone and sharp on either edge. The horizontal striations left by passing glaciers are plainly visible across the face.

An hour or two later, Anderson snapped another photo, this one looking back, and down, toward Waterton Lake, filling a valley and running almost due north back toward Waterton Township. From this vantage point, perhaps 500 vertical feet above the edge of the lake, the boys could see that despite the relatively light snowfall thus far in the season, there was in fact considerably more snow above the tree line than there was below. More snow than they had planned on seeing, period. The months of fabulous fall climbing weather had apparently come to an end. The Cleveland climb could no longer be thought of as a late-autumn expedition. This was winter.

The lake itself looked battleship gray. Alf Baker and his boat were long gone. Ice could be seen inexorably creeping its way from the edges of the lake toward the middle; in another couple of weeks, the lake would be completely iced over, the last access to Mount Cleveland shut down until June.

Unshouldering his pack during a break in the woods, Pogreba gave Martin his camera and asked for a photo of the team checking their gear. Martin's pack, larger than the others, carried a set of ski poles in addition to a sleeping bag, and Mark Levitan, still carrying his pack, held ski poles of his own. Whether the boys were skiing at this point is impossible to tell; now that they were climbing more steadily, perhaps they left their skis down low and were using the poles only as walking sticks. Kanzler and Pogreba were both wearing high lace-up leather boots, and were not skiing; although they packed snowshoes, the snow was not deep enough, here under the trees, to merit their use. Levitan wore black plastic glasses beneath a light green hat, and an orange ski suit, a heavy coil of climbing rope strapped to the top of his green pack. Anderson's ice ax, sticking straight up from the top of his pack, looks like an antenna poking out from a military-issue pack radio. Kanzler, his blue winter jacket looking thin and dusted with snow, carried a double load. His own orange pack was strapped atop his father's old green Kelty like a koala cub clinging to the back of its parent.

But rather than following this creek to the west face, the boys followed another line—along Cleveland Creek—to the north face instead. They moved ahead with their plan to climb the Great Face of Cleveland. They would take the elevator of snow rather than the parabolic mirror, and try to make some history.

By the end of the day, after a four-mile walk fully loaded with gear, the Mount Cleveland team reached the base of the north face, and set up a base camp. What they saw could not have been inviting: snow clouds covered the mountain's summit, and snow had begun to accumulate on the north face, with loose powder avalanches regularly scrubbing it clean as quickly as the snow built up. Beneath the face, and out of reach of the avalanches, the boys decided to build three snow caves in case the weather turned much colder. Snow is a far better insulator than the nylon walls of their mountain tents, and for a short stay, a snow cave can be a cozy place to ride out a storm. There, beneath the frigid stone of the north face, they spent the night.

The next day, Sunday the twenty-eighth, with snow still falling on the upper reaches of the mountain, the team began to discuss their options for the most difficult leg of the trip: the final approach and climb of the mountain's most vertical upper reaches. Up until now, the team had found shelter in the trees below the mountain's shoulders, and had had little difficulty in their approach. Now, however, the going would get steep, and treacherous. Two routes presented themselves: the north face, their original goal, and the west face. The north face would demand their most exquisite technical climbing skills, skills that at least two of the team, Jim Anderson and Mark Levitan, did not possess. The north face would require the full use of ropes and climbing hardware. The lead climber, moving like a spider, would inch his way up, hammer pitons into the frozen rock, and run his rope through an aluminum carabiner. The chill of the rock would be unforgiving, the footing slick, and the handholds, where they existed at all, unreliable. The north face, in summer, was more than any but the country's best climbers would even consider. In winter, it seemed impossible, especially with a pair of climbers who would literally be learning their first steps on the icy face.

A far more tenable route would take the boys along the serrated knife's edge of the northwest ridge, which would take them over to the west face and an easier, if still challenging, way to the top. The west face, although at 35 degrees not nearly as steep as the virtually vertical north face, would still require utter vigilance from the team. Ropes would be used not to clip into the rock, but to hold the team together, in case someone slipped on the ice. If one of the team slipped, the others would hold fast and hope they weren't dragged down as well.

The team's decisions were not casually made. With the weather always threatening to turn, the boys wanted to get up and down the mountain without delay. As they made their way up, step by step, they checked constantly for settling and cracking snow underfoot, to gauge the tension in the snowpack; even if the snow down low was thin, it was still useful as a predictor of the deeper stuff up high. Their cheeks picked up any shifts in the wind, helping determine which angles in the mountain would be covered in deeper, wind-blown snow. They listened to their footsteps, making sure not only that the snow immediately beneath them felt solid, but that any unstable layers buried underneath would support their weight as well. They listened as their footsteps fell for any sounds of sudden settling, the ominous "whoompf" of a weak layer of invisible depth hoar giving way under their weight.

The climbing was plainly using every bit of energy the boys could muster; a photograph taken during the trip showed them sitting under a ledge, visibly freezing and physically spent. Jerry Kanzler, leaning forward, holds his face in his left hand.

Even with the boys less than halfway into their journey, those most concerned for their safe return began nervously checking the skies. Back at St. Mary, Bob Frauson drove to a spot near Cardston, Canada, to look at the peaks and assess the weather. He reported seeing a heavy cloud cap hovering above Mount Cleveland, although the Stoney Indian Peaks to the south were clear. George Ostrom and his brother had flown up to their ranch near the Canadian border, and upon reaching it they looked back toward the mountains of Glacier. Even from a distance, they noticed the unmistakable plumes of avalanches cascading "all over." As an inveterate hiker himself, Ostrom was no stranger to avalanches; he tells stories of seeing slides "that would make Niagara Falls look like spilled teacups." Once, hearing an avalanche begin while hiking on Mount Grinnell, he looked at an adjacent slope and saw a herd of mountain goats standing in the direct path of the slide. At the last minute, the avalanche turned and went to the east, just missing the goats, who had not moved. "That thing fell like thunder, but the goats knew it would turn," he said. "How the hell did they know?"

Any new snow on Mount Cleveland, of course, would add weight to the existing snowpack, which may have been unstable to begin with. New snow is a common cause of avalanches, particularly in the hours during and immediately following a storm. Those watching the peaks from afar knew this, and prayed the boys did too. Out on Mount Cleveland, though, at least one of the climbers had something on his mind in addition to the deteriorating weather.

The next day, Monday, December 29, would have been Hal Kanzler's forty-ninth birthday.

Part 2

Track

Chapter 10

❄

*The power of such a mountain is so great and
yet so subtle that, without compulsion, people
are drawn to it from near and far, as if by the
force of some invisible magnet; and they will
undergo untold hardships and privations in
their inexplicable urge to approach and to
worship the center of this sacred power.
Nobody has conferred the title of sacredness
on such a mountain, and yet everybody
recognizes it; nobody has to defend its claim,
because nobody doubts it; nobody has to
organize its worship, because people are
overwhelmed by the mere presence of such a
mountain and cannot express their feelings
other than by worship.*

— Lama Anagarika Govinda,
The Way of the White Clouds

Mountains have not always been places for people to prove their
might or seek their destiny. Monks and medicine men in many spiritual traditions have chosen deserts and mountains as the places in which to shed the influences of human endeavor, and to meditate or commune with the holy. A
Hindu sage once wrote that a hundred ages of the gods would be insufficient to
tell the glories of the Himalayas, and he was not talking about the glories of
man. The Dravidians of ancient India spoke of a lone, naked yogi, the physical
embodiment of the Absolute, sitting atop Mount Meru (known also as Mount
Kailash) in perpetual contemplation of eternity. Buddhist mythology allows
that the human realm is represented by four islands surrounding Mount Meru,
which rises into the sky and is occupied by deities whose holiness increases
with elevation. Floating above the mountain are four heavens, the highest of
which serves as the home of Maitreya, the future Buddha. Pilgrims do not
climb this mountain, they circle around it—often on hands and knees. Indeed,

if Nepalese Sherpas rush to assist western climbers on Everest expeditions, they would not consider desecrating a holy mountain like Kailash, which half a billion of the world's people consider to be among the holiest places on earth. It is the home from which the Hindu god Shiva and his wife, Parvati, gaze down on the joys and sorrows of humanity. Tibetans revere Kailash as the peak on which the great yogi Milarepa triumphed in a contest of supernatural powers with a priest from the native Bon religion and secured the peak as eternally Buddhist. Three peaks around Kailash provide homes for Manjushri, Vajrapani, and Avalokitesvara, who symbolize respectively the wisdom, power, and compassion required of all those seeking enlightenment.

The Native American Hopi tribe consider Mount Meru to be the other end of the earth's spine, which in their country juts up through the Black Mesa. Native Americans have always told creation stories about the world's high places, but they, too, rarely climbed them for sport; hunters in some tribes would abandon expeditions rather than follow their prey into a holy mountain's upper sanctuaries. The Sioux, the Cheyenne, and the Crow, among other tribes, climbed sacred mountains only during vision quests, when they hoped to push through their experience of the temporal world to find the strength and wisdom of the holy. "The harshness of the environment on the summit of a mountain also contributed to the ordeal of self-inflicted suffering that some tribes made an essential part of the undertaking," Edwin Bernbaum writes in his wonderful study *Sacred Mountains of the World*. "To demonstrate their commitment and willingness to sacrifice everything for a vision, the Crow would even cut out strips of their flesh and chop off joints of their fingers." Those without proper ritual preparation were forbidden from entering certain mountains. A Sioux legend has it that Custer died in his battle with Crazy Horse because he had climbed Bear Butte just prior to the Battle of Little Big Horn.

Mount Kenya, the world's only mountain with a country named for it, has long been revered by native Kikuyu as being the home of their god Ngai. The Masai worship Ol Doinyo Lengai, in Tanzania, as the home of the god Engai, Bernbam writes, and the Chagga regard Mount Kilimanjaro as "the divine embodiment of all that was exalted, eternal, and nourishing." Likewise, the Chinese consider mountains to be divine sources of water; the clouds and mists that surround them are the mountains' holy respiration. The Taoist term for an immortal, *hsien,* is composed of two pictographs, one of a man, one of a mountain.

In ancient Europe and the Middle East, mountains, or mountaintops, at least, were also once considered sacred; like Gothic cathedrals, with their vaulted ceilings, they offered invitations to look skyward for salvation. Greek gods inhabited Mount Parnassus and Mount Olympus; Prometheus first stole fire from atop the Caucasus. Moses received the Ten Commandments atop Mount Sinai. Noah landed his ark atop Mount Ararat. David built his capital on Mount Zion. Muhammad saw the angel Gabriel on Mount Hira. Jesus delivered the Sermon on the Mount. But more broadly, mountains—and wilderness generally—have traditionally inspired fear in western minds; Eden, a garden called by the Hebrew word for *delight,* was notably lacking in uncharted territory. There was no wilderness in paradise. The Greeks, British essayist John Ruskin wrote, considered mountains beneath their aesthetic consideration. "They carved, or variously represented, men, and horses, and beasts, and birds, and all kinds of living creatures—yes, even down to cuttlefish; but not so much as the outline of a mountain." The Romans either ignored mountains—Catullus, Virgil, and Horace rarely mention them—or considered them inhospitable and hostile. Titus Lucretius Carus, writing in the first century B.C., felt it was a "defect" for the earth to be so "greedily possessed by mountains and the forests of wild beasts." The earth, he wrote, "is filled full of restless dread throughout her woods, her mighty mountains and deep forests."

The wandering experience of the Israelites gave wilderness a new meaning, one that lingers today, as a sanctuary from which to escape the sins and persecutions of society, as a place in which men test themselves against inhospitable forces, and as a place in which to get closer to God. For the early Christian, wilderness represented the moral chaos of an unregenerate world, with primeval forests the domain of demons and spirits all too eager to steal a good man's soul. In the Middle Ages, the saga of Beowulf depicted

> *Wolf-haunted valleys, perilous fen paths*
> *And windswept headlands, where the mountain stream*
> *Descends beneath the shadow of the cliffs,*
> *A torrent down the crags . . .*
>   *T'is not a pleasant spot;*
> *Dark toward the clouds the turmoil of the waves*
> *Leaps upward from it, until the heaven grows dark*
> *And the skies weep.*

When Petrarch climbed Mount Ventoux in 1336—considered by some to have been the first recreational climb—he found great pleasure in wandering "free and alone, among the mountains, forests and streams." But rather than delight in the view from the summit, Petrarch took out a copy of St. Augustine's *Confessions,* which he habitually carried, and was disheartened to read that good Christians should not take pleasure in the wonders of the world, but should concentrate wholly on their own salvation. "I was abashed, and . . . I closed the book, angry with myself for not ceasing to admire things of the earth, instead of remembering that the human soul is beyond comparison the subject for admiration. Once again, as I descended, I gazed back, and the lofty summit of the mountain seemed to me scarcely a cubit high, compared with the sublime dignity of man."

In the 1600s, Europeans preferred that nature be tame, cultivated, charming—not wild and unruly. God, they reasoned, had made the earth a perfectly symmetrical oval, a "mundane egg"; the scars and blemishes of mountains were somehow caused by human depravity. A majority of Christian thinkers blamed mountains on the sins of Cain, Marjorie Hope Nicolson writes in *Mountain Gloom and Mountain Glory.* Even more frequent, it would seem, was the belief that "mountains, like other distortions of the earth, were an immediate result of the sin of Adam and Eve. Tenfold punishments were inflicted at that time on Adam, on Eve, and on the serpent, and—according to some interpretations—on earth also." Mont Blanc, the highest peak in the Alps, was until the eighteenth century known to locals as Mont Maillet or Mont Maudit—"Accursed Mountain"—in part because Satan had been banished to the mountain's interior after a failed battle with St. Bernard.

It was only during the Enlightenment, with geologists, philosophers, and astronomers pointing out the harmony and complexity of the universe, that Europeans first began to associate nature with the holy. Mountains in the early seventeenth century were still regarded as "warts, wens, blisters, and imposthumes," but by the 1680s and 1690s books were appearing with titles like *The Sacred Theory of the Earth* and *The Wisdom of God Manifested in the Works of the Creation.* Awe, once reserved for God, began to apply to His natural works—from the cosmos straight down to the mountains, oceans, and deserts. Over the next hundred years, philosophers like Edmund Burke and Immanuel Kant advanced the idea of the "sublime," which associated nature directly with God, and assured Europeans that rather than terror, awe and exhilaration could be found in wild nature. Part of this philosophical shift, then as now, stemmed from the anxiety of urban dwellers over their increasingly mechanized and polluted cities. Suddenly, to the overwrought cog in the wheel of the Industrial Revolution, a walk in the woods didn't seem so bad.

From the late 1700s forward, Romantic painters began "traversing the wildest places of the globe in order to obtain subjects with craggy foregrounds and purple distances," Ruskin wrote. "Some few of them remain content with pollards and flat land; but these are always men of third-rate order; and the leading masters, while they do not reject the beauty of the low grounds, reserve their highest powers to paint Alpine peaks or Italian promontories." Suddenly, nature was worthy of worship, and a generation of Romantic poets in the early nineteenth century—Wordsworth, Shelley, Keats, Byron, and Coleridge—began to sing its praises. In "Mont Blanc: Lines Written in the Vale of Chamouni," Shelley wrote in 1816 of a mountain that had first been climbed just a generation before.

> *Far, far above, piercing the infinite sky,*
> *Mont Blanc appears—still, snowy and serene—*
> *Its subject mountains their unearthly forms*
> *Pile around it, ice and rock; broad vales between*
> *Of frozen floods, unfathomable deeps,*
> *A desert peopled by the storms alone,*
> *Blue as the overhanging heaven, that spread*
> *And wind among the accumulated steeps;*
> *Save when the eagle brings some hunter's bone*
> *And the wolf tracks her there—how hideously*
> *Its shapes are heap'd around! rude, bare, and high*
> *Ghastly, and scarred, and riven.—Is this the scene*
> *Where the old Earthquake-daemon taught her young*
> *Ruin? Were these her toys? or did a sea*
> *Of fire envelop once this silent snow?*
> *None can reply—all seems eternal now.*

Across the Atlantic, Romantic voices were echoed and inflected by the American Transcendentalists, particularly Emerson, Thoreau, and Whitman, who were also steeped in Buddhist and Hindu philosophies of nature. Broadly conceived, these traditions have always placed mankind within rather than above the natural world, and have offered a useful counterpoint to western notions of mountains and wilderness. Petrarch's hand-wringing over his delight in the mountains is emblematic of the West's troubled relationship with the natural world. The view that the earth is somehow blemished, or inherently flawed, has for years led scholars to point a finger at Judeo-Christian tradition as having contributed to the West's shortsighted attitude toward all things ecological. The landmark essay "The Historical Roots of Our Ecological Crisis" published by Lynn White in 1967 blamed the Judeo-Christian notion of linear, rather than cyclical, time: since heaven awaits, in other words, why bother preserving this world? "Christianity, in absolute contrast to ancient paganism and Asia's religions, not only established a dualism of man and nature but insisted that it is God's will that man exploit nature for his proper ends," White wrote. If such polemic overlooked other roots of western exploitation, like two centuries of unbridled capitalism, and turned a blind eye to Asia's own intense industrialization and urbanization as well, it nonetheless provides an interesting light in which to think about mountain climbing as a sport that glorifies man rather than mountains, at its root a decidedly western idea.

The civilizations that grew up in and around the world's highest mountain ranges—the Incas in the Andes, the Tibetans in the Himalayas, the Mexicans in the southern Sierra Nevada, the Navajo, Hopi, and Pueblo groups of the southern Rockies—worshiped high places as the centers of the universe or the hubs of creation; Chinese and Japanese painters celebrated nature more than a thousand years before western artists. Ancient European and Middle Eastern cultures, by contrast, developed in river valleys, deserts, and pasturelands— far from the wilds of the mountains—and were thus easily able to conjure terrors that existed in the high places. Indeed, contemporary Buddhist thinkers, it seems, are less than pleased with the mountaineering craze, which has swept Japan as ferociously as it has the West. "In these prosaic days of ours, there is a craze among the young men of Japan for climbing high mountains just for the sake of climbing, and they call this 'conquering the mountains.' What a desecration!" the Zen scholar D. T. Suzuki wrote in 1959. "This is a fashion no doubt imported from the West along with many others not always worth while learning." The Judeo-Christian notion of mankind's having "dominion" over nature has contributed immeasurably to his sense of isolation and alienation from the natural world, Suzuki writes, and the image of a mountaineer "conquering" a mountain can only be seen as a predictably neurotic outgrowth of this. "We of the Orient have never conceived Nature in the form of an opposing power. On the contrary, Nature has been our constant friend and companion, who is to be constantly trusted in spite of the frequent earthquakes assailing this country of ours. The idea of conquest is abhorrent."

———

Like much of the history of world exploration, the story of mountaineering is largely a story of Europeans—and later, Americans—traveling farther and farther afield in search of new routes to discovery, gold, and celebrity. "In keeping with the individualistic nature of their sport, climbers tend to view mountains as centers in a personal rather than a cosmic sense," Edwin Bernbaum writes. "Many of them order their lives around a peak that has become the focal point of their attention, subordinating everything to the task of reaching its summit. The mountain becomes the central preoccupation of their waking thoughts and the recurring image of their nightly dreams." Reinhold Messner, the twentieth century's most admired mountaineer and certainly one of its most studied historians, considers Antoine de Ville's ascent of France's Mont Aiguille in 1492—the same year Columbus arrived in the Americas—to have marked the advent of sport climbing. "Was it just a whim? Surely not. Curiosity? A lust for conquest? Perhaps. At the beginning of the New Age the idea of conquest spread like wildfire in the Occident. Man wanted to rule the earth once and for all: the philosophy was perceived as a religious mission by Europeans. . . . In doing so, discovery had not been his impulse, nor the exploration of the mountain, nor the opening of access to it. Only conquest, in its own right. Nothing else." Although the Spanish documented a climb of Ecuador's volcano Pichincha in 1582, archaeological evidence suggests that several high peaks in the Andes were climbed by natives well before this; with their reputed sixteenth-century ascent of the 22,000-foot Chilean volcano Llullaillaco, Atamaca Indian climbers apparently made it higher than anyone in the world until Europeans climbed the Himalayan peak Abi Gamin three hundred years later.

By most accounts, it wasn't until 1741 that a group of Englishmen climbed Montenvers in Chamonix, France, that sport climbing began in earnest. The Genevese scholar Saussure offered a reward in 1760 for the first climb of Mont Blanc; the first serious attempt, in 1775, ended in failure when the four climbers returned almost snow-blind. The peak remained unscaled until 1786, when Dr. Michel-Gabriel Paccard and Jacques Balmat, a local chamois and crystal hunter, made the first ascent; following the ordeal, Balmat stated that "my eyes were red, my face black and my lips blue. Every time I laughed or yawned the blood spouted from my lips and cheeks, and, in addition, I was half blind."

With the exploration of mountains came dangers more real than those of superstitions, particularly in winter, when the strange vagaries of snow added to the troubles of backcountry travel. Colin Fraser's opulent *Avalanches and*

Snow Safety, though sadly out of print, brims over with incredible accounts of mountain tragedy and heroism. His book compiles centuries of anecdotes dug out of the archives of the Swiss Federal Institute for Snow and Avalanche Research and Britain's Royal Geographic Society and Alpine Club; the result is a vivid history of avalanches and man's efforts to survive them. Although soldiers and explorers had been dying in the world's mountain ranges for millennia, it wasn't until August 20, 1820, that a councillor to the emperor of Russia named Dr. Hamel became the first tourist to die in the mountains, in an avalanche on Mont Blanc. Dr. Hamel decided to climb the mountain with an optician from Geneva named Selligue, who hoped to try out a homemade barometer. They were joined by two Oxford students, along with 12 guides.

Their first night out they were hammered by a severe storm, which forced them to stay in place for another day and night. Dr. Hamel, according to one account, insisted that the group continue, despite the dramatic premonitions of one guide, who, weeping hysterically during the preceding night, had thrown himself into the arms of a friend and cried out, "It's all over with me! I shall be killed up there!" Selligue and two guides remained behind. Dr. Hamel and the rest continued. Among their gear was a pigeon in a cooking pot, cooing contentedly as the group prepared for the final ascent. Suddenly, the snow released from its fragile mooring, and the entire group was engulfed by an avalanche 70 yards wide. The first three climbers in the line were swept down a crevasse and buried. The fourth and fifth were flung across the first crevasse and buried in a second one, but later managed to escape. The remaining members of the party were only partly buried, and little hurt. Forty-three years later, in the Glacier des Bossons just above Chamonix, there appeared pieces of skull complete with hair, an arm, a foot severed below the calf, a large piece of a man's back, an intact compass, and a frozen pigeon in a pot.

From the mid–nineteenth century forward, mountaineering developed into the established sport it remains, with climbers scrambling to have their names affixed to first ascents and ever more dangerous routes. Just as fine artists, who once painted anonymously for popes or kings, gradually became celebrities in their own right and created cultures of narcissism around themselves entirely apart from their work, mountaineers initially drawn to the quiet mysteries of the mountains were now beginning to climb to bring celebrity to themselves, and their countries. Even the language used to describe first ascents had the ring of colonialism. The British "claimed" Mount Elbrus, Europe's highest mountain, in 1868; the Germans "took" Kilimanjaro in 1889; South America's Aconcagua "fell" to the British in 1897; Mount McKinley "went" to the Americans in 1913. When Edmund Hillary, a New Zealand beekeeper, and Tensing Norgay, his Nepalese teammate, climbed Everest in 1953, word of their achievement reached England on the eve of Queen Elizabeth's coronation, and offered the beleaguered, post-Imperial British a chance to once again claim world supremacy. With each ascent, the rhetoric the climbers used to describe their exploits grew ever more dramatic. Perhaps it was their experience of oxygen depletion, perhaps it was the unprecedented depth of the visual field; in any case, the language of high mountain exploration took on a mystical glow.

"I felt as though I were plunging into something new and quite abnormal," wrote Maurice Herzog, in his report on the 1950 ascent of the Himalayan mountain Annapurna, the first 8,000-meter (25,000-foot) peak ever climbed. "I had the strangest and most vivid impressions, such as I had never before known in the mountains. . . . This diaphanous landscape, this quintessence of purity—these were not the mountains I knew: they were the mountains of my dreams. . . . I had never seen such complete transparency, and I was living in a world of crystal. . . . An astonishing happiness welled up in me." After seven unsuccessful attempts, the British climber Edward Whymper and several partners first climbed the Matterhorn in 1865 and became major celebrities in the process. On the way down, however, Whymper watched helplessly as four members of his team fell off a 4,000-foot precipice; when he returned to England he was greeted with criticism and a query from Queen Victoria about whether a law should be passed banning mountaineering. Whymper's book *Scrambles Amongst the Alps* contains a poignancy all too familiar to veteran mountaineers. "Still, the last sad memory hovers round, and sometimes drifts across like floating mist, cutting off sunshine and chilling the remembrance of happier times," Whymper wrote. "There have been joys too great to be described in words, and there have been griefs upon which I have not dared to dwell; and with these in mind I say: Climb if you will, but remember that courage and strength are nought without prudence, and that a momentary negligence may destroy the happiness of a lifetime. Do nothing in haste; look well to each step; and from the beginning think what may be the end." Rather than dampen the British enthusiasm for climbing, the Matterhorn incident—like all mountaineering tragedies, it seems—only served to enflame it.

The new heroism also cultivated an entire genre of wilderness writing, in which explorers outdid themselves describing their harrowing adventures. If, as some say, romantic love did not exist before poets came up with the words to describe it, danger in the mountains found vivid expression in the words of mountaineers who put themselves in harm's way and came home with fabulous stories to tell. "It may be admitted that the mountains occasionally push things a trifle too far, and bring before their votaries a vision of the imminence of dissolution that the hangman himself, with all his paraphernalia of scaffold, gallows, and drop, could hardly hope to excel," wrote Albert Mummery, one of Britain's most celebrated climbers, in 1895. "But grim and hopeless as the cliffs may sometimes look when ebbing twilight is chased by shrieking wind and snow and the furies are in mad hunt along the ridges, there is ever the feeling that brave companions and a constant spirit will cut the gathering web of peril."

Predictably, the heroic impulse of the middle and late nineteenth century caught the attention of satirists as well, who saw in all the far-flung expeditions no small hint of self-aggrandizement. John Ruskin wrote that his contemporaries looked upon the Alps as "soaped poles in a bear garden, which you set yourselves to climb and slide down again, with shrieks of delight. . . . You rush home, red with cutaneous eruption of conceit, and voluble with convulsive hiccough of satisfaction." Mark Twain, in his 1880 tale *A Tramp Abroad,* described the hoopla surrounding the great climb of "The Riffleberg." Organizing a team of 51 animals (44 mules and seven cows), 154 men (including 17 guides, 15 barkeepers, 12 waiters, and four pastry chefs), the team leader assembles the gear (including 22 barrels of whiskey, 2,000 cigars, 154 umbrellas, and 143 pairs of crutches), and sets off. After a series of narrow escapes, the leader makes it to the grand summit—in full formal attire. "Yes, I had made the great ascent," Twain writes, "but it was a mistake to do it in evening dress. The plug hats were battered, the swallowtails were fluttering rags, mud added no grace, the general effect was unpleasant and even disreputable."

Across the Atlantic, the craze advanced more slowly. Although a climber named Darby Field and two perplexed Native Americans climbed New Hampshire's Mount Washington in 1642, the honor for North America's first "high mountain ascent" is generally accorded Edwin James for his climb of Pike's Peak in 1820. Far from the romance of the Alps, Americans in the nineteenth century looked to their western mountains not as places in which to find God but places to find gold. "The absorbing pursuit of money, the strangely practical character of the American mind, so averse to anything merely visionary, are quite sufficient to account for the absence of that *passion des montagnes* which is so often to be met with in older communities," wrote Edmund Coleman, an English mountaineer who had scaled Washington's Mount Baker in

1868. "Those who come out to the Western States do so either to make money, or to build up a home for themselves and families; consequently, they have neither the time nor the money to spend in what is generally considered to be a visionary, if not a foolhardy pursuit."

In the twentieth century, all this changed. As Americans settled in high mountain mining camps in Colorado and California, they gradually learned to climb for sport, and soon created their own gallery of first ascents: Mount Rainier, 1870; Grand Teton, 1898; Mount Logan, Canada's highest peak, 1925. As Europeans and their American and Canadian heirs explored more and more of the continent's high peaks, the challenge for sport climbers became one of finding new and more difficult ways to climb the same peaks—with harder routes, less equipment, or more adverse winter conditions. Part of this was made possible by the arrival of European climbing gear like slings, pitons, and carabiners, which opened up the mountains on this continent to a whole new array of possible approaches. Finding new routes up familiar peaks became a kind of exploration in miniature, like finding new territory on a vertical plane. With no more continents to tame, and all too few peaks left to climb for the first time, mountaineers challenged themselves the way gymnasts, or divers, or skaters do: they upped their skill levels and did things—on the same peaks as their forebears—in challenging and stylish ways that left their peers breathless. Three French alpinists made the first winter ascent of Mount Rainier in 1922; a pair of German brothers named Stettner took technical climbing to a new level in 1927 with an ascent of the east face of Colorado's 14,256-foot Longs Peak, the highest in Rocky Mountain National Park. Paul Petzoldt and two others made the first winter ascent of the Grand Teton in 1935. In addition to the challenges of cold weather climbing, like the constant dangers of hypothermia and frostbite, and the dangers of frozen terrain, like avalanches and crevasses, winter climbing offered climbers the chance to experience, at home, some of the trials of the famous climbs being attempted in the Himalayas. If there was no need to carry oxygen to the top of the Tetons, mastering the use of ice axes and crampons—metal, toothy plates attached to the bottom of climbing boots—at least allowed ambitious climbers a new opportunity to make headlines.

With the rise of affluence and the return of American mountain troops, American climbing took off after the Second World War. Rock climbing clubs began springing up in California's Sierra Nevada particularly, and Yosemite National Park became the new mecca for young climbers. By the late 1950s, Royal Robbins and Warren Harding took the sport of "big wall" climbing to new heights with their first-ever ascents of Yosemite's Half Dome and El Capitan—respectively 2,000 and 3,000 feet of heart-stoppingly vertical rock. Yvon Chouinard, another Yosemite legend, who had once been hauled off to jail for eighteen days in Winslow, Arizona, for vagrancy, joined Robbins, Chuck Pratt, and Tom Frost as the first to climb the North American Wall of El Cap. Once penniless and haggard, Chouinard, who had been selling improvised climbing hardware out of his truck around the time of his arrest, would go on to become a celebrated manufacturer of climbing gear and the founder of the Patagonia clothing company. (Robbins started his own clothing company as well, named it for himself, and by the mid-1990s was selling some ten million dollars' worth of clothes a year.) In 1963, seven Harvard students took a route straight up the center of 14,000-foot Wickersham Wall on Mount McKinley. But that same year it was an American ascent of Mount Everest that gave young American climbers a new generation of heroes.

Ten years after Edmund Hillary and Tenzing Norgay's first ascent—and just three weeks after a Seattle climber named Jim Whittaker became the first American to climb it—a thirty-six-year-old professor of theology named Willi Unsoeld and a thirty-two-year-old doctor named Tom Hornbein reached the roof of the world via Everest's West Ridge, considerably more challenging than either of the two routes previously accomplished. Along the way, the two climbers were forced to spend the night without shelter above 28,000 feet— the highest bivouac in history at the time—and although both men survived, Unsoeld would lose his toes to frostbite. Worse yet, one of their teammates, Jake Breitenbach, was killed in an avalanche on the mountain's notorious Icefall, the first of 19 people killed on that slope alone.

The story of avalanches in the United States in many ways parallels the story of American mountains themselves, and largely follows the same course of westward exploration. Because the great eastern mountain chains—the Smokies, the Blue Ridge, the Catskills, the Green Mountains, the White Mountains, the Adirondacks—are relatively tame and lush, they have historically been explored and even settled with little trouble from snowslides. The regional literature reflects this. Thoreau considered winter "a cabinet of curiosities, full of dried specimens, in their natural order and position"; Emerson, during a winter walk, discovered an image that would serve as the basis for much of his Transcendental thought: "Crossing a bare common, in snow puddles, at twilight, under a clouded sky, without having in my thoughts any occurrence of special good fortune, I have enjoyed a perfect exhilaration. . . . I became a transparent eyeball; I am nothing; I see all." Hawthorne considered winter storms an excuse to get cozy. "Gloomy as it may seem, there is an influence productive of cheerfulness and favorable to imaginative thought, in the atmosphere of a snowy day," he wrote in an essay entitled "Snow-flakes." "Blessed, therefore, and reverently welcomed by me, her trueborn son, be New England's winter, which makes us, one and all, the nurselings of the storm and sings a familiar lullaby even in the wildest shriek of the December blast."

It was only when pioneers began to move west, into bigger ranges that captured and held more snow, that American mountains turned ominous. Native Americans took to the high country to escape the heat of summer, but once the aspens began to turn gold in the fall, they would leave the hills and head back to the plains, following herds of elk and pronghorn. This all changed, as wilderness often does, with the discovery that some mountains contained limitless mineral riches, or simply stood in the way of Manifest Destiny. Snow suddenly became an impediment, something to be cleared from the road so the business of exploration, commerce, and settlement could continue. Some 280 patents for snowplows were taken out in the late nineteenth century, the *Railroad Gazette* reported in 1891. "They include devices to plow the snow, to remove it with knives and spoons and buckets and wheels." The construction of the transcontinental railroad in the 1860s introduced engineers to the hazards of snow and avalanche-prone mountain slopes; their solution was to build sugar pine snowsheds over the tracks to keep cascading snow from derailing passing trains.

The first non–Native Americans to explore—and die in—American mountains were settlers and trappers, but few historical accounts survive of their experiences with avalanches. In contrast to European villages, which suffered because of extensive residential development on mountain slopes, the first large-scale avalanche catastrophes in the United States occurred with the advent of commercial development, which especially early on meant that the highest number of victims were those looking for silver and gold. Extracting the Comstock Lode, some miners acknowledged the damage they were doing to the mountains. "It was as if a wondrous battle raged in which the combatants were man and earth," wrote a visitor to Virginia City, Nevada. "Myriads of dust-covered men are piercing into the grim old mountains, ripping them open, thrusting murderous holes through their naked bodies." The mountains often repaid this violence in kind. *The Avalanche Book,* quoting nineteenth-century newspaper reports, recounts the story of the winter of 1883–84, in which 100 people were killed in Colorado, including 20 in the San Juan Mountains in the southern part of the state. Badly hit was the Virginius Mine, perched on a steep, 12,000-foot mountain above the town of Ouray. December 1883 had brought continuous snow for three days; late in the storm an avalanche barreled into the mine's boarding house, "carrying death and destruction in the mighty embrace," according to a newspaper account in *The Solid Muldoon*. Four men were killed, and rescuers took twenty-four hours to find the last two survivors. The following day, 32 men from nearby mines came to Virginius to help recover the bodies; as they pulled the "sled hearses" beneath a particularly steep slope, they were engulfed in another avalanche, this one nearly a quarter mile wide.

Photographs of avalanche rescuers from this era show men dressed in three-piece woolen suits, complete with hats and neckties, standing in a line in the snow. At their feet are wooden sleds bearing the bodies of avalanche victims, covered in canvas. The rescuers, formal in their attire as if they have just performed a makeshift funeral, appear stunned.

As mines began to close early in the twentieth century, the number of avalanche deaths dropped accordingly. It would not be until a second wave of commercial development—and mountain recreation—started that people would again begin dying in large numbers. As Americans began moving into cities in ever greater numbers in the late nineteenth century, there arose another in a series of "back to nature" movements, with city dwellers looking to the mountains, even in winter, for escape from crowds and noise. Although people in Scandinavia, Russia, and Hungary had been hunting and traveling on skis for six thousand years (the modern version of the word *ski* comes from the Latin *scindere,* for "split," since skis were split from solid logs) and had developed skiing into a sport in the early nineteenth century, it would not become popular in the United States until a hundred years later. The first American ski book was published in 1905, and downhill skiing as it is practiced today did not gather momentum for another thirty years. Along with its growth came anxiety about people's changing relationships with the winter mountains. A debate over the development of a ski area on Oregon's Mount Hood in the late 1920s made local residents contemplate the meaning of wilderness, of allowing "the sophisticated and man-dominated region of every-day life into the borders of an ultimate and essentially untamed alpine wilderness of rock and snow and ice." If a resort would make some people rich and make the Mount Hood region a major draw for tourists, shaving away the mountain's trees and replacing them with hotels and cable cars would compromise its natural integrity. Averell Harriman's resort in Sun Valley, Idaho—known as the St. Moritz of America before it was even finished being built—is generally given credit as opening the modern alpine skiing era in the United States; his complex, which he built in part to lure people onto his Union Pacific Railroad, included Austrian ski instructors, luxury accommodations, and, most important, mechanized lifts. For the first time in history, people could get to the top of a mountain without having to climb it.

Over the next twenty years, the federal government began subsidizing American skiing by building roads and leasing land to private developers. Shortly before World War II, Felix Koziol, the supervisor of the Wasatch National Forest in Utah, joined with Alf Engen, a legendary early skier, to build Alta, outside Salt Lake City; they would hire Monty Atwater in 1945, in the resort's seventh season, to oversee avalanche control. All over New England and the West, ski tourists began crawling over the mountains. From the beginning, downhill skiing was a sport largely enjoyed by the well-to-do; wealthy skiers learned the sport in the Alps and then came home to practice on slopes in Massachusetts and New Hampshire and Vermont. "Ski trains" began shuttling weekenders to the Berkshires and the Green Mountains, where first towropes and then mechanical lifts would take them to the top of the mountains. The peaks had been tamed, some thought for the worse. "The whole business of skiing was becoming too much like the day-to-day business of life," the ski historian E. John B. Allen writes. "Parking lots filled up, the line for a ski tow paralleled the one for train tickets earlier in the day. An extra rope tow had to be put into operation to handle 'rush hour.'" It would not be long before bumper stickers appeared in New Hampshire reporting that THIS CAR CLIMBED MOUNT WASHINGTON, and before helicopters annually began dropping hundreds of wealthy skiers atop peaks in the Canadian Rockies that even today may actually have been climbed by less than a dozen people.

By the 1960s, ski resorts in the United States began flourishing in full, and media superstars like the French alpine champion Jean-Claude Killy became household names. "To say the least Killy is very—how yu say eet in Engleesh—hot," burst out a satiric piece in *The Denver Post,* with an overwrought stylistic nod to Tom Wolfe. "He's sensational! Extraordinaire! A gas! He's Jean-Claude Killy, the greatest superhero since Charlemagne, or at least since Ally Khan. . . . See Killy challenge Mt. Ngauruhoe, 7,515 feet of rumbling volcano in New Zealand! Watch the daredevil fight mad bulls on the French Riviera! Weewowzakboomsisba!" Killy's success had an enormous impact on the skiing industry in France, and the world. In a rush to capture the sport's newfound popularity, France poured money into old resorts like Val d'Isere, overlooking the fact that the venue was smack in the middle of three converging valleys and would serve as a natural catch basin for avalanches from all sides. On February 10, 1970, an avalanche rumbled over a building occupied by 280 children, killing 39 and injuring many others. American resorts, and the upscale housing communities that accompanied them, would soon find themselves confronting tragedies on a similar scale.

In northwestern Montana, meanwhile, the climbing and skiing communities were still relatively quiet. If Yosemite and the Grand Tetons had become the places of pilgrimage for hotshot young climbers, and Alta, Sun Valley, Aspen, and Vail were the equivalent for skiing, Glacier National Park and its environs remained comparatively unexplored. The Kanzler family represented the hub of a small local climbing group that remained removed from the rest of the world. No one was coming to Glacier to break world records. "We'd been trying to keep all this quiet," Jim Kanzler said. "There's nothing in *Climbing in North America* about us—we were out on the fringe. A friend of mine who had gone to the National Outdoor Leadership School [in Lander, Wyoming] and climbed with Galen Rowell came over from Yosemite and told us we were in the backwater of climbing. That's when we got the idea that we weren't going to talk about it. Anything we did in Montana we were going to keep in the verbal tradition. Once you write about it, every idiot for miles will try to climb where we've been climbing. We wanted to keep it quiet. We didn't care about being famous."

Hal Kanzler and his two sons, Jim (front) and Jerry, hiking in 1959 near Glacier National Park's Boulder Pass, just east of the Continental Divide. The north and west faces of Mount Cleveland dominate the distant view to the east. Ten years later, Jerry would die on Mount Cleveland, and Jim would risk his life trying to save him.

PHOTO BY HAL KANZLER, COURTESY OF JEAN KANZLER

Jerry Kanzler, age thirteen, on a hiking trip in the Bob Marshall Wilderness, south of Glacier National Park, 1964. Thanks to the inspiration of his father, Jerry became one of northern Montana's finest young climbers in the 1960s and, along with his older brother, Jim, and friends Ray Martin and Clare Pogreba, explored much of the northern Rocky Mountain wilderness.

Jim Kanzler on cliffs above Hidden Lake in Glacier National Park, 1963. Jim has spent much of his life in the mountains of Montana and Wyoming, and in recent years has become one of the country's top climbing guides. During the winter, he works as an avalanche forecaster in the Tetons.

Clare Pogreba (fourth from left) and Ray Martin (behind him) were inseparable friends and climbing partners in Butte. Here they are shown with other members of the Montana Tech Climbing Club.

Two years before they made their attempt on Mount Cleveland, Jim and Jerry Kanzler, Clare Pogreba, and Ray Martin became the first ever to climb Citadel Spire, a rocky pinnacle in Glacier National Park. On their way, Jerry Kanzler took this photograph of his climbing companions with Mount Cleveland in the background. Cleveland's north face is visible to the left of the center ridgeline; the west face bowl is to the right.

Clare Pogreba, with ropes and ice ax, during winter climb. Pogreba was so enamored of ice climbing that in order to practice his skills in winter, he would flood the steps of his college football stadium to create steep sheets of ice.

The 1969 expedition to Mount Cleveland began with a boat trip from Waterton Townsite, Canada, south across the border to the Goat Haunt ranger station in Glacier National Park, Montana. Jerry Kanzler (left) and Clare Pogreba, along with Ray Martin, were the most skilled climbers in the group. Two other young climbers, Jim Anderson and Mark Levitan, were experienced but had little knowledge of winter camping or technical rope climbing. This photo and the four that follow were discovered in a camera found by the search party.

Clare Pogreba pulls the boat ashore to unload ski poles, showshoes, and other gear at Goat Haunt. To the right, Ray Martin checks his backpack and skis on the dock.

Mark Levitan, Ray Martin, and Jerry Kanzler on the dock as boat captain Alf Baker leaves for home. Baker was the last man to see them alive.

The boys' ski tracks leading from the lake toward the 4,000-vertical-foot north face of Mount Cleveland, which had never before been climbed.

The team stops for a gear check. From left, Jerry Kanzler, Jim Anderson, Clare Pogreba, and Mark Levitan on the way to the foot of Mount Cleveland. This is one of the last images of the boys taken before they disappeared.

Less than a week after the boys left, family members notified the Park Service that the team had not returned, and a massive search began. Two dozen men began looking for the boys in early January 1970. Most of their supplies had to be ferried by boat from Waterton to Goat Haunt, until bitter temperatures and ice forming on the lake made such efforts impossible.

The rescue team in a probe line at the base of the north face of Mount Cleveland. Each searcher would plunge a probe deep into the snow, hoping to hit a buried body. The step-by-step pace of the search was agonizingly slow.

One of two cameras discovered during the search. Color film found inside was flown overnight to a developer in Vancouver and returned the next day, but provided little insight. Exposed black-and-white film found in a canister proved more useful, however, and seemed to indicate that conditions on the mountain were far worse than the rangers—or the boys—had anticipated. As the winter weather grew worse, the search ultimately had to be abandoned until the spring thaw.

Ski patrollers use a variety of explosives to release avalanches before they endanger paying customers. Here, patrollers at a Colorado resort shoot an avalauncher, a modified mortar that was known as a "soup gun" in the 1960s because it was first tested by firing cans of soup.

Colorado ski patrollers watch as a hand charge explodes on a small slope. Forty years ago, explosives with ignition caps and fuses replaced electronic bombs that required dozens of yards of wiring; the pioneering snow ranger Monty Atwater said that a ski patroller could suddenly throw explosives "like a newsboy delivering papers."

In June 1970, the search for the missing boy continued. George Ostrom and a ranger hiked up the west face, hoping to discover some clues in the melting snow. Here, the ranger stops by Camp Creek. Although he and Ostrom did not know it, the boys were buried in the snowfield visible just above the waterfall.

Not long after Ostrom and the ranger abandoned their search, another team, led by ranger Jerry DeSanto, climbed higher on the west face and, peering into a cave hollowed out by spring runoff, discovered Ray Martin's body suspended from the cave's ceiling.

Once Martin's body was discovered, rangers began digging deep trenches to locate the others. The slope on which they worked was so steep that a loose cartload of snow nearly knocked the park superintendent over a cliff.

After days of trenching, a ranger stands nearly eighteen feet below the surface. At his feet is a body bag.

Another ranger follows a red climbing rope into a hole. At the ends of the rope were Ray Martin and Jerry Kanzler.

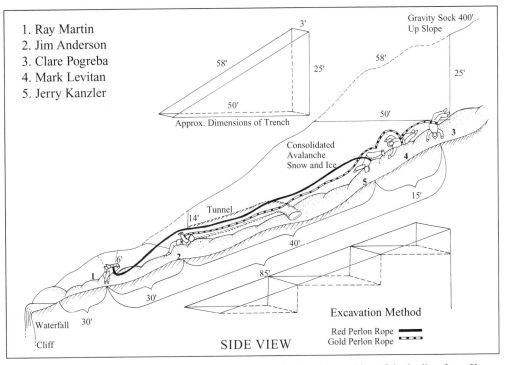

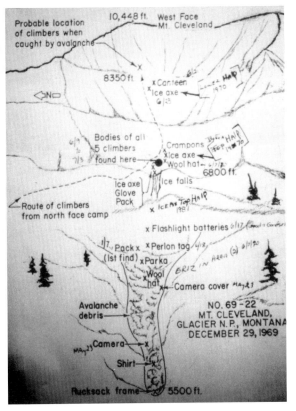

1. Ray Martin
2. Jim Anderson
3. Clare Pogreba
4. Mark Levitan
5. Jerry Kanzler

Approx. Dimensions of Trench

Consolidated Avalanche Snow and Ice

Tunnel

Excavation Method

Red Perlon Rope
Gold Perlon Rope

Gravity Sock 400' Up Slope

Waterfall
Cliff
SIDE VIEW

A schematic diagram of the trenches, and the location and final resting position of the bodies. Jerry Kanzler and Ray Martin were discovered attached to a red climbing rope; Jim Anderson, Clare Pogreba, and Mark Levitan to a gold rope.

10,448 ft. West Face Mt. Cleveland

Probable location of climbers when caught by avalanche

8350 ft
Canteen
Ice axe

Bodies of all 5 climbers found here
Crampons
Ice axe
Wool hat
6800 ft.
Ice falls

Route of climbers from north face camp

Ice axe
Glove
Pack

Flashlight batteries

Pack (1st find)
Perlon tag
Parka
Wool hat
Camera cover

Avalanche debris
NO. 69-22
MT. CLEVELAND,
GLACIER N. P., MONTANA
DECEMBER 29, 1969

Camera
Shirt
Rucksack frame
5500 ft.

A diagram of the west face of Mount Cleveland, showing where the bodies and the boys' gear were discovered. Rescue personnel estimated that the boys made it above 8,300 feet before being caught in a massive avalanche. Their bodies were carried some 1,500 vertical feet by the slide; their gear was deposited over more than a mile.

Rescue pilot Jim Kruger leaving the west face in his Bell helicopter. Attached to his landing gear are two body bags.

The rescue team found the varnished half of this ice ax during the search, and gave it to Bob Frauson. Frauson kept it in his office until, a year later, the other, weathered half was found; the two pieces fit together perfectly. The photograph shows the west face of Mount Cleveland, with the left-hand arrows indicating where the two halves of the ax were found. The right-hand arrow shows where the bodies were discovered.

The north face of Mount Cleveland, which Jim Kanzler, Terry Kennedy, and Steve Jackson climbed in 1976, becoming the first ever to do so. On the way down the west face they stopped near the site where the five boys had perished.

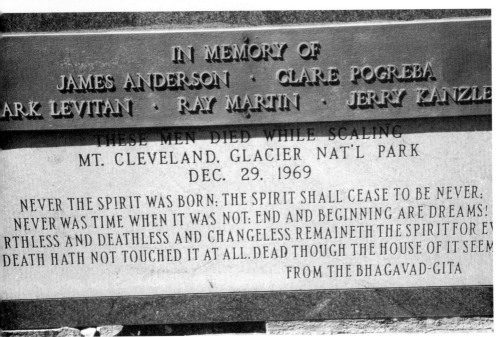

IN MEMORY OF
JAMES ANDERSON · CLARE POGREBA
ARK LEVITAN · RAY MARTIN · JERRY KANZLE

THESE MEN DIED WHILE SCALING
MT. CLEVELAND. GLACIER NAT'L PARK
DEC. 29. 1969

NEVER THE SPIRIT WAS BORN: THE SPIRIT SHALL CEASE TO BE NEVER:
NEVER WAS TIME WHEN IT WAS NOT: END AND BEGINNING ARE DREAMS!
RTHLESS AND DEATHLESS AND CHANGELESS REMAINETH THE SPIRIT FOR E
DEATH HATH NOT TOUCHED IT AT ALL. DEAD THOUGH THE HOUSE OF IT SEEM
FROM THE BHAGAVAD-GITA

A memorial plaque in honor of the boys, near the shore of Flathead Lake. Jim Anderson's father, a mason, built the memorial, along with a stone bridge, near the lake's Yellow Bay.

Bob Frauson, leader of the Mount Cleveland search effort, at home in northwest Montana, 1999. Frauson, a veteran of the Tenth Mountain Division during World War II, became one of the country's early experts in winter mountaineering and backcountry rescue. He worked for decades as a ranger for the National Park Service in Wyoming, Colorado, and Montana.

Chapter 11

❄

*I think there is no difference if you die at
twenty or at sixty. It's more difficult for a wife
or a child or a mother to understand it than
for a climber himself; it's never a tragedy for
the one who dies, because the one who dies is
not living the tragedy. The tragedy is only with
those who survive.*

— Reinhold Messner,
quoted in Nicholas
O'Connell, *Beyond Risk:
Conversations with Climbers*

On Tuesday, December 30, Bob Frauson left St. Mary for a scheduled few days of skiing at Big Mountain, directly on the opposite side of the park. As he left his station, he noticed that extremely high winds had begun buffeting the mountains. It was an ominous sign: winds have a way of piling up and cementing vast quantities of ground snow, contributing significantly to slab formation on leeward slopes, particularly at higher elevations like the upper bowl of Mount Cleveland's west face. If a weak layer of depth hoar lay underneath the new snow, Frauson knew, the wind-blown layer could become just heavy enough to precipitate a major slide.

Frauson was not the only one concerned by the weather. Bud Anderson, James's older brother and a recreational pilot, had hoped to fly a single-engine plane over the Mount Cleveland area to chart the boys' progress; four days into their trip, they would be plainly visible somewhere along the north face.

He hoped, perhaps, to rock his wings at them as a sign of encouragement, or congratulations, depending on how far they had gotten. But as the day progressed, the winds became so strong, and the cloud cover up high so thick and cottony, that Anderson was unable to make the flight.

The next day, New Year's Eve, Anderson's luck changed. Flying over Mount Cleveland, he spied what looked like tracks leading along the lower reaches of the mountain's west face, which he thought odd, given the boys' north face itinerary. Perhaps they had changed their minds when they realized how much snow had fallen, or maybe the north face had proven too tough. As he looked closer at the tracks, though, his breath caught. The tracks ended at the unmistakable edge of a massive fresh avalanche, about halfway up the mountain. Strangely, Anderson also thought he saw tracks leading away from the debris, and thus, perhaps unconsciously, convinced himself that the group had managed to avoid disaster and continue on its way. Perhaps the team had crossed the face before the avalanche had hit, and the avalanche had simply covered up their footprints. Surely the boys were by now already on their way back to the Goat Haunt ranger station, and would be checking in by morning. Nonetheless, his anxiety grew.

"We had a bad feeling about it really. My brother Don and I both felt that something was wrong," Anderson said. "It had been a really mild winter. There probably wasn't eight inches of snow on the ground when they left." It was only once he was up in his airplane, however, that Anderson realized that when the boys began their trip there was in fact a full three feet of snow up on the west face, and more had begun falling almost as soon as they left. If they had tried the north face, they would have found themselves constantly bombarded by small avalanches, as the vertical slope cleansed itself of powdered snow before it could build up. If, on the other hand, they had chosen the bowl of the west face, they would have found themselves in a different kind of danger, since the amassing snow would have posed a serious threat of releasing as a slab. Given the way the weather had played out in the late fall and early winter—light snow, followed by cold temperatures—the snowpack on the west face of Mount Cleveland had become a textbook example of depth hoar formation.

If Bud was worried about his kid brother, he remained confident that the boys' collective training would convince them to turn around if things got too sketchy. To Jerry DeSanto, a Glacier ranger, the Mount Cleveland group should never have tried such a difficult climb in winter, especially once they had been told how perilous the upper reaches of the mountain had become.

DeSanto had been the summer ranger at Goat Haunt for three years, but the day the word came in that the boys were out past their return time, he was working at park headquarters in West Glacier, and had not known of the boys' expedition. "The sign of a true mountaineer is one who can get to within 100 yards of the top and turn around, even if there's no danger," he said. "These kids were looking up, even after 20 inches of snow had fallen, and they couldn't resist."

DeSanto had climbed Mount Cleveland, and knew its dangers. A veteran mountaineer and experienced rescue worker, DeSanto grew up in Duluth, Minnesota, but came west in 1949. After bouncing around a couple of universities in the southwest, he graduated from the University of Colorado at Boulder, and later made it halfway to a Ph.D. in medieval history—another in a long line of climber-scholars who gravitate to the West's vast wildernesses. He worked seasonally in Yellowstone in 1952 and came to Glacier in 1966, where, in addition to his Park Service work, he drove down to Missoula once a week from his post in East Glacier to do graduate work in botany.

All told, he spent twenty-one years working in the field as a Park Service ranger; every time he was asked to "move up" to a desk job, with better pay and less risk to life and limb, DeSanto would demur and head back into the mountains. He received high marks for his work in all areas but one. Park rangers in previous years had been encouraged to wear German forest sweaters: good, thick clothing that protected them against the changeable weather. But with more rangers spending more time doing office work, dress requirements changed as well; you can always tell a ranger's habitat by looking at his shoes. DeSanto passively protested, refused to trade in his well-worn boots and field clothes, and—after he was given the lowest possible mark for attire on an annual review—was finally told that he had the worst uniform in the park. DeSanto now says that he "was as proud of that zero as of anything in my career."

Eventually, DeSanto's refusal to come in from the mountains caught up with him. One summer he received a call that a couple of kids from Great Falls had gone camping up the North Fork of the Flathead; one had come back and reported the other one missing, and DeSanto was told to go find him. He drove to the end of the service road, which ended at Kintla Lake, and started hiking down the Boulder Pass Trail, which had been closed for the search. Coming around a bend in the trail, DeSanto was confronted with one of the park's most dangerous situations: a sow grizzly and a pair of little cubs.

———

Grizzly bears are, along with the peaks, Glacier's most majestic in-habitants. More than any other creature in North America—more than wolves, more than eagles, more than wild mustangs—grizzlies are the living symbol and embodiment of wilderness. Requiring vast areas in which to forage and breed, grizzlies have been shoved farther and farther back from the rest of the Lower 48, and now only occupy land that is either utterly inhospitable or legally restricted from human habitation. Grizzlies are alone in their position at the top of the food chain, and few are the hikers in bear country who are not conscious of this. Walking through a thicket of huckleberry bushes, one is all too aware of the rather astonishing physical attributes of grizzlies: reaching weights of up to 900 pounds, they can nonetheless run faster than a quarter horse; some estimate that in a 100-yard dash they would beat the world's fastest human by 35 yards, or, in a mile run, by half a mile. Their strength has also been well documented; grizzlies have been known to fracture the head of a bull moose or full-grown horse with a single blow. But more than their physical profile, it is a simple and uncompromising need for open space that has made grizzlies such a difficult animal for humans to accommodate. In some ways, grizzlies are like the rock climbers with whom they share remote mountain terrain: pushed to the edge of the North American continent, they have been forced into places that others consider too wild, too unforgiving, too dangerous. The image of a grizzly forced to look for food above the tree line is not far different from rock climbers pushing to test their skills on vertical cliffs that will kill them with the slightest mistake. Both are quite literally up against the country's walls. A dedicated rock climber would have about as much chance as a grizzly of surviving in a world of golf courses, manicured subdivisions, and shopping malls.

In the first thirty years of Glacier National Park's existence, only one per-son, in 1939, was killed by a grizzly, largely because the park had so few visi-tors, and the second attack didn't occur until seventeen years later. By the time ten more years had passed, however, the number of visitors to Glacier had grown to more than one million per year, and nine more people were attacked, three seriously. Over the next three decades, as people continued to pour into Glacier every summer, tromping through the park's backcountry in record numbers and leaving garbage and food waste in their wake, bears became in-creasingly used to thinking of people as sources of easy meals. Bear-human encounters continued to increase, occasionally with tragic results for both people and bears. But as late as the 1960s, grizzlies were not considered a regular threat. "If you set up a danger index ranging from zero to ten, where the butterfly is zero and the rattlesnake is ten, the grizzlies of Glacier National Park would have to rate somewhere between zero and one," a ranger in the 1960s told the writer Jack Olson. "The rattlesnake kills about ten Americans a year. The grizzly kills about none. It's foolish to talk about the grizzly menace to human life."

As a frequent guest in grizzly bear country, Jerry DeSanto knew how to move among them without getting himself into trouble, and for a moment, when confronted by the family of bears, DeSanto thought he would be okay. Rangers in Glacier know grizzly bears like rangers in other parks know raccoons, and DeSanto stayed calm, averting his eyes, and making himself appear as nonthreatening as he could. Unlike raccoons, however, grizzlies occasionally allow their curiosity to supersede their natural fear of humans, and suddenly, one of the grizzly cubs came bounding up the trail toward DeSanto. He immediately tried climbing a tree, but the mother ran right at him and started clawing at his leg. With a swipe, she tore his shoe off, grabbed him by the calf, and jerked him out of the tree. Once on the ground, DeSanto rolled into a ball, waiting for the inevitable. The mother bear clamped her jaws down on his wrist right by his watchband, and bit down hard, puncturing his wrist to the bone. For some reason, perhaps because they prefer to intimidate rather than kill, grizzlies often leave an attack well short of a mortal mauling, and this bear let go of DeSanto's wrist and started to walk away, apparently satisfied that DeSanto had been properly humbled. DeSanto apparently thought otherwise; as the bear walked away, he yelled out an oath and swung his day pack like a club, banging it into the retreating bear. "To be perfectly frank, she was just as scared as I was," DeSanto said.

In any case, the bear decided to leave well enough alone, gathered her rambunctious charges, and walked off into the woods. But DeSanto's plight was far from over. Bleeding heavily from his punctured wrist, he had to walk two miles back to the lake's patrol cabin, where he found some rags and bandaged his wrist. He then took a boat eight miles across the lake, where he finally found a couple of campers, and told them he was in trouble. They piled him into their car and drove him five miles to a field known as Round Prairie, where he radioed for help. By now the loss of blood had DeSanto falling into a state of shock. The rescue helicopter arrived in time to fly him to the hospital in Kalispell, where a doctor sewed him up and released him, with a scar and a good story to tell. The boy DeSanto had hoped to find, it turned out, popped up in Kintla Lake days later, a drowning victim.

What DeSanto took from the Kintla Lake incident, beyond further evidence of the unpredictability of grizzly bears, is something only the wisest back-country experts know: that the best thing wilderness experience can teach you is humility. "I always get so mad at the people over in headquarters. They think that if you have experience you have all the answers," he says. "The fact is, the more experience you have, the more you realize you *don't* have the answers."

DeSanto's sentiments, of course, apply broadly in the backcountry, as perhaps they do in life generally: only the foolish can convince themselves that they know everything, or even *can* know everything. Life, for those willing to learn, has a way of teaching the value of *not* knowing—bowing respectfully before forces more powerful or mysterious than might even be imagined. The idea of "conquering" a mountain, to someone like DeSanto, is ludicrous. Indeed, the very idea of achieving notoriety by climbing mountains is, to those who spend their lives saving the unsuccessful, a dangerous impulse. Whether climbers broadcast their achievements to the world's mountaineering press, or merely, in hushed and somber tones, tell each other, they are still risking their lives for a version of celebrity. If the park's paper pushers ("rangers who sit in front of computers all day") frustrate field men like DeSanto, brash, so-called extreme climbers plainly scare them. Backpackers and climbers who push the limits of their expertise endanger not only themselves but the rangers who must remain constantly on alert in case they get in over their heads. "These new guys are more intent on conquering mountains. The older guys were just outdoor-sort-of-guys—they might have wanted to get to the top of a mountain, but they wouldn't try to do it the most difficult way. These sport climbers *drive* to the bottom of a face and then climb it. They don't walk there. That's rock gymnastics, to my mind. It used to be that getting to the mountain was as much trouble as climbing it."

When William Briggle, the park superintendent, called DeSanto into his office, he wanted to know what one of his top rangers thought about the boys. When DeSanto gave his opinion—that the boys were climbing in dangerous avalanche country, and might well have been caught—his boss seemed reluctant to agree. "He didn't believe it could have been an avalanche—he thought it was too early in the season," DeSanto said. "I said it sure as hell could have been."

The uncertainty among even the most skilled backcountry rangers over the conditions on the upper shoulders of Mount Cleveland was not unusual. Forecasting avalanches, especially for those out in the field, remains a difficult, mysterious business; even physicists, working in the safety of cold-room laboratories with sophisticated computer models, often find themselves scratching their heads. For backcountry skiers and winter mountaineers, for whom avalanches are an ever-present danger, diagnosing the characteristics of a mountain slope is parallel to getting out of the canoe and reading a rapid before descending a particularly dangerous stretch of river. In both cases, one can get a fair sense of the potential danger just by observing flow dynamics. Signs of previous avalanches are an important factor: treeless slopes, broken or scarred trees, or "flag" trees with branches torn off on all but one side are clear indications that masses of snow have torn their way down. Sluffs of small loose-snow avalanches indicate instability, as do large snowballs rolling down a slope. Cracks or fissure lines running horizontally across a slope indicate a slab that has already fractured and may release with the slightest trigger.

There are no guarantees, and no certain safe zones. One might think that hiking or skiing along a sunny slope would be safest, since the wetter snow might be more likely to settle and stabilize. This is true, except after a storm, when the rapid warming may get the snowpack to start creeping downhill; if the creep is sufficient, the elasticity of the snow may become stretched to the point of snapping off a large slab. So, given the choice, particularly after a storm, one might choose a shady slope, since the snow would tend to be cooler and less prone to slide. Perhaps. Cool upper layers, as noted, often draw moisture from those lower down, and contribute to the formation of the faceted or cupped crystals of depth hoar.

A slope that is overloaded by new snow can slide at any time. Even if it hasn't snowed in weeks, a slope that has had a new layer deposited by wind becomes dramatically less stable. Snow falling off cornices can trigger an avalanche; so can snow falling from the branches of trees. The shape of a slope also matters. Hiking across or just below the hump of a convex slope is trouble, as is hiking anywhere in the upper reaches of a concave bowl. Better in either case to hike low, below possible fracture zones, or above, along a ridgeline that is immune to sliding. Traveling across a steep slope, hikers may find temporary havens from avalanches among outcroppings of rocks or trees, known as "islands of safety." But if a large slide should suddenly occur uphill—perhaps triggered even by a footstep far below—it could easily flow over and engulf the island and its inhabitants like a tidal wave washing out a tiny atoll. Snow is often weakest next to these little islands, and fractures begun by a step near a "safe" bush may trigger an avalanche that carries away the entire slope. In the winter of 1996, two experienced avalanche rangers on a bombing run at the Solitude resort in Utah came to a stop on a flat plateau above a sharp slope; one stood next to a tree and one just five feet away. When one of their hand charges triggered a huge slab avalanche, which broke right through the tree where the two were standing, the ranger closest to the tree was spared but his companion was not. Carried over a cliff and down 800 vertical feet, he was buried vertically, head up, with his mouth just 18 inches below the surface. Although he was rescued after only fifteen minutes, the ranger later died in the hospital.

If simply gazing on a slope was all it took to tell if it was safe, hundreds of people would not die from avalanches every year. Once, while teaching a course on route-finding after a heavy snowstorm near Jackson Hole, Rod Newcomb of the American Avalanche Institute took his students to a ridge above a large bowl. The weather was sunny, the powder light and fluffy. Just to make sure the run below was safe, Newcomb had his students dig a snow pit, to look at a core sample—a biopsy—of the snowpack. They found a major layer of instability less than three feet below the surface. As they were discussing what this could mean—that it might release at any time—a fissure suddenly yawned open, and ran directly through the pit they had just dug. With a "crack!" a massive slab broke off and took the bottom half of the pit's wall down the path the group had planned to ski. The lesson, it is fair to say, was learned.

In addition to judging a slope by its cover, there are a number of techniques one can use to help determine the strength and stability of a given snowpack. To judge the hardness or compaction of the snow, a hiker can punch his fist in the snow; if it penetrates that particular layer of snow, it is considered, in forecasting language, "very soft." If the snow resists, but gives way to four fingers, it is "soft." If it can be penetrated only by one finger, it is "medium hard," by a pencil, "hard," and by a knife blade "very hard." Of course, it is not simply the density of individual layers that is of interest, but also what may lie below these layers—or what may be trapped between them. Two perfectly hard, compacted layers mean anything but safe travel if they are sandwiched around a crumbly layer of ball bearings soft enough to put your fist through.

The first thing experienced backcountry skiers will do is dig a snow pit, as Newcomb did, to get a close-up look at the profile of the layers of snow beneath the surface. Like the rings in a tree stump, which can reveal fifty-year-old seasons of drought and rain as accurately as a farmer's almanac, individual layers of snow provide detailed evidence of a snowpack's formation. An hour-long heavy dump of snow followed by a few days of frigid weather followed by a light layer of surface hoar can be examined, in cross section, as fruitfully as a highway road cut, passing through a mountain, that reveals millions of years of rock formation. A number of simple techniques have evolved for diagnosing the personality of snow. The "burp test" consists of cutting a one-foot block of snow out of the pack and tapping the bottom of the shovel to see if and where the block fractures. When the snow is unstable, one can see smooth fracture lines between weaker and stronger layers. Similarly, in a "compression test," one taps the *top* of a block to see if any of the layers give way; the easier a layer shears or collapses, the more dangerous the snowpack. In the "shovel shear" test, one digs a small pit, isolates a column of snow, then uses the shovel to gently pull forward, to see how easily the block shears loose. Slab layers will frequently shear off in a clean plane.

Some more refined avalanche hunters use small paintbrushes to tease out individual layers; others go so far as to use a 15- or 20-power magnifying glass to examine the differences between snow layers. Grains that appear largest and loosest are indications of depth hoar; thin layers covered by new snow point to surface hoar. Layers of "graupel," or pellet snow, can cause snow to act like marbles on a slanted asphalt playground.

As thorough as these tests may seem, they are ultimately only reliable for the precise section of snow one is examining. If a skier planned to remain within the one-foot-square snow pit, in other words, he could feel quite safe. But since the characteristics of snow change so easily, given the shade of a stand of trees or the angle of a slope or the orientation of a face, one would have to dig a snow pit every ten yards to feel secure. And even then there would be no absolute certainty, given the vagaries of the deep, invisible snowpack. Perhaps the safest diagnostic technique, propounded in early English skiing manuals, is the "cow test." According to a certain expert named Professor Roget, quoted by Colin Fraser, "when in doubt, the ski-runner should ask himself: Are cows as I know them likely to feel comfortable when standing on this slope in summer? If an affirmative answer can be given in a *bona fide* manner, the slope is not dangerous."

Even the sheer, unpredictable frequency of avalanches should be enough to make backcountry explorers think twice about precarious slopes. Avalanches are among the most ubiquitous occurrences in the winter mountains. It is not unusual, after a single snowfall, for contemporary backcountry ski patrollers to observe hundreds of avalanches in a single week; from the air, they might observe thousands. The Westwide Avalanche Network, which compiles avalanche data from a number of American sources, records some 9,000 observed avalanches per year in the United States, but since so many avalanches occur beyond the sight of man, this must be considered a small fraction of the number that actually take place. Betsy Armstrong and Knox Williams, in their compelling volume *The Avalanche Book,* estimate that at least 100,000 avalanches occur every year in this country alone, and a similar number in the Alps, the Himalayas, and the Andes. Adding smaller mountain ranges in Scandinavia, Canada, Russia, and New Zealand, they figure that something on the order of one million avalanches fall somewhere each year. Given the snow that was beginning to fall in the northern Rockies, the team making the approach to Mount Cleveland was certain to encounter at least a few of them.

Since the boys had told their families not to worry until January 2, Bud Anderson spent New Year's Day at home. But early the next morning, he and Canadian warden Jack Christiansen took the boat to Goat Haunt for what they expected to be the triumphant return of the group. There was no one waiting for him at the dock. There were not even any tracks leading to the dock. The boys had not returned.

Hiking around the ranger station, Anderson and Christiansen did come across some ski tracks climbing up through the timber leading to the bottom of the north face. Following them, they found abandoned skis and snowshoes about a mile and a half from the lake, leading toward the north face and just about at the timberline. It appeared as if the boys had decided to make an attempt on the north face after all; their skis and snowshoes, once the going got too steep, were shed as cumbersome and useless. Regardless of the route up, the abandoned gear struck Anderson and Christiansen as an ominous sign. The boys had not returned to pick it up. They were still out there on the mountain.

Shortly after 9:00 A.M., Anderson called Glacier National Park chief ranger Ruben Hart to express concern. He told him of his flight two days earlier, and of seeing the strange footprints disappearing into, and then leading out of, the avalanche on the west face. The Park Service, knowing full well the dangers of backcountry travel in the Montana winter, kicked into full swing. Hart told Anderson to wait at the warden's office for a return call, and phoned Park Superintendent Briggle and Willie Colony, a supervisory ranger. Briggle dispatched Ranger Joseph Ries from St. Mary to Waterton Townsite to help coordinate the search and rescue efforts, and to provide radio communication between park headquarters and the rangers in the field. Briggle also called Chief Warden Bud Armstrong at Waterton Lakes National Park. Because the boys had begun their expedition on the Canadian side of the park, Canadian wardens were immediately notified of the team's disappearance. They would be a welcome addition to the rescue effort. As a group, the Canadians received backcountry training superior to that of their American peers; after the Second World War, several of the wardens had been hired from Austria, Switzerland, and Germany, where they had been steeped in the European tradition of alpine training. The Canadian Rockies are a vast alpine region, stretching from the United States border 1,100 miles north to the Alaskan border and comprising a wilderness far larger than anything in the Lower 48. To patrol such an expanse, Canadian park officials had decided to create a group of backcountry experts with the title "Alpine Specialists," who would combine deep experience, acute judgment, and strong wilderness leadership abilities. The position paid enough to attract people who otherwise would have been professional guides, and, given the country's fondness for the outdoors, offered them a kind of national celebrity that outstripped that given to their American peers. Jerry DeSanto had been through several training sessions in Canada, and in many cases considered Canadian wardens far better trained than his American colleagues.

As the situation grew increasingly foreboding, park officials called the Midwest Regional Office at 10:30 A.M. The decision was made to begin an aerial search through Malmstrom Air Force Base at Great Falls; officials there then called the Western Air Search Center at Hamilton Army Airfield in California. Park Superintendent Briggle also arranged through the Montana Aeronautical Commission in Helena for a fixed-wing aircraft search to be made. A plane was dispatched from Cut Bank, a small town on the prairie east of the park, but the pilot reported no signs of the climbers. He did report possible signs of tracks and a small snowslide on the mountain's northwest face, but he was unable to tell if the tracks had been left by humans or animals. Since the weather was extremely turbulent, with high winds ricocheting off the higher peaks, the pilot returned to Cut Bank and recommended against further flights.

At 3:00 P.M., Ranger Joe Ries was dispatched to the Goat Haunt station with a radio and told to stay overnight, in case the boys returned. By midafternoon, rangers had decided that a helicopter would be more versatile in a high mountain search than a small plane, and a call to the Western Air Search Center secured one for the following day. After Anderson and Christiansen had returned with their report of the skis, five rangers from each side of the border were told to be prepared to leave on a full-fledged search and rescue mission the following day.

On January 3, a day after the boys' planned return, two teams of rescuers gathered at Waterton Townsite to pack their gear—climbing skis, ice axes, probe poles, and ropes. Americans Jerry DeSanto and Doug Erskine, who had worked previously in Yosemite and Rainier, joined Canadian wardens Larry Tremblay, Christiansen, and a naturalist named Kurt Seel; despite the Park Service's reluctance to work with family members of missing climbers, Bud Anderson was allowed to join the group as well. The two teams of three caught a boat across the increasingly iced-over Waterton Lake, unloaded their gear at Goat Haunt, and hiked and skied their way to the north face of Cleveland and the beginning point of what appeared to be the boys' final ascent. DeSanto, Erskine, and Tremblay were to climb the northwest ridge route, to see if the boys had decided to veer off and try the western bowl. The second group, Anderson, Christiansen, and Seel, proceeding slowly on skis, found the group's tracks headed directly toward the north face, the more dangerous route Bob Frauson had warned against. The first few hours of the search were charged with nervous optimism. Perhaps, rather than return home to schoolwork and army recruiters, the boys had decided to stay out an extra day or two to revel in their triumphant climb. Even if they had gotten into trouble, as long as the boys were not in some sort of critical condition, they were probably all right. If, for example, one of the team had broken an ankle, or sustained some frostbite to his feet, they would probably have rationed their food for the extended trip home. Perhaps the rescue team would find the boys huddled around a fire, or meet half the team hiking out to seek help from rangers. No matter how they found them, the rangers wanted to find them alive. Search and rescue is a whole lot more heroic and rewarding work than body recovery.

Meanwhile, a military Huey helicopter from Malmstrom Air Force Base arrived at the Star School Strip, a few miles outside of Browning, at 9:20 A.M. A veteran ranger named Willie Colony met the helicopter, and flew back to the Waterton ranger station. When he arrived at 10:18, Colony was officially put in charge of the Mount Cleveland search and rescue mission.

Colony already had more than a decade of mountain rescue experience under his belt. He had known Jerry DeSanto at the University of Colorado at Boulder, which DeSanto described as being, even then, "full of a lot of earth mamas and guys with long hair clunking around in hiking boots." While still an undergraduate, Colony got some training through the Rocky Mountain Rescue Group, where students got paid for going out on forest fires and gave half their wages back to the group to buy equipment. They were also sent out to clean up plane crashes. "Some of those wrecks were so dirty and ugly they didn't want to use paid deputies," Colony said. "They'd call us in to pull the chestnuts out of the fire."

Before coming to Glacier, Colony had helped the Park Service work the big fire near the North Fork of Colorado's Big Thompson River in 1956. Like Bob Frauson before him, he had worked for the service at Longs Peak in Rocky Mountain National Park, which, at 14,256 feet, is both the highest peak in the park and a haven for big wall climbers. Colony came to Glacier in 1962. He spent his first summers as the ranger at Goat Haunt, and his winters in East Glacier doing winter mountain patrols, cracking down on big-game poachers, and training for winter rescues. A quiet man, whose black horn-rims gave him the appearance of a young Allen Ginsberg, Colony had always worn his hair closely cropped, except for one brief flirtation with fashion. Earlier, in the sixties, he tried letting his hair grow, but when it got in his eyes while he was doing his ranger work he marched into a barbershop and told the barber to "cut this crap off."

An articulate man given to wearing suspenders and bolo ties, Colony, like emergency room doctors, occasionally lapses into ironic rhetorical flourishes that reveal some of the tragedy he has seen in his work. Describing a climber who fell to his death on Longs Peak, for example, he uses the term "tomatoed out." As soon as he heard of the Mount Cleveland search, he feared that it would not end happily, for the boys or for the rangers looking for them. "I was never wild about winter mountaineering, but attacking it from the angle [the boys] did was just asking for trouble."

Chapter 12

❄

*The unknown, the remote and inaccessible
places of the earth have, to be sure, always
had the power to stir the human imagination,
but far more often to awe and dread than
inquiry and action. Modern man, staring at
the horizon, sees beyond it a challenge and a
promise; his ancestors, with rare exceptions,
saw only darkness. The cross-legged Buddha
was born into the world long before the
wandering Faust.*

— James Ramsey Ullman,
The Age of Mountaineering

From the beginning, Bob Frauson—among the country's most
highly trained winter mountaineers after completing his stint in the 10th
Mountain Division—knew the Mount Cleveland search would stretch the capacities of the Glacier National Park rangers. They had never been confronted
with so many missing people in the dead of winter; indeed, with so few cold-
weather visitors, winter search and rescue was a rarity in the park. How the
rangers, most of whose experience was limited to summer emergencies,
would respond to the crisis was entirely uncertain. Called back from his ski
vacation, Frauson began outfitting his rescue team, which he could tell immediately was short on the gear required for what could be an exhausting and
dangerous search effort. He called Ome Daiber, a cofounder of the national
Mountain Rescue Council in Seattle, and ordered special mountaineering
tents and equipment for the team. The gear was flown to Kalispell, but, with
stormy weather moving in from the northwest and shrouding the mountains

in thick clouds, the gear had to be driven up to Waterton. By this time, the deteriorating weather complicated the search in other ways as well; the temperature had dropped so quickly that two inches of new ice had formed on Waterton Lake, and boats could no longer get searchers and their gear into Goat Haunt. Horses were considered but decided against; horses need to be housed and fed, and one thing the Park Service did not have in abundance, out at the far end of the lake, was shelter. Rangers arranged for several snowmobiles instead.

At the request of Superintendent Briggle, the air corridor above Mount Cleveland was closed to all nonemergency flights, to prevent media or other commercial planes from interfering with the rescue helicopter. Briggle planned to go on television to plead with local pilots not to volunteer their help; he was afraid their helicopters might, with the downdrafts from their rotors, "knock our people off the mountain." Briggle also had to smooth over an odd bureaucratic hurdle: since the rescue helicopters belonged to the American military, they were not allowed to land on Canadian soil without technically constituting an act of war.

With light snow falling at St. Mary, however, even the rescue helicopter was grounded for an hour, as the pilot and rangers waited for a break in the clouds. Winds began kicking up to 25 knots, which dropped the windchill to 44 below. Chief Ranger Ruben Hart said he doubted the actual temperatures would drop below zero, but added that "that can be mighty cold when you can't move around, and moving around is a problem on a steep rock face." The cloud cover hung so thickly over the mountain that it occluded its upper half entirely; rescuers could see nothing from above the clouds and couldn't fly sufficiently high enough beneath them. "The days are so short in winter, and there was so little time to search, we had to be really efficient," Colony said. "We had to get the guys loaded into the helicopter, help them on with their packs, and get them up in the air as fast as possible."

What this weather would have meant to the boys, presuming they were still high on the mountain, was perhaps better left undiscussed. After several days of exposure to such extreme conditions, even the hardiest climbers, with plenty of food, begin to succumb to exhaustion. Winter climbing places unusually high caloric demands on a body, just to stay warm; cold weather campers, feeling their bodies run out of heating fuel, have been known to eat entire blocks of cheese, or gulp mouthfuls of cooking oil, just to take in enough fat to keep the body's fires burning. Hypothermia, the result of a body's core temperature dropping to ever cooler levels, is one of winter's most common killers. Absent concentrated vigilance on the part of all members of a climbing party, each one checking the others for chattering teeth, blue lips, or muddled conversation, hypothermia will kill just as surely as a heart attack. The difference is that hypothermia kills slowly. Just 1.5 degrees below the normal body temperature of 98.6, the brain starts to fail: judgment falters, survival instincts disappear. Early on, shivering starts slowly, then intensifies, then stops, as the victim drops into the fetal position and becomes unable to talk. At 86 degrees, the body becomes what wilderness rescuers call a "metabolic icebox": unconscious, ashen gray, and apparently pulseless. How long this takes depends on a number of factors. Even falling out of a canoe on a warm summer evening can become risky if there are no warm clothes around; damp skin can drop a body's temperature very quickly. All this would happen much quicker on a January night in Montana. As the hours and days ticked by, the chances that the boys would even have enough food left to survive such cold weather grew dimmer.

With the weather keeping them socked in, rangers anxiously stomped around waiting for even the smallest break in the clouds, known as a "sucker hole." Suddenly, someone pointed skyward and yelled, "Let's go!" and Willie Colony hopped aboard. "Once you get up there you see why they call it a sucker hole," Colony said. "They have a tendency to close up on you." Although the sky was overcast, the helicopter pilot was able to fly close up under the ceiling—so close, in fact, that the helicopter blades "started to suck clouds down into him," Colony said. "We'd have to drop down again, get as close as we could to the mountain, without getting stuck in the clouds. We could see enough to see their tracks in the snow." Indeed, Colony found what he thought was the best evidence that the boys had made it to the top of the north face: tracks that looked to be human leading down the northwest ridge from the top of the north col. Perhaps the boys had made it to the top after all; perhaps they had then climbed down the west side, and left the tracks that Bud Anderson had seen earlier. Surely no other climbers had been up this far; few other climbers would have had the temerity even to try. But where were the boys now? Colony could see the two ground parties making their way below, but there was no sign of the boys. It was from the air that Colony became aware of just how massive the search teams' job would be. "It's really a huge goddamn mountain," Colony said. "People just look like ants."

The Huey helicopters, in use because they were the nearest government-issued aircraft, were proving to be less than ideal as airborne observation posts, since they were built to transport troops or medical teams and had few usable windows. Colony was also troubled by another problem with the Hueys: the vibrations sent out by their heavy blades, which make an unmistakably deep, thundering "whumpawhumpawhumpa," were beginning to cause avalanches of their own.

Following the ski tracks from the lake toward the mountain, at about 10:30 A.M. the team of Anderson, Christiansen, and Seel found something remarkable, and haunting: the remains of a fire, coals still smoldering near the base of the north face, about a half mile above the spot where the abandoned gear had been discovered. They had located the base camp. There they found two backpacks, four cargo packs with aluminum frames, two tents, a cache of food, and an array of gear: hard hats, a stove, seven carabiners, six pitons, food for four meals, webbing, socks, three foam pads, five sleeping bags, a wool jacket, 200 feet of avalanche cord, and a roll of film. Leading away from the camp were not one but two sets of footprints; one led to the north face, the others led to the west face. Apparently, the boys had split up. On the face of it, this was not surprising. Most likely the boys, divided as they were in the level of their mountaineering skills, had separated to attack the mountain from two angles. But their progress was impossible to map: beyond the base of the north face, the tracks became mixed with the countless tracks of mountain goats, who, Seel reported, were "all over that mountain."

Following the boys' tracks toward a cirque below the north face, the team found two snowcaves, although, oddly, neither seemed to have been used. "They weren't big enough for a man to sleep in, and besides, when you've been climbing as long as I have you can just tell whether a snow cave has been used much," Seel said. One cave had a candy wrapper and some snowballs inside; perhaps Jerry Kanzler, squatting in the cave and thinking back on the days when he and his friends had built snow forts back in Columbia Falls, had built up an arsenal to use once Pogreba or Martin had turned their backs. Beyond these clues, however, the rescue team came up short. Tracks leading away from the caves gave no indication about the boys' progress. If they had tried the north face, why would the caves have appeared so little used? Wouldn't they have used the caves as a base camp from which to scout the face? The north face climb would have taken a maximum of a couple of days. Assuming that Anderson and Levitan had opted not to test their skills on the face, might they not have remained in the caves as a support team? Was it possible that at least some of the boys had climbed the north face, returned the same way they went up, and made their way back to the lake? They had initially told Bob Frauson that the north face was their intended route. Had the steepness of the face and the deadly conditions convinced them to try another route, or perhaps to abandon the climb altogether?

The day's findings convinced the ground rescue teams that the climbers had run into serious trouble, and a full-scale search was planned for the next day. Because of the forbidding terrain, the Park Service decided to call in Canadian alpine specialists from Banff, who were dispatched to Waterton with their climbing gear and avalanche rescue equipment. After a debriefing, one of the Banff team requested additional skilled Canadian support from Jasper, four hours to the north. Colony also asked for help from a group of climbers from Grand Teton National Park, and from the support parties whose names had been left by the boys with Bob Frauson. The Teton group—George Lowe, Mike Lowe, Richard Reese, and Jock Glidden—would be particularly welcome. George Lowe, who with his cousin Mike was part of one of the most talented climbing families in the United States, had already, by his early twenties, become one the country's finest winter climbers. Like Willi Unsoeld, Pat Callis, and any number of other top climbers, George Lowe was also to become a scholar, a systems analyst with a Ph.D. in physics; like Unsoeld, he would go on to pioneer one of the most difficult routes up Mount Everest. Lowe had climbed with a number of the world's finest mountaineers, and impressed them with his endurance in extreme conditions. "My strength is probably my determination," he once told an interviewer. "My weakness— judgment, going on too long." Looking for the Montana boys may have carried an extra poignancy for Lowe, who just a few years before had been climbing in Utah's Little Cottonwood Canyon when his partner, just seventeen, had fallen and died. Two weeks before arriving in Glacier, Lowe had been with Peter Lev in the Tetons, when they kicked down the avalanche that nearly buried Jerry Kanzler and Pat Callis.

Despite the expertise of the Teton climbers, Willie Colony remained skeptical of the chances for a live rescue. He had worked at Longs Peak in Colorado, and had scraped the bodies of some very fine climbers off the floor below the notorious Diamond Face. He was afraid that the Teton group would see the north face as a climbing challenge as much as a rescue mission, and give it a try even if it meant putting themselves at great risk. At 4,000 vertical feet and now fully iced over, Colony felt, the north face might even be beyond the talents of the most daring climbers of the time. Rock faces, like whitewater rivers, are categorized by class, with higher numbers attached to more difficult climbs. A Class 1 climb is literally a walk in the park, requiring nothing more than a pair of shoes and a smile. Class 2 requires some scrambling; Class 3 a bit of vertical climbing, and the use of a rope for beginners. Class 4 climbs require the use of a belay, in which a stationary climber, either above or below a partner on the rock face, takes up the slack of the rope. If the climbing partner slips, the stationary climber is able to arrest the fall.

Class 5 climbs require the use of "protection," meaning that ropes are attached to fixed objects from above, like trees or boulders, or to pitons hammered into the rock face, to help arrest falls. The use of "protection" does not mean that climbers rely on hardware to assist in their ascent; it only means they will be protected if they fall. A Class 6 climb is one that cannot be carried out without the use of artificial assistance, like a fixed rope hung down from above, or stirrups drilled in the rock by a previous climber. "Free" climbers, those who operate without the use of mechanical aids, have pushed themselves to such remarkable levels that they have to keep adding degrees of Class 5 to accommodate their accomplishments. A 5.0 climb is one for which there are at least two handholds and two footholds available for every move; a 5.8 has only two of these four, meaning that the climber might have a place to put one foot and one hand, but nowhere to put the others. A 5.12 is a face that is smooth as glass, with no apparent holds of any kind; a 5.13 is the same, except that it is located under an overhang. In recent years, climbers have discovered different grades of overhung glass: Class 5.13 climbs have now themselves been broken down into degrees of difficulty—5.13a, 5.13b, and so on. Climbers have refined their technical skills to such a degree—just short, it seems, of shooting webs out of their fingertips—that it seems hard to imagine what geologic geometry will exceed their grasp.

The north face of Mount Cleveland, Colony felt sure, was somewhere in the upper atmosphere of Class 5. "If these people can make it then we can use one team of technical climbers and they could possibly look at some of that technical stuff up there," he told Briggle. "If the Teton [men] are really red hot, they might be able to climb, but I would rather take the group up and show them what is there. As to this Class 6 stuff—a lot of stuff on Everest would only be Class 3 or 4. It's hard to [explain this] to nonclimbers, but the north face of that mountain is suicide. The only possible reason they could have had for wanting to do it is the glory."

At the end of the day, the two search parties returned to the Waterton station, and the helicopter returned to Great Falls. If the weather permitted, the helicopter would be used again the next day. If not, the rescue would have to continue as well as it could on the ground. Colony was not optimistic, since it was still unclear even which approach to the mountain the boys had taken.

Even though the boys had spoken with Frauson about the north face, Colony doubted that they had taken his warnings to heart. Moreover, he worried about the gear the rangers were *not* finding; if the boys had indeed tried the north face, surely they would have unburdened themselves of more gear that such a climb did not require: backpacks, ski poles, snowshoes. If the boys had made a run at the north face, Colony told Briggle, "they went in to make a quick attempt to climb the mountain and get out. Chances are very much against this. Apparently they did the same thing on Wilbur and lucked out. They should have realized from their overnight on Wilbur. They should have known what they were getting into—80-mile-an-hour winds there, they said. The chances are only 1 to 2 percent of their being alive. I am very pessimistic about it."

Briggle and Colony then did their best to buoy each other's spirits. "Be optimistic," Briggle said. "Keep your spirits up," Colony replied. "You have the best operation going that is possible. You can look anybody right square in the eye, Mr. Briggle, as you have asked for the best climbers in North America."

Looking people in the eye and assuring them that the Park Service had things under control was not a matter of small concern to Briggle. Soon after the search began, the press started calling, and first among the press was Hal Kanzler's old friend George Ostrom. "I understand that George Ostrom is coming up," Briggle told his team. "We are to cooperate with them, but they are not to interfere or press demands on an already overworked staff. If they want to go up to the head of the lake they will have to find their own transportation."

The prospect of George Ostrom arriving at the scene gave the Park Service more than a few jitters. During the Mount Cleveland rescue operation, he had been providing live broadcasts over KOFI radio and wrote columns and notes from the field to the *Hungry Horse News;* later, for a stretch in the 1970s and early 1980s, he would own and publish the tiny *Kalispell Weekly News,* nurturing it along from a four-page sheet that sold 1,000 copies to a 30-page paper with 20,000 copies. In much of his work as a writer and professional curmudgeon, Ostrom used the National Park Service as his whipping post. He was not just an armchair critic of wilderness policy. He had hiked much of the park and, like Kanzler, had become a highly regarded wildlife photographer. In a previous professional life he had been an instructor for Montana's celebrated smoke jumpers, parachuting firemen trained to fight forest fires. He had also worked as a legislative assistant for U.S. Senator Lee Metcalf during a time when another Montana senator, Mike Mansfield, was majority leader; during his tenure he helped write landmark legislation granting federal protection to both wilderness areas and wild and scenic rivers. During the Mount Cleveland mystery, he saw his role, as both public critic of the Park Service and as close friend of one of the missing boys, as central to the search.

Ostrom told Briggle that he would contact the boys' families. In addition to Ostrom, among the first to call was Mel Ruder, a writer and photographer from the *Hungry Horse News*. "Mel, the position to take is prudently optimistic," Briggle told him. "The public opinion is that the kids didn't belong there. It's not like bears and girls in sleeping bags."

The bitter sarcasm in Briggle's comment was not lost on Ruder, as it would not have been lost on Ostrom. Just two years before, a pair of gruesome grizzly attacks had caused the park public relations headaches from which they were still reeling. Early in the summer of 1967, a number of campers began seeing what appeared to be an emaciated, misshapen, and apparently sick bear digging in the garbage cans around their cabins on the northwestern edge of Lake McDonald. Although the campers told park rangers of their fears, they were apparently dismissed. "When his illness makes him go berserk, we'll do something about him," one ranger was quoted as saying. On June 25, a week later, at a campground four miles away near Trout Lake, two other campers watched a grizzly walk into their campsite and begin tearing open tin cans with his teeth. When the couple ran from the camp, the bear set about shredding their tent and their clothing, crunched their backpacks, and opened all but two of their 15 cans of food. When the couple reported the incident, they, too, were brushed off. For the next month, visitors to the Lake McDonald and Trout Lake spots consistently reported seeing the scraggly bear, but the bear, which showed startlingly little fear of man, never threatened anyone directly.

Although the rules of the park clearly stated that any bear that consistently hassled campers must be shot, nothing was done, even after the bear trailed a biology teacher and his two small children, treed a pair of hikers from California, and chased a pair of fourteen-year-old Montana boys away from their trout dinner. Rangers had intended to shoot the bear, these people were told, but they had not had time.

While all this was going on, another bear had begun menacing people near the Granite Park Chalet, about nine miles from Trout Lake. The couple in charge of the chalet for the summer had taken to putting their garbage out in a dump about 50 yards away from the chalet. Predictably, grizzlies started to show up for regular meals. At first, the three dozen or so tourists loved it— they could watch as first two bears and then a third ambled up to the dump, and then look on with fearful exhilaration as the bears fought for dibs on the food waste. Once, fighting over two pounds of spoiled bacon, the two bigger bears got into a frightful battle, roaring and swinging wildly at each other. Watching safely from the chalet, the guests applauded; the fights became so popular that the chalet's manager began adding bacon to the garbage regularly. Although rangers and park naturalists frequently slept at the chalet and knew about the bear fights, little was done to stop the dumping. It got to the point that the managers could predict the bears' arrival within ten minutes, every day.

After midnight on Sunday, August 13, Michele Koons, a nineteen-year-old California Western University sophomore from San Diego who worked in the Lake McDonald gift shop and had been hiking with four other concessionaire employees, was mutilated beyond recognition near Trout Lake. Incredibly, that same night, just nine miles away, Julie Helgeson, a nineteen-year-old University of Minnesota sophomore who worked in the laundry room at East Glacier Lodge, was killed in a campground near the Granite Park Chalet.

Over the following couple of days, rangers went on a spree, killing four bears, including the mother of two cubs that had not been seen before. When the bodies of the dead bears were examined later, only the Trout Lake bear had evidence of human remains in its stomach.

Ostrom had criticized park officials for years before the bear attacks for allowing bears to be fed at Granite Park. When he went up to the Granite Park Chalet a couple of days after the incident, and met the hunters who had killed the mother bear, he asked about the two cubs. When the hunters explained that they had tried to kill the cubs as well, since they had grown accustomed to eating garbage, Ostrom exploded. "God damn it! The cubs won't come back to the garbage if there isn't any garbage to come back to! It's that goddamn simple!" Later, rangers saw the two cubs bawling next to their dead mother, and only convinced them to leave after they poured lye over the carcass. Park biologists, watching through binoculars as the cubs walked away from their mother, saw one of them repeatedly dipping its head in a creek. Part of its jaw had been shot away.

Less than a month after the double killing, a grizzly mauled the face and head of a hunter from California before being killed by the man's companions; the next spring, an amateur photographer was chased up a tree by a mother sow trying to protect her cub; the man was only slightly hurt. When Glacier National Park opened for the summer of 1968, rangers had been given carte blanche to shoot any troublesome bears; trails were closed the instant a bear was sighted; campsites were closed until foraging bears had moved on; all dumps were cleared. The strict regime took a particularly heavy toll on black bears: rangers killed 20 that summer, three times the average. Only two grizzlies were killed, including the cub with the shattered jaw who had somehow managed to survive the winter despite being unable to properly feed itself.

With the Night of the Grizzlies still fresh in their minds, the Glacier rangers desperately wanted the Mount Cleveland search to have a less tragic ending, one that at least did not reflect badly on their reaction time or preparedness. During the early part of the search, news accounts trickling out of the park made it clear that rangers remained hopeful that the boys would be found. "They must be somewhere in the clouds," park spokesman Dan Nelson said. "We don't know if they're still climbing up, coming down, or stuck up there."

"All we know now is they're lost somewhere in the rocks above the camp we discovered today," Chief Ranger Ruben Hart said. "That covers several square miles. The problem is compounded by the fact that the rocky terrain is shaded by the mountains and hence quite black. It's difficult to spot anything. We know now they have concentrated their climbing efforts on the north slope. If they do return to either of their base camps they will see our tracks and surely know we are looking for them. And even if they can't return under their own power, it's highly probable they have heard our aircraft circling the peak."

As soon as they got word from the Park Service, relatives of the five boys began an anxious pilgrimage to northwest Montana. "I had worked late that night, and I had just gone to bed about 8:00 A.M., when I heard the phone ring, and something told me there was a problem," Ruby Martin, Ray's mother, would say later. "I got up, and boy, was there a problem. It was devastating."

When he got back to Kalispell after his reconnaissance flight, Bud Anderson called his father, who was spending the winter down in Quartzide, Arizona, and told him of the search effort. Dr. Levitan came up from Helena. Lynn Pogreba, Clare's brother, drove all the way from Phoenix to Butte without stopping for a rest. Once home, he picked up his parents and Ruby Martin, and the four of them drove to Waterton together; Arthur Martin had left earlier on his own, and met the others when they arrived. Settling into makeshift accommodations in Waterton, the families were confronted with more than just dread: weather forecasters were predicting that temperatures would be 15 to 20 degrees below normal for the next five days. Already, at 6,000 feet, thermometers were registering nighttime temperatures of 30 below zero. If the boys were still up there, and were somehow able to hunker down in snow caves and ride out the cold snap, their food supplies would by now almost certainly be gone.

The town of Waterton, small and modest even during the height of the summer season, had long since begun shutting down for the winter when the families arrived. Rangers arranged for the families to set up a makeshift shelter in the town's Lions Club hall, with sleeping bags on the floor the only comfort against the freezing temperatures. "It was cold, cold, cold," Clare Pogreba's mother, Esther, said. "There must have been some heat in the building, but I don't remember it." No restaurants were open, so most meals were taken at the Waterton ranger station, but the women in town made the group coffee and sandwiches, and offered their homes as places to visit and share their fears. "They treated us so graciously, and seemed to feel a bond for the boys," Mrs. Martin said. "They all had kids and knew how it was."

Esther Pogreba remembers walking around the small town, "watching the mountain and waiting for news." For distraction, she and others would buy apples at the grocery store and feed them to the elk and deer that routinely walked through town. To outsiders, the scene at the townsite was heartbreaking. "That was the saddest thing, the families all standing there in the bitter, bitter cold and staring up at that mountain," George Ostrom recalled. "Each hour that passed, their hope would decrease." The *Hungry Horse News* reported that Arthur Martin, who had survived decades working deep in Butte's copper mines, and his friend and doctor, Morton Levitan, who had survived the assault on Mount Belvedere as well as being taken as a prisoner of war, "spent hours sitting near the foot of the lake in a pickup looking at Mount Cleveland." As the families saw reporters taking pictures, they welcomed them into their cars. Arthur Martin opened his door to a reporter for the *Hungry Horse News*. "Come in, get warm," he said. A photograph in the newspaper shows the shuttle *Elizabeth II,* a low-slung boat with three square windows on either side of its cabin, tied up at the dock; toward the right, Dr. Levitan is shown assisting workers in hard hats.

Jean Kanzler, widowed just three years before, could not bear to go to Waterton, and awaited the news at her home in Bozeman. Her son Jim reacted differently. He contacted his friends and climbing companions Peter Lev and Pat Callis at Montana State and drove off to join the search team. "When they left they were laughing, saying they were going to bring them back," Jean says. "But as soon as Jimmy left I knew. You know when you've lost a child. A mother has this feeling, that a connection has been snapped." Over the next week, the phone at Jean's house would ring incessantly, with updates from the mountain and from neighbors checking on a woman facing the loss of a son.

A number of volunteer climbers arrived from Butte, including the faculty adviser to the university climbing club. Arthur Martin volunteered to help despite his emphysema, as did Clare Pogreba's brother Lynn, despite his utter exhaustion after driving all the way from Phoenix. The determination of friends and family members to help in the search was not completely welcomed by the professional team assembling at Waterton. One news report noted that, in contrast to the opinions of the wardens and park rangers, "there was general agreement" among the nonprofessional climbers "that the mountain was in fine condition to be scaled," and could be combed over with little danger. Kurt Seel, the Canadian naturalist, demurred, saying even the most experienced climber can't live through an avalanche. "There's just no way, not when you've got thousands of tons of snow on you."

Willie Colony knew how dire the situation had become, and he told Superintendent Briggle so. "Personally, I feel after we have used ground parties for three days, they will have done all they are capable of doing. Temperatures are zero and colder. There is quite a bit of wind, and at this latitude this is tougher than any 14,000-foot peak in Colorado or California. My personal opinion is that they have been avalanched. The whole party."

Chapter 13

❄

Climb higher and gaze into the distance,
Your heart will be gripped with fear.
Cirques of chasms surrounded by peaks,
Frowning cliffs all around;
Loose rocks that lean over the abyss,
Escarpments that overhang each other . . .

Clinging like a climbing bear,
You remain frozen in place,
Perspiration dripping down to your feet.
You feel yourself lost, reeling,
Transfixed with anguish, out of yourself;
And your spirit, shaken loose,
Plunges into terrors without cause.

— from "A Poetic Description of
the High Tower," attributed to
Sung Yu, fourth century B.C.,
quoted in Edwin Bernbaum,
Sacred Mountains of the World

By all accounts, the family member who arrived with the greatest determination to find the boys—his younger brother and two of his best
friends—was Jim Kanzler, who had begun work just three weeks before as a
ski instructor at the Bridger Bowl. The moment he heard about the search, he
bolted for Mount Cleveland with a small group from Bozeman, including
Peter Lev and Pat Callis, the chemistry professor from Montana State who had
become a mentor and climbing companion of the boys. Lev, twenty-nine,
spent his summers working as a mountain guide for the Glenn Exum School in
Jackson, Wyoming. During the school year, he taught mountaineering at Montana State and provided technical support for backcountry snow research conducted by the university's engineering department.

The trio joined the group from Butte at Bob Frauson's station at St. Mary,
where the five missing boys had begun their trip, and were fed breakfast. Jim
Kanzler, a climber with as much technical skill as most of the rangers, could

barely contain himself. Still deeply wounded by the death of his father, he now sat, and waited, while plans were made to search for his younger brother. Jim and Jerry had been climbing mountains together since they could walk; the idea of losing half of his remaining family was intolerable. "Jimmy was almost irrationally affected by the disappearance of his brother," George Ostrom recalled. Frauson, like several other rangers, was concerned that Kanzler, more than any of the others, might be difficult to handle. "It bothered me greatly that a family member was involved—they tend to jeopardize the rest of the group," Frauson said.

Indeed, the prospect of including a family member in the search for the boys took some of the rescuers aback. "I had a hell of a time keeping Jimmy Kanzler off the mountain," Willie Colony said. "His father was dead, it looked like his brother was dead, but I told him he was all his mother had left." In a conversation with Briggle, Colony related his fears. "If our people can control Kanzler's group then we can put them to work. We can put them to work and they will have eyes and ears open there, therefore they will be quite useful, but I would still rather have only our people. But I will not let them get in our way." If allowing a family member to take part in a dangerous search is highly unusual, it is also rare that a family member has as much skill as most of the professional rangers. Between them, Jim Kanzler, Callis, and Lev had technical climbing experience that outstripped many of the assembled search team. Granted, rangers need to know a good deal more than how to navigate their way up a sheer rock face, but given the current crisis, the three men from Bozeman would have to be considered worth the risk. They were not, after all, day hikers.

As the afternoon of January 4 progressed, crack winter-rescue personnel began arriving at Waterton Townsite from up and down the Rocky Mountains. They were soon joined by Kanzler, Lev, and Callis, who, after gathering available avalanche equipment from the park supplies at St. Mary, had driven with the rest of the volunteer climbers to Waterton, about 50 miles around the perimeter of Glacier National Park to the northwest. When they arrived, Kanzler produced two photographs of the north face of Mount Cleveland, which his brother Jerry had taken two years before. He marked the photos with the routes that the boys had discussed, and the team began formulating their plan. Having spent so much time climbing in the fine Rocky Mountain weather of the last six months, Callis, Lev, and Kanzler figured one of the boys must have suffered a fall, or fallen ill; at no point were they thinking about avalanches. There simply hadn't been enough snow.

Running the rescue operation out of the Waterton ranger station, on the north side of Waterton Lake, required skills not usually associated with backcountry work. Finding food and cooking supplies for several dozen men with appetites sharpened by extreme exertion in frigid weather became a serious issue; moreover, the team needed a cook who could run a generator and keep it going in the most severe conditions. With ration supplies at the ranger station being stretched by the arrival of the new rescue team, some in the support group had to be held at the townsite to await arrival of more supplies. The Park Service in fact had very few backcountry supplies available for the arriving team—there were only three tents, for example, which could seriously limit a rescue effort that required a full day's walk simply to get back and forth from the Goat Haunt ranger station on the lake's south side to the mountain. In a conversation with Bob Frauson, William Briggle reminded him to "be careful, as we don't have any money. Only order what you absolutely have to."

By late in the day—even though full rations had not arrived—Colony took the entire group by boat from Waterton to the Goat Haunt station, along with gasoline lanterns, stoves, tents, shovels, and cooking gear. The move was risky, since the weather bureau had begun issuing ominous forecasts for the Waterton area, showing signs of a serious change with the approach of a Pacific front within the next twelve hours. Flying in food stores by helicopter might be impossible, and, with the eight-mile-long lake freezing over, providing supplies to the rescue team was proving more difficult the longer the search went on. Nonetheless, Warden Peter Fuhrmann's equipment was advanced to the site of the missing climbers' tent in preparation for a reconnaissance of the north face by the Canadians from Banff. All available personnel were used to carry equipment from the ranger station to this camp.

Focusing the entire team's attention on the north face bothered Frauson, who had advised the boys to try the southwest ridge instead, and he cautioned Briggle about "putting all their eggs in one basket." Frauson had told the boys to avoid the north face; he'd told them to avoid the climb altogether, truth be told. Even if the evidence appeared otherwise, even if it looked as if they had chosen the north face after all, Frauson advised that the rangers spread out and cast their eyes over the entire mountain.

As the two talked, they also acknowledged that the search might well stretch the team to its limits. Working from sunup to sundown in freezing, snowy weather, on steep, unstable slopes, all the while looking for what increasingly looked like a doomed group of boys, even the strongest members of the search team would begin to wear down from exhaustion. A clipped exchange between the team leader and the park superintendent spoke, in code, of decisions neither one wanted to make.

"This could build up for one or two weeks," Frauson said. "Doesn't look like it'll be a short one."

"This thing is going to track out because of the weather," Briggle replied. "If it goes longer, then we're looking for something else. We can't jeopardize these people who are working up there."

Despite the fogged-in skies, park officials were still trying to arrange for a private helicopter, which would be expensive—$120 an hour—but far better suited for searching the mountains than the clumsy Hueys. Helicopters, Butch Farabee, Glacier National Park's assistant superintendent, has written, are, "with the possible exception of the two-way radio and the continuing refinement of emergency medicine," the greatest advance in the evolution of wilderness search and rescue. Although the German-made Focke-Wulf first flew in 1936, it wasn't until 1944 that a Coast Guard pilot performed America's first helicopter rescue mission—delivering blood plasma to 100 badly burned men who had been aboard a burning ship in New York Harbor. Four years later, the Forest Service used a Bell helicopter to pull a radio operator out of the California woods ahead of an advancing forest fire. In 1949, a helicopter flew into an active volcano in Hawaii to help retrieve the body of a disoriented soldier who had fallen into the 500-foot-deep crater.

In addition to their usefulness as observation posts and vehicles of body recovery, helicopters, the American ranger suggested, could be used for another purpose high on the slopes of Mount Cleveland: dropping explosives on the snow to clean out the bowls and make the going safer for the rescue teams. During the debate, the Canadians were quiet on the subject, but later, when the Americans were out of earshot, they cracked jokes about Vietnam-obsessed Americans "bombing the mountain." The idea was not pursued further.

With the search beginning in earnest, then, the Park Service had its team: Bob Frauson in charge of organizing the team and the flow of supplies at Waterton Townsite; Willie Colony coordinating the search teams at Goat Haunt; Management Assistant Jack Wheat assigned to handle press and public relations for both parks from the townsite. Park Ranger Robert Morey served as headquarters liaison officer with the search coordinator. Briggle handled press relations from the park's main office, and spoke regularly with Waterton Superintendent Tom Ross at Waterton. Park Ranger Riley McClelland was dispatched from West Glacier to handle timekeeping and search records at Waterton station.

The job of handling the distraught families, then, fell to Frauson, who did his best to address their fears, while reminding them of the dangers his men faced up on the mountain. Talking to Morton Levitan, a fellow 10th Mountain Division veteran, was particularly trying, since Levitan, of all people, knew the dangers of high mountain rescue operations. He'd been at Camp Hale, where men far more rigorously trained than most park rangers had collapsed from the rigors of mountain work. He'd been on Mount Belvedere, and seen men die. But as a doctor he also knew of the protocol of triage, when rescue officials must make decisions that put the least number of people at risk. Frauson explained this to the assembled families. "You've each got a son up there, but I've got 35 sons up there."

Frauson knew from long experience as well as anecdote that risks to rescue personnel have always been acute. High mountain rescue had been evolving in the United States almost as long as there had been people to rescue. In 1925, while trying to save a climber attempting to become the first woman to ascend Colorado's Longs Peak, Herb Sortland became the first official rescuer to be killed in a national park. When Yellowstone opened as the country's first national park in 1872, just 300 visitors came; by the early 1960s, some 80 million people were visiting American national parks each year. By the end of the century, this number is expected to reach 350 million, according to *Death, Daring, and Disaster,* Butch Farabee's compendious accounting of search and rescue missions in the national parks. In 1997 alone, 4,500 visitors to the park system's 84 million acres had to be rescued, 14,000 required emergency medical attention, and some 300 died.

What is notable in Farabee's history is the relatively few winter accidents that took place during the national park system's early years. In January 1936, a man became lost while trying to become the first to climb Washington's Mount Rainier; after two weeks of intensive searching, his frozen body was spotted from the air by Ome Daiber, a founding father of American mountain rescue. Daiber and Bob Frauson's father-in-law, John Davis, had been pioneering rescuers on Mount Rainier in the 1920s. Two decades later, Daiber organized local climbers into a band of volunteer rescuers, and finally founded the Pacific Northwest's Mountain Rescue and Safety Council in 1948—a group that would become the nationwide Mountain Rescue Association. That same year, at the Dartmouth Mountaineering Club, John Montagne, a Teton ranger and Dartmouth alumnus who would later become a mentor to the Kanzler boys, established one of the first alpine safety programs on the East Coast.

The return from the war of mountain troops like Frauson and Montagne dramatically increased the number of the country's expert mountain rescue personnel, and from the late 1940s through the early 1960s, rescue teams were formed in Oregon, California, Colorado, and Arizona. The first "ranger school" was established in Yosemite in 1957; a year later, a benchmark new book, *Mountain Search and Rescue Operations,* defined the new field. Given the growth of outdoor recreation that accompanied this burgeoning of rescue expertise, it came just in time. Americans were heading into the mountains in ever greater numbers; many of them were looking for something more than just a peaceful respite from their urban lives. The hair-raising exploits that Royal Robbins and Warren Harding were promoting on the granite walls of Yosemite were only the most sensational of a new brand of recreation that lured more and more campers with less and less experience into the American wilderness. In response to this trend, which expert backwoodsmen looked upon with some ambivalence, training programs like Paul Petzoldt's National Outdoor Leadership School (NOLS) began to pop up around the western states. If this new popularity meant that the American backcountry would become more crowded, and less the domain of the vagabond climbers who had come to think of it as their own, at least veteran climbers could try and ensure that the new crop of outdoor enthusiasts would treat the wilderness—and themselves—with some humility and respect. In addition to technical climbing skills, NOLS trained its students to tread lightly in the woods, to leave no trace of their travels, and, above all, to use their heads when confronted with adverse conditions. Petzoldt, a 10th Mountain Division veteran and one of the country's leading climbers, knew all too well what would happen if thousands of untrained people lit out for the country with experience limited to a subscription to *National Geographic* magazine.

Predictably, given the growth of outdoor recreation, the 1960s ushered in a period of intensifying rescue activity that continues today. The decade began with what *Life* magazine called "the most massive mountaineering rescue operation in U.S. history": nine days in May 1960, during which 65 highly trained mountaineers and 23 world-record high-altitude aircraft landings were used to assist injured climbers on the country's tallest mountain, Alaska's 20,320-foot Denali. For the first time, two separate climbing teams had made it to the summit of Denali at the same time. Hours after they reached the summit, four men from one party suffered a massive fall and lay in a pile at 17,500 feet; Helga Bading, a climber trying to become the second woman to reach the top, lay 1,000 feet below that with a dangerous swelling of the brain brought on by the altitude. These were highly accomplished climbers: one of the four men in the first group was Jim Whittaker, who three years later would become the first American atop Everest; another was Pete Schoening, who had climbed K2 seven years before. But a third man, John Day, had snapped one ankle and ruptured the ligaments in the other, and was unable to move down the mountain.

Top-flight rescuers began to gather from all over the Northwest, including many from Ome Daiber's group; during the search, a rescue plane with a pilot and an army-trained high altitude specialist crashed and burned just 250 feet from the foursome. Later, at 13,000 feet, another team got trapped by a forty-hour storm that sent winds of 135 miles per hour whistling past the rescue site. Finally, after a week and a half, the climbers and the rescuers got down in one piece.

The same day that the story made the front page of *The New York Times,* the paper also reported that a Soviet-Chinese team claimed to have reached the top of Mount Everest and a joint British-Nepalese-Indian team had made it to the top of Annapurna II, at over 26,000 feet the third-highest unclimbed mountain of the time. Seven years later, in 1967, seven of 12 climbers would die on another Denali expedition in what one survivor would call "the most severe high altitude windstorm in the entire history of mountaineering," with winds reaching 200 miles per hour. None of the seven climbers who died was ever found.

If the innumerable threats of a high mountain rescue in the middle of winter were daunting to the Mount Cleveland team, they were not enough to intimidate the arriving expert climbers, most of whom seemed to have spent more time in the backcountry than they had in civilization. Whether they came to their profession from the 10th Mountain Division, or straight out of college, or from unsatisfying lives in other parts of the world, rangers and wardens, like the climbers they were called upon to rescue, often combine an affection for mountains with a barely concealed disdain for all things urban. The word *hermit,* which we think of as defining a man withdrawn to a mountain hut, originally derives from the Greek word *eremite,* for "desert dweller"; both refer to those who have withdrawn from the world to pursue lives of singular devotion. Indeed, some members of the rescue team seemed awkward being indoors at all. One of the most respected Canadian wardens in the group, Willie Pfisterer, once told Jerry DeSanto that he hadn't spent a night inside a building for a year. Jerry DeSanto himself spends so little time near town that to reach him, Bob Frauson says, "you have to send up smoke signals."

———

By the morning of January 5, with time running out on any chance of finding the boys alive, the rescue team organized into five groups. A team of Canadian wardens attempted a climbing reconnaissance of the north face. Three other Canadians set off onto the northwest ridge to look at the tracks spotted from the air on the previous day. Three American rangers looked again at the lower portion of the west side, while another ranger took a group of volunteers, along with two telescopes and a pair of binoculars, to the southwest ridge of Goat Haunt Mountain to establish an observation post from which they could keep their eyes on any avalanche activity on the north face. The last group—Peter Lev, Pat Callis, and Jim Kanzler—were told to climb the bowl on the west face, what Bob Frauson had called the "parabolic mirror." This was the safest place for them, the rangers felt, and would keep them out of the way of the professional search team—and out of the way of the most likely disposition of the boys' bodies, if in fact they had been killed on the north face. Despite their climbing expertise, the fact that the Kanzler-Lev-Callis team had personal ties to the boys made the rangers uncomfortable. More than technique, rescue work in the high mountains, especially given uncertain weather, requires clarity of mind and precision of judgment, and the emotional strain that the Bozeman team carried was certainly enough to compromise their efforts. The plan, the rangers said, was for the three friends to go fast and light, with no sleeping bags, stoves, or any other overnight gear. They were to get as high up on the west face as they could and then descend to the base of the face by nightfall, where they would be met by a support team with tents, sleeping bags, and dinner.

Callis, the Gandolph of Montana climbing, refused to go along with this plan. None of the team was familiar with the terrain of the west face, he told the rangers, and no one could predict what sort of hardships or bad weather might be encountered on the way up or down. Climbing with no overnight gear meant that if they did happen to get stuck up there on the mountain overnight, they would be in for serious trouble. What Callis did not discuss was that he, Lev, and Jim Kanzler represented the finest technical climbing skill that western Montana had to offer. They, collectively, had taught the five younger boys most of what they knew about mountaineering. Setting out to look for such a large number of their friends was a grim project that none could have imagined, but it was also somehow darkly compelling. While the rangers were looking for five lost boys, Callis, Kanzler, and Lev were searching for their closest companions and friends. If Frauson and Colony were right to think that the personal connection might cloud the trio's judgment, or drive them to take undue risks, there was also the chance that the team's intensity would drive them to make a useful discovery.

After some hard debate, the team decided to take full backpacks, with sleeping bags, a stove, a shovel, and two days' worth of food. They did not bring a tent. If they were to spend the night on the mountain, they would dig themselves a cave in the snow and ride it out. On the way up the west face, looking for the little brother with whom he'd climbed so many peaks, Jim Kanzler cried.

The efforts of the professional ground teams were hampered by the on-going reluctance of the military to donate helicopters to the search team. Bob Frauson had been in contact with Malmstrom Air Force Base, but the military would not commit until the weather cleared. When a helicopter finally arrived from Great Falls at 11:30 A.M.—three and a half hours after the ground team was ready—it was nearly out of fuel. Since the military refused to put a service truck at the townsite, the helicopter had to fly to Star Strip to refuel, and lost still another hour. More frustrating, air force regulations prevented the team from hauling supplies and men from the townsite, since it was across the Canadian border.

When the military helicopter, with Pfisterer and DeSanto aboard, finally finished refueling at Star Strip, it flew the Belly River, Stoney Indian Pass, and the Waterton trail, looking for any sign of the boys and mapping snow conditions up high. With the Canadian team still climbing the north face, the helicopter crew was advised not to fly over, for fear of releasing further snowslides. "Let's don't let the 'copter knock our people off the mountain," Briggle warned.

No more human tracks were seen. By this time Pfisterer had voiced his frustration about the difficulties of doing reconnaissance from the Huey, and the team put in a call to Johnson Flying Service, a private group of crack pilots from Missoula. They asked for the best man available, and within hours, Bob Schellinger was on his way.

A rugged man more at home in the air over mountains than under a roof, Schellinger, when he was single, had lived in a trailer and used his oven as a storage locker for his camera gear; his wife, Bonnie, a secretary at Yellowstone National Park, said she agreed to marry him only if he would allow her to replace his lenses with pot roasts. Schellinger routinely pulled injured hunters out of the Bob Marshall Wilderness, helped locate lost hikers in Yellowstone and the Bitterroots, and pulled blackened smoke jumpers from forest fires. He had herded elk, antelope, and mountain goats from the air, hovered, blades whirring, over cherry trees to dry them out after severe rainstorms, and dropped hundreds of pounds of pine seeds over burned-out or clear-cut mountain land. He had also flown newlyweds away from Missoula's Florence Hotel, delivered an outhouse to a fire lookout, and taken Marlon Perkins, host of *Mutual of Omaha's Wild Kingdom,* in search of mountain sheep. In 1965, while flying in Wyoming, he had been called in to take two injured climbers off a ledge at 9,700 feet in the dead of night; flying through the mountains in complete darkness, with no moon and no ground reference points until he reached a road forty-five minutes from the peaks, he managed to get the climbers to the hospital in time to save their lives. For this mission he had been named Pilot of the Year by the Helicopter Association of America.

Two years later—in August 1967, two years before the Mount Cleveland call—Schellinger took part in one of the most dramatic rescue missions in U.S. mountaineering history. Two climbers, Gaylord Campbell and Lorri Hough, had been attempting an ascent of the north face of Grand Teton when, about 900 feet from the top, a rock the size of a cannonball came crashing down and exploded on the ledge on which Campbell was standing, knocking him head over heels to another ledge 20 feet below. When he jerked to a stop on the table-sized platform, Campbell had bones sticking out of his leg and was rapidly losing blood. Somehow, he managed to force the broken bones together, and splinted his leg with an ice ax. As darkness set in, they tried signaling with their flashlight, but their batteries died. There, exposed to the night air and in unimaginable distress, the two spent the night.

At dawn, Park Ranger Ralph Tingey scanned the north face with his binoculars and noticed the two in trouble. An emergency call brought a dozen men to the mountain, many of them highly skilled rangers and former guides, and Schellinger, who had been fighting one of the worst fires in fifty years over in the nearby Shoshone National Forest. Schellinger began shuttling the team to a camp on the south slope. The flying was dangerous—13,000 feet was considered the maximum altitude at which the helicopter could safely operate, and Schellinger had to scan continually for updrafts that would boost him up the precipitous slopes.

After reaching the peak, the rescue team traversed 1,400 feet across an icy, fractured cliff, then made a series of rappels hundreds of feet down to the ledge where Campbell and Hough were waiting. They touched down at 4:00 P.M., and it took three more hours to get Hough to a support party from the base camp. At such a late hour, moving Campbell was impossible; the only way to get the immobile climber down was somehow to lower him 1,800 feet—the equivalent of 150 stories—to a glacier below. As evening fell, Schellinger delivered an aluminum litter, ropes, and two 150-foot steel cables to the team, but—his helicopter's weight restrictions already taxed with the gear—was unable to deliver sleeping bags. Worse still, he handed over only a few C-rations and candy bars to get the three rescuers and Campbell through the night.

The next morning, as the helicopter hovered next to the ledge, a park ranger tossed some morphine right into Ranger Leigh Ortenburger's lap. The four men who had taken Hough to the upper saddle the day before rappelled back down to join the others on the ledge. Once Campbell had been anesthetized and placed in the rescue litter—his leg in an inflation splint—Ranger Ted Wilson was roped into the litter in a sitting position, to shield Campbell from falling rocks and keep him from careening into the rock wall. The team began lowering the litter over the ledge, with another climber rappelling down beside to balance it and keep it from swinging; they managed to descend about 400 feet before running out of visible ledges on which to stop and reset their rappels. To judge the distance to the Grandstand, a ledge they knew to be somewhere below, Ortenburger dropped a stone over the side and listened—six seconds, he figured, six hundred feet. His calculation needed to be precise; given the 150-foot lengths of their ropes, the team could only operate between ledges less than 300 feet apart; miscalculating the distance to the Grandstand could mean leaving the litter swinging in the wind overnight.

Ortenburger's calculation turned out to be right on the money. After a harrowing few hours, Campbell and two rescuers reached the ledge and hunkered down for another night, with only a four-ounce can of chili between them. The others, tying themselves into ledges above and below them, had only jelly beans and candy mints. Worse, the upper ledge was too narrow for the team to lie down; they tied themselves to the mountain and tried to rest standing up. By noon the next day, after another 800-foot descent, the team and their charge were on the glacier. Schellinger waited for them in a narrow, dead-end canyon, where he somehow had to turn around without smashing his rotor against a wall, which would have sent the helicopter careening. He flew Campbell to the hospital in Jackson, where he recovered so fully that he was back climbing a year later. Two years after that, the Mount Cleveland search, for Schellinger, would seem safe by comparison.

———

By the middle of the day, after four hours of climbing, Canadian warden Peter Fuhrmann had climbed partway up the chute of Mount Cleveland's north face. The going was treacherous; hard-packed snow within the chute had been formed by recent avalanches cascading off the mountaintop. High on the face, Fuhrmann found in the snow what looked to be marks left by the climbers, but quickly decided they were simply prints left by falling rocks. By this time, Schellinger's helicopter had reached the base of the north face. After he descended, Fuhrmann climbed in and the pair flew directly up the chute for another look. Although the visibility was good, he was unable to see any further signs of the boys' ascent. Perhaps their tracks had been wiped clean by later avalanches. Fuhrmann's progress was plainly visible to the Erskine group on Goat Haunt Ridge.

Over on the northwest ridge, a Canadian search party had also discovered tracks. One set, those leading down from the ridge, which had been seen earlier from the air, turned out to be goat tracks. But a second set were more promising. These appeared to be made by one or two men, leading out of the north col, where they milled about on the ridge before descending down the col again. On the ridge, a warden found what appeared to be human urine marks. The party continued to work high on the northwest ridge, but despite good tracking conditions, found no further tracks leading down to the west side. Clearly, they figured, some of the boys had decided to stick to their original plans of climbing the north face; the tracks on the northwest ridge, as proposed earlier, must have been made by part of the team acting in support of the more experienced climbers. Anderson and Levitan, less experienced than the others, must have forgone the north face and moved up the northwest ridge to set up an observation point—or, perhaps, to fix ropes near the top of the north face for the other three to use in case of an emergency—and wait for the others to make their ascent. The urine must have marked the point at which the boys had stood and watched. Or, perhaps, one or two boys had climbed the ridge to scope out the north face, to check on the snow conditions up high, which were invisible from below. Either way, the north face was the place to concentrate the search.

During their ascent of the west face, which continued late into the afternoon, Jim Kanzler, Peter Lev, and Pat Callis were spotted from the air by Willie Pfisterer, who reported their progress by radio to base camp. After considering the danger of continuing upward so late in the day, with stormy weather predicted at any time, rangers at the base as well as from the lower west face radioed Lev and tried to order the three men back. The orders, for

some time, were not received. As the rest of the rescue team returned by helicopter to Goat Haunt, Kanzler, Lev, and Callis continued to climb. After
scrambling up the scree field at the base of the face, they moved up to about
6,000 feet, where the slope became suddenly steeper. If the walking got increasingly arduous, it wasn't because of snow; especially for the middle of
winter, the snow cover seemed remarkably thin. "There was no more than six
inches of powdery snow off to one side at 6,000 feet before you started up any
semblance of a face above the scree field," Callis recalled. "That's so unusual
you can't imagine. Usually it would have been *feet*." The light snow cover was
disconcerting to the members of the west face team, who like the others were
trying to figure out how much snow there really had been in the mountain's
upper reaches. Was there so little snow because so little snow had fallen, or
because lots had fallen and the west face bowl, the parabolic mirror, had
cleansed itself with a massive slide? Had they indeed attempted the west face,
the fate of the five boys clearly would have hung in the balance.

Down below, anxieties about the pending storm were alleviated somewhat
by the arrival of the Grand Teton climbers. Support functions back at Waterton
continued throughout the day, with several of the Butte volunteers helping to
move supplies to the search teams. The Waterton Lake boat made two trips
from the townsite to Goat Haunt, but navigation had become increasingly difficult as ice began to form on the lake. A photograph in the *Hungry Horse
News* showed warden Al Sturko and mechanic Bud Sloan scraping ice from
the hull of the 27-foot, steel-hulled *Elizabeth II;* one trip took rescuers three
hours to negotiate the seven-mile, ice-encrusted lake. The cold was also af-
fecting the health of the boat's engine. Sloan had to run the engine day and
night to prevent the propeller from freezing solid, and continually had to chip
ice off the steering mechanism. Finally, the boat had to be removed from the
water in Waterton and put in dry dock. All supplies would now have to be
moved by helicopter, snowmobile, or on the backs of the rescuers. Bob
Schellinger's air shuttle offered the most efficient, fastest service. His helicopter, with aluminum side panels and an oversized glass-bubble cockpit,
would zip back and forth from the mountain to Waterton, where it would
touch down and load up on gear or newly arrived rangers. When Schellinger
needed to refuel, rangers would back up a green Forest Service Chevrolet
pickup truck, outfitted with 55-gallon gasoline drums, and run a fuel line into
the blue-and-white tank, with JOHNSON FLYING SERVICE stenciled on the side,
on the top of the helicopter.

It quickly became apparent that yet another of these options might have to be eliminated. On the last flight of the day, Bob Schellinger developed a sinus blockage in his ear canals that had resulted from a persistent head cold. Every time he descended through 10,000 feet, the expanding air inside Schellinger's ears would become excruciatingly trapped by his swollen glands. Finally, still unable to clear his head as he descended toward the townsite, Schellinger decided to punch through the 10,000-foot floor, and nearly blacked out from the pain. Rather than pausing before touching down, he landed hard—in airmen's terms, he "went through his cushion"—and hit the ground with a bang, safe but unsteady. The pain, he told Frauson, "about blew my head off." The rescue team was now faced with a boat that couldn't float and a pilot who couldn't fly. The boys had now been out ten full days. If they were still alive, somewhere out there on the mountain, they would now be in extreme danger; they had packed some extra food, they said, but even this would likely have run out by now.

Back in Waterton, Frauson and Superintendent Briggle met with the parents and friends of the boys, to keep them apprised of the search efforts and of "the dim outlook of finding the climbers alive." News of the search had spread all over Montana, and papers in Spokane, Washington, had also begun to follow the daily reports of the rescue team. In Bozeman, Jean Kanzler told a newspaper reporter that "we've had no official news, but we still have great hopes they'll be found." Newspaper headlines, which had become increasingly dramatic as the search continued, took a turn for the grim. HOPE FADES OF MISSING CLIMBERS, the *Daily Inter Lake* announced, RANGERS ENTER THIRD DAY OF SEARCH FOR FIVE YOUTHS IN GLACIER PARK. For the first time, Briggle began to express publicly his fears of risking the lives of searchers in the weather. "We'll continue searching as long as we dare," he said. "But, at the same time, we must consider the safety of our rescue teams."

Briggle's comments were emblematic of the credo among wilderness rescue experts that in the backcountry, safety for the rescue team must be considered before the safety of the victims; injured or dead searchers are of little use to those awaiting their help. "Rescuers must resist desires to move quickly in a rescue operation," according to the Wilderness Medical Society. "Hero mentality can lead to disaster. Hazards must be thoroughly assessed. Each rescue leader and rescue member must be capable of saying 'no go.' "

Back on the middle reaches of the west face, meanwhile, the day had grown very late for Jim Kanzler, Peter Lev, and Pat Callis, and still the rangers down below were unable to reach them by radio. On their way up the west face, the three had followed the northwest ridge for a stretch, and then worked their way across toward the middle of the bowl, where they had begun to follow a slightly diagonal line from left to right. Searching into the early evening, they climbed up past the low-lying scree field, then up a ramp to the left of a ledge that in summer supported a waterfall, and across a small flat area just above it. Although the west face did not require the technical climbing gear that an attempt on the north face would have, it was still a high-altitude climb carried out in dangerously cold conditions. They were climbing at upward of 7,000 to 8,000 feet, on an utterly exposed rock face, with no tree cover, in the middle of winter. A slip of the foot would have carried any one of them careening down the bowl and over the frozen waterfall below, which on its own was a 30-foot vertical drop. Beyond this, of course, was the inexpressible trauma of looking for their five friends, with whom they had spent so many months and years sharing a love of the mountains. It must have seemed impossible to believe that Jerry Kanzler wouldn't, at any moment, pop his head out from behind a drift and hurl a snowball at his older brother. Just like the old days.

The west face team, physically and emotionally wrung out, peered into the diminishing light to look for the tiniest protrusion from the slope's thin snow cover, for anything that might turn out to be the tip of an ice ax, the end of a climbing rope, or a piece of discarded clothing. Initially, there was very little snow—just a few inches of light powder under their feet. It wasn't until they got up several hundred feet above the waterfall that the snow started to get deeper, apparently carried over from the surrounding peaks and dumped in the west face bowl. Wind-loaded snow, as it is called, has come to be known as one of the most dangerous contributors to slab avalanches, since—even in the absence of new precipitation—it can tightly pack layers of blowing snow on top of already existing layers of depth hoar. Once the depth hoar—the invisible layer of marbles—is sufficiently loaded, it is only a matter of time before it releases. Thus can massive high-altitude avalanches build up enormous energy without the addition of a single flake of new snow. At the time, this particularly indirect dynamic was not fully understood. "It hadn't occurred to us that you could have calm conditions down below and have windblown snow up top," Callis said. "That's something people didn't think about."

On the way, they walked across the path of a three-pronged avalanche, but since there still didn't seem to be much snow under their feet—they could still see bare rock poking through the snow—they figured it had been a small one.

When they came to the middle reaches of the bowl, however, they encountered something that left them chilled: a "crown face," or fracture line, some two to three feet deep and extending all the way across the bowl. A massive slab avalanche had clearly broken off above them and, spreading across just below the ridgeline, had caused the entire bowl to release. Looking at the slope below, Kanzler, Callis, and Lev could now see why there had been so little snow under their feet on the way up. Everything in the bowl—three feet deep and nearly a half mile across—had slid down the mountain.

"When we got there we could see the fracture lines all along the rim. A slab had come down all at once," Lev recalls. "The fractures were all connected. The runout zone way below was completely level, and 60 feet deep. Just the disturbance of walking can transmit a fracture hundreds of feet above you. Then, of course, it's curtains."

To Pat Callis, the evidence of the recent slide provoked a sense of horror. At no point in their ascent of the west face had they even considered finding an avalanche. There had been so little snow at the bottom. How could there possibly have been enough up top to form such a massive slide? "We could have seen it from the bottom with binoculars, but we never thought to look," he said. "Pete Lev was an extremely accomplished avalanche forecaster, Kanzler was a ski patroller, and I had years of training myself. We were going up there not having much of an idea that that was where the group was, and we weren't even thinking about avalanches. As soon as we realized there had been an avalanche, you couldn't imagine a bigger change in our behavior. All of a sudden we were just creeping up the ridge. There was this incredible mosaic of fracture lines. I was shocked to realize how careless we had been, the three of us, in walking right into the middle of a potential slab avalanche. We all three should have known, but it was just not in our minds to be thinking about avalanches."

When the search leaders down below in Goat Haunt finally got through to the west face team, it was too late for Callis, Lev, and Kanzler to return before dark, and the air was getting colder. As night began to fall, temperatures back at Waterton, which sits at an elevation of 4,193 feet, dropped to zero degrees; up high, temperatures on Mount Cleveland were estimated to be three to five degrees colder for every 1,000 feet in elevation. Up where Kanzler, Lev, and Callis planned to camp, temperatures would have been no warmer than 5 below zero, with windchill dipping at least into the negative 30s. With the weather deteriorating, they decided they would hunker down in snow caves and try to ride out the cold. For Jim Kanzler, it was a long night. His father was dead. His brother was missing and presumed dead. So were two of his best friends. Now, in the thrall of a Montana winter night, exposed to the wind and cold of a mountain peak, he and two of the few remaining members of the small Montana climbing community faced extinction themselves.

Chapter 14

❄

*Here, as though fixed in the jaws of death,
we remained in peril of death by night and by
day. . . . When these fervent devotions were
taking place in church a most sorrowful
lament sounded through the village, for, as the
marones were advancing out of the village in
one another's steps, an enormous mass of
snow like a mountain slipped from the rocks
and carried them away, as it seemed to the
depths of Hell. Those who had been aware
of the mysterious disaster had made a hasty
and furious dash to the murderous spot and
having dug out the marones were carrying
back some of them quite lifeless, and others
half dead upon poles, and dragging others
with broken limbs.*

— Rudolf, the Abbot of
St. Trond, A.D. 1128,
quoted in Colin Fraser,
Avalanches and Snow Safety

Tuesday, January 6, broke overcast, with temperatures at the town-site pinned at ten below zero and the forecast calling for more snow. Chuck Trail, a replacement pilot who had flown with Bob Schellinger in Missoula, arrived at the townsite early for a debriefing. A former navy pilot, Trail had lit-tle experience flying in the peaks, and had to be brought up to speed on the winter winds howling through the mountains. After his introduction, Trail left for the ranger station and began shuttling equipment and rangers, including the new recruits from the Tetons, to the foot of the north face avalanche. After days of fruitless searching, they had decided to look for the boys in a new place: under the snow.

Undertaking an avalanche probe several days into a search, the rescue team had tempered hopes. The average avalanche victim is buried in five feet of snow, an intimidating statistic when one considers that no one in the United States has ever survived being buried in seven feet. (In Switzerland, a mountain guide survived being buried in 22 feet and was pulled out after four hours of digging by rescuers.) Avalanche rescue depends critically on the speed of the search team's response. Nearly two thirds of those who have survived burial—ranging from those with critical injuries to those facing suffocation— have depended on the efforts of searchers within their own parties. Only one in five has been saved by an organized rescue team. Rescuers arriving at an avalanche site typically carry a backpack filled with specialty gear: a small shovel, two-way radios, headlamps, flares, medical kits, surveyor's plastic flagging tape to mark the borders of the slide. One of the most primitive—and effective—pieces of avalanche rescue gear remains the probe pole, which has been in use in mountain regions for centuries. Usually resembling a jointed aluminum tent pole, with an elastic connecting each of the pole's collapsible sections, probes were once one-piece lengths of wood or metal that rescuers jammed into the snow in hopes of hitting a buried victim. Probes slip through all but the hardest snowpack with little trouble; the feel of a solid object several feet beneath the snow is similar to hammering a nail through wallboard and hitting a wooden two-by-four.

The Greek geographer Strabo wrote of seeing wooden staffs carried by inhabitants of the Caucasus Mountains near the Black Sea, but he assumed that they were used not by searchers but by people caught in avalanches, who presumably would push their staffs up through the snow to alert rescuers. How these victims knew which way was up is hard to know. Perhaps they knew to spit. More typical was a rescue carried out in December 1886, when a young Swiss man named Franz Josef was buried after setting out to deliver a load of flour to a nearby village. Because it was snowing heavily, he decided to turn his horse around, only to find the way blocked by an avalanche. As he shoved his way through, a second avalanche fell on top of both horse and rider. A policeman found the horse and alerted rescuers, and the next day, after the weather cleared, about 40 people, thinking the man was dead, began probing for his body. Meanwhile, below the snow, Franz Josef was alive but worried— he knew the searchers were using heavy, two-person probes used to locate roads and houses, and feared that where he had so far survived an avalanche he might not survive a goring, however well-intentioned. He listened intently as the probing grew louder. When a probe grazed his shoulder, he somehow managed to grab it and hold on. The workers could not understand their difficulty in removing the probe, and began jerking on it. Franz Josef was freed after nearly twenty-nine hours.

Roping themselves together to direct their progress and to make sure they covered every square foot, the north face team began probing the snow with 12-foot-long collapsible poles brought in by the Canadians; the outmoded American one-piece poles had proven too long to fit inside the helicopter. Step by step, yard by yard, they progressed across the snowfield, hoping against formidable odds to feel a body or a ski or a backpack buried under the snow. Wearing a rainbow of ski sweaters, wool knickers, and orange or blue one-piece ski suits, the probers, eyes at their feet, looked from behind like they were searching for someone's lost car keys. One Canadian warden used a magnetometer to try to detect metal beneath the snow, hoping to speed up the laborious and time-consuming probing process.

Given the huge breadth of snow that avalanches can spread over the base of a slope, locating a buried victim can be exceedingly difficult. The first step for a rescue party is to make what has become known as a "hasty search." By locating the Place Last Seen—the point at which the hiker or skier was last seen above the snowpack—rescuers first look around to see if another slide is imminent; avalanches frequently come in a series, particularly if they find their start in a bowl, where the snowpack is connected across a broad expanse and may or may not release all at once. Posting a lookout to warn of other slides makes sense if manpower allows it. Next comes a search of the avalanche debris for any signs of a victim. This includes probing around any pieces of equipment that may have come to rest above the surface. If someone happens to find a daypack, for example, they must avoid the temptation to run it over to a fellow rescuer, since in so doing they might lose the one spot that indicates where the victim is buried. Despite what might be a logical first impulse, rescuers typically don't begin digging immediately below the find; since surface snow slides faster than snow below the surface, the chances are better that the victim is buried uphill of his gear. Moving snow follows laws similar to those of a river, with places of deceleration, like the outside of curves, and unseen obstacles that can catch and hold a victim.

Establishing a trajectory of the victim's most likely descent, from the Place Last Seen to the avalanche runout, helps rescuers chart a likely area in which to begin probing. At this point, they must decide whether to send for help. Is there time? Are there people to spare? Emergency rescue personnel working in urban areas and along the nation's highways speak of the "Golden Hour"—the clock starts ticking the moment of the gunshot or the car crash, and stops inside the emergency room—in which they can reasonably expect to save a victim's life. Any longer than this and the trauma, whether it is brain damage or loss of blood, begins to take an irreversible toll. Searching an avalanche, rescue teams typically have only fifteen to thirty minutes in which to recover a buried victim alive. In addition to the physical trauma, like organ damage and broken backs, which avalanche victims suffer as they are smashed over rocks and tree stumps on the way down a slope, there are also the dangers of drowning, more familiar to lifeguards. With snow both flying through the air and flowing like liquid around them, avalanche victims are always in danger of inhaling snow or having it form an ice mask over their mouths. The faster a rescue team can free a victim's breathing passages, the greater the chance that they will not suffer permanent brain damage from lying buried too long without oxygen.

Thus, given the premium on time, rescuers probing with those already at the scene for as long as possible is considered the most promising of the few available options. The hasty search uses all available searchers to scratch over the surface, looking for any clues—clothing, equipment, a protruding leg—and to spot-probe likely burial areas using anything they can, including ski poles or, as has proven successful in several emergencies, tree branches.

If, after a period of desperate probing—thirty minutes, an hour—the team has had no success, the hasty search shifts into a "coarse probe." Rescuers line up elbow to elbow with hands on hips (called "close order") or fingertip to fingertip (called "wide order") if there are too few of them. In a coarse probe, the search begins at the bottom of the runout zone—the delta of snow found at the bottom of a slide—and works uphill toward the Place Last Seen. In a close-order probe, searchers spread their feet and drive in their probes once between their legs, about six feet deep. In the wide-order probe, each person probes three times—left, center, and right of their feet—at two-foot intervals. The group then moves forward as a unit, about two feet, and repeats the procedure. The probe line moves as quickly as possible, with probers thrusting in sync. Since the victim is most likely buried in one of the spots of heaviest deposition, along the flatter portions of the runout zone, success most likely comes early, or not at all. If a strike occurs, a shovel crew following the probe crew digs down while the probers continue. Shovelers also zigzag around behind probers to check snow for clues of its path and depth.

Ideally, a probe line brought to a scene from outside includes 20 or more searchers armed with probes about ten feet long. As the probe line advances uphill, the flanks of the probe are marked by flags or surveyor's tape to show what has been, or won't be, searched. Occasionally a string is stretched across the toes of searchers to keep the line straight and systematic.

With a full complement of 20 trained probers, it will take about four hours to coarse-probe an area a bit larger than a football field. The probability of finding a completely buried victim, dead or alive, using the coarse probe depends in part on the angle in which the body has come to rest. On the back or stomach, 95 percent; on the side, 75 percent; in the vertical position, that is, standing on feet or head, 20 percent. About seven in ten bodies buried in less than ten feet of snow are found by coarse probers—how many of these bodies are still breathing depends entirely on chance.

If, after several hours of searching, the coarse probe fails, searchers start all over again with a "fine probe." Searchers must return to the bottom of the suspected area of burial, and begin their search all over again in smaller increments. Moving forward a foot at a time, probers sink their pole three times each—once on either side of their feet, and once straight down between them. With that same team of 20 probers, it will take between sixteen and twenty hours to fine-probe the same area that took four hours with the coarse probe. The chances of the victim being found alive is almost nil, but the theoretical probability of at least finding the body nears 100 percent. Even in an age of technology, probe lines have found more buried people than any other method, but of the 140 people found on American slopes by probers since 1950, 121 were already dead.

One of the great stresses of probe lines is the conflict between the need for speed and the need for thoroughness, particularly at the beginning of a search. Early on, the hasty search and even the coarse probe can be done rapidly, in the hopes of not only finding a body but finding a living body. By the time several hours have passed, the chances of survival have become so diminished that fine probers can slow down. At this point they are concentrating less on rescue and more on body recovery.

If the bodies are buried too deep—below the reach of a 12-foot pole—the best chance a team has of finding the victim is by digging a trench, deep and long, along the probable line of descent. Dug five or six feet apart, wide enough to stand in, and to a depth of 15 to 20 feet, depending on the depth of the runout, trenches take days to complete and require the removal of thousands of cubic feet of heavy, compacted snow. While standing deep inside a trench, searchers use poles to fine-probe the walls on either side, on the off chance that the body has come to rest directly parallel to the hole in the snow. It is best understood at the beginning that the chances of finding someone alive this way are close to zero.

The only other way to speed up an avalanche search is with a specially trained dog, which by itself can cover in twenty-five minutes the same area that takes 20 men four hours. Avalanche rescue dogs have been in use in the Alps for nearly three hundred years, since residents of Switzerland's St. Bernard Hospice began using dogs—long since named for the hospice—to assist travelers crossing the Alps. Saint Bernards may have descended from Tibetan mastiffs; Xerxes apparently brought them over to Greece in about 485 B.C. These early dogs were recruited to guard the mountain hospice from highwaymen, but mountain guides also took them on outings as companions and for their uncanny ability to find their way in adverse conditions. One famous Saint Bernard who lived in the St. Bernard Hospice in the nineteenth century, Barry I, is credited with saving more than 40 lives, including that of a young child he found lying in the snow. Barry I—whose name came from the German word *bari,* meaning "little bear"—reportedly licked the boy's face until he regained consciousness and was able to cling to the dog, which half dragged, half carried him back to safety. Contrary to popular legend, Saint Bernards do their work without the help of distilled spirits. Colin Fraser calls the image of a St. Bernard carrying a keg of brandy to avalanche victims "the figment of someone's imagination, perhaps that of the erstwhile publicity manager of a certain brandy manufacturer." The romantic legend may have emerged from people embroidering stories about saddle-bearing dogs who had been trained to fetch milk from a cowshed.

Legend has it that it was in fact not a Saint Bernard but a terrier that first pioneered the use of dogs in modern avalanche search. In 1937, when a Swiss rescue team went looking for avalanche survivors, one of the rescuers took along his dog Moritizli. All the victims had been discovered except one when it was noticed that Moritizli kept sniffing around and returning to the same spot in the snow. When he began to bark and whine, the rescuers began to dig and found the last victim—alive. In 1982, when an avalanche descended on the California ski resort of Alpine Meadows, a dog located a woman buried for five days inside a demolished building; miraculously, she too was alive, protected from suffocation by air spaces inside the building. Seven years later, a slide buried a snowplow operator near Colorado's Wolf Creek Pass. A trainer named Susan Lester and her dog Avy—who picked up a scent from inside the cab of the plow—found the man outside his plow within minutes. Because he had managed to get a hand in front of his mouth, the man lived despite being buried for three hours.

Dogs are able to find avalanche victims, dead or alive, about 50 percent of the time, depending on the consistency of the snow; the wetter and denser the snowpack, the harder it is to pick up a scent. Not all dogs are suited for the work. Some have better heads, some have better hearts, some have better noses. Labrador retrievers have considerable drive and endurance; golden retrievers are meticulous but not quite as fast. No matter how smart or strong, if a dog can't pick up a scent, it is useless; trainers talk about dogs that couldn't locate a pound of ground chuck in a phone booth. Deb Frauson, Bob Frauson's daughter, has worked in mountain rescue in the Tetons for years. She has a German shepherd named Loki that has, simply by sniffing from a boat, found three drowning victims six feet under the Snake River. Deb Frauson trains her dogs in stages of hide-and-seek. Dogs are first asked to run to find their master standing in plain sight; then their master hiding behind a bush; then their master buried in snow. This last is a practice that is not for the faint of heart, or for those inclined toward claustrophobia. Team members dig a pit in the snow, one volunteer lies down in the frozen grave, and is covered completely with snow. "You trade off being the victim with other dog trainers," Deb Frauson says. "I've been buried in five or six feet for thirty minutes. You have a radio and a transceiver and a Therm-a-Rest to lie on—it's very comfortable. I've been in situations where a person we'd buried said, 'I need out! I need out now!' I've seen other times where we dug at the Point Last Seen and the person wasn't there. We had to probe to find her."

Dogs have found people buried under 15 feet of snow. Just six months before the boys left for Mount Cleveland, a man buried under five feet on Mount Rainier was located by an avalanche dog—the first success for the German Shepherd Search Dog Committee of Washington, one of a pair of groups that would later evolve into national organizations training search and rescue dogs. In fact, dogs are trained not so much to find bodies as to find scents. Their technique is not always to find an isolated object but a trail, not unlike birds of prey who are able to see linear tracks of urine rather than individual mice. Human beings shed tens of thousands of skin cells every minute, and each cell, as it deteriorates and is consumed by bacteria, gives off pungent gases that are unique to each individual. Dogs, equipped with noses full of scent receptors and tiny cilia that collect passing molecules, are on the order of 10,000 times more sensitive to smell than humans, and can pick up odors as they percolate up through the snow.

Corpses are a different story. Decomposing bodies all smell the same. Dogs trained to find cadavers are given altogether different instructions when they are out on a slope looking for buried victims: find dead people. In fact, during training, dog handlers use something called Pseudo Corpse, manufactured for one purpose by the Sigma Chemical Company. Dogs are presented with a noseful of Pseudo Corpse and then told to go find the smell again, buried somewhere in the snow. Plainly, not all of this is fun for rescue dogs. Especially during body recovery missions, when dogs are fully tuned into the despair of their human companions, handlers are careful to attend to their dogs' emotional states. Although trainers say that search dogs generally enjoy search missions for the game of hide-and-seek rather than the heroism of the live discovery, they are also certain that dogs in traumatic searches suffer from psychological distress. Rescue dogs used to search the rubble of the recent Oklahoma City bombing presented unmistakable signs of depression.

Although a trainer in Kirkland, Washington, agreed to send three dogs and three handlers to Mount Cleveland at no charge save the cost of transportation and expenses, rangers decided against it, since each passing hour decreased the chance that the boys would be found alive. The boys had gotten out of Alf Baker's boat ten days before. Adding a whole new crew of dogs and handlers seemed useless and even dangerous, since every additional person on the mountain meant one more possible casualty.

Chuck Trail and Willie Colony followed their shuttles to the base of the north face with close reconnaissance flights up and down the face itself, checking the boys' proposed climbing route, but found nothing. They then flew to the top of the mountain, where Colony hoped to check the climbing register to see if the boys had in fact reached the summit, but heavy winds prevented their landing. They were, however, able to chart the progress of Kanzler, Lev, and Callis, who by now were on their way down the west face after a hellish night in the cold. Asked later about their experience that night, the three climbers demurred, it not being in their nature to add rhetorical melodrama to what everyone knew to have been an awful experience. It was cold, they said, but not intolerable. "We were quite comfortable," was all Jim Kanzler would say. George Ostrom, ever voluble, described the scene more vividly in a newspaper column. "The next time the temperature drops to 30 below zero and wind is howling, go up and spend the night on the roof of your house and you'll have some idea of how Dr. Callis, Pete Lev, and Jim Kanzler spent January 5, 1970."

During the descent, Kanzler and his team were asked to do a more thorough search of the massive avalanche path they had noticed on the way up. As they descended, they spotted one of the Canadian searchers standing near the toe of the avalanche below them. They yelled to him about the fracture lines they had seen all along the west face, the size of the slide that must have been released, and the fact that despite its appearance, the snowpack was easily deep enough to have buried five climbers. The rescuer, still convinced the snow was too thin, remained incredulous. "That?" he said. "That couldn't have done a thing."

"No one realized the depth of the slide above the cliff," Callis said. "Here's this highly accomplished alpine specialist from Canada, whom I have the highest respect for, and he was not impressed with this avalanche."

Assessing the terrain on the west face, Peter Lev felt certain that the boys had also had no idea what kind of danger they were in. "These guys gave considerable thought to using the terrain to their advantage," Lev says. "They were trying to be clever, by climbing up the north edge of the face. They thought they were staying out of the middle of the bowl. They just didn't realize how much snow was above them, or how the weak layer had set up a booby trap. When they looked up, all they saw was rock. No snow. They were sucked in. Looking up, it doesn't seem that dangerous. Walking in, kicking bushes and two inches of snow on the ground, they must have been thinking, 'There's no avalanche danger.' But as they got higher, the wind would have deposited more snow. It would have been fairly stiff on top, but underneath it was totally hollow."

Frustrated by the fruitless searching, Callis kept walking down the west face. Suddenly, in a skiff of snow that had dusted the surface debris of the avalanche, he reached down and pulled up a small backpack. In that moment, the entire search changed. The boys had not gone up the north face after all. The search party had been looking on the wrong side of the mountain. "Up to that point I was such an optimist about this," Callis said. "Until I saw the pack I couldn't handle the idea that something had happened to them. When we had just arrived in Waterton, I told Mark's father that there was no problem. He said, 'There's a problem. Something bad has happened.' He knew. But even with that I couldn't think that way."

In the moment that Callis discovered the backpack, his team realized that the boys had indeed been swept down the west face, and they were almost instantly able to reconstruct what had happened. Although it was possible that the boys had triggered the avalanche on their way *down* the mountain—

perhaps from "glissading," a frolicsome romping and sliding down a slope that can be easier than walking—it was more likely that the avalanche had released above them on their way up. Most likely, they had crunched through to a layer of depth hoar and sent a fracture line running uphill. Eventually, the fracture would have reached a weak spot in the terrain—a dip in the face, a rock outcropping—and broken off completely. All this would have happened in an instant, and without the boys ever seeing it. When it released, the avalanche would have caught the boys utterly unawares.

Terry Kennedy, a close friend and climbing partner of Jim Kanzler's who worked as a seasonal ranger in Glacier in the early 1980s, called the predicament the boys must have found themselves in the "foreshortening effect"—a kind of optical illusion that occurs when, to a climber standing at the bottom of a mountain, the top appears closer or more accessible than it really is.

"Imagine yourself standing on a football field looking up at wooden bleachers that are painted the school colors—let's say blue and white. The vertical steps are blue and the horizontal surfaces where you place your feet and sit are painted white. From the field what do you see? Answer: blue. You don't see the white. It doesn't matter how steep the overall angle is, you only see blue. If you were at the top of the bleachers and looked down you'd only see white. If you were in the middle and looked up: blue. Down: white. Now, this phenomenon happens in all mountains, but it is especially apparent with Glacier's characteristic horizontal strata. Many is the time the mountain scrambler approaches the base of the mountain only to be psyched out because he looks up and sees only the cliffs and thinks the face is much steeper, but is not fully aware that between each ten foot cliff is a twenty-foot-wide ledge and the overall slope is only 30 to 35 degrees. One guy chickens out and goes home and his buddy goes there and climbs the route without a rope."

The reverse, which can have far deadlier repercussions, also holds true, Kennedy said. When he was a seasonal ranger in Glacier he recovered more than a few bodies of climbers who had apparently tried to take a shortcut, thinking they had an easy slope to descend and got quickly into trouble on steep, high cliffs they couldn't tell were there.

"The Cleveland five approached the north face. At the base there was very little snowpack. Looking up at the mighty north face, they weren't going to see much either. The lower angle pockets of the north face might have been loaded and dangerously slabbed, but one viewing the face from the base would see only dry cliffs for the most part. They wisely decided the intimidating north face is too big of a project for them at the time. So here they are. The north face is out. What to do? The five regroup and follow a gully onto the ridge, ascend it a ways, then begin a long but easy traverse to the middle of the west face under several thousand feet of cliffs that would be challenging and doable (and less likely to avalanche) but serious and would require a bivouac with a large party and short days. The logical thing is to keep traversing to the center of the west face and do the standard route. They go. The snow becomes deeper.

"They look up and what do they see? Answer: dry cliffs. What they don't see is the full breadth of the middle part of the slope above them that is loaded with snow that has been transported by wind to that region and dangerously soft slabbed. At some point the series of short cliffs disappear and they find themselves on even easier terrain that only warrants plodding through it. Maybe they recognize soft slab and maybe they don't. Their awareness is jaded by rapid progress and the likelihood that by then the day was waning quickly just a week after the solstice and if victory is to be they are going to have to keep the pace stiff to get up and down by nightfall. Up they go, breathing hard, their attention on the summit, not the plates of snow fracturing underfoot."

Although it is impossible to know precisely the boys' final moments in late December, it is most likely that the avalanche caught them in a flash. If there is anything typical about the way in which man and avalanche meet, Monty Atwater has written, it is the total surprise of the victim. If the majority of people entering the mountains cannot be expected to be fully trained in avalanche forecasting, they should at least be aware, "as the mariner does with the ocean, that snow can turn from friend to enemy in the blink of an eye."

One of Atwater's close friends, John Hermann, once attempted to make a film about avalanches for Disney on Colorado's Berthoud Pass in 1957. A week of snow had loaded the slopes, and Hermann set up three cameras along the highway, which had not been hit by an avalanche in twenty-four years. A shot from a 75-mm howitzer released a slide from a 50-acre start zone; it came down at 100 miles per hour, threw up a cloud hundreds of feet in the air, and snapped fully grown trees. Hermann got one of the finest avalanche sequences ever filmed, but died in the process, buried along with a twenty-one-year-old highway employee in 15 feet of snow. A photograph of his excavated body shows him frozen as if running. On his face, Atwater wrote, was an expression of "complete astonishment."

Indeed, if avalanche research was still in its formative years in the late 1960s, one thing the west face team knew was the unlikelihood of surviving one. Once caught in a cascade of snow, there are limited choices, and even more limited time in which to choose. Whether buried under six inches or six feet of snow, especially snow that has compacted into cement after its crystals are smashed together during a slide, the chances of someone surviving a burial are about four in ten.

If the boys on the west face were somehow able to hear the avalanche bearing down on top of them, they might well have initially tried to leap on top of it before it bowled them over. Or perhaps they tried to run out of its track, but found it moving too quickly. Once they were knocked down, they likely tried to grab their ice axes and go into a "self-arrest" by holding tight to the top of the ax and jamming it into the slope. Even if they had the time to do this, the chances of scraping to a stop as the wall of snow crushed over them would have been remote. Perhaps they then tried swimming out of the slide, furiously waving their arms and kicking their boots to thrust themselves out of the surging snow. Or perhaps they tried barrel-rolling sideways, in an effort to move faster than the snow and get out of its teeth.

None of this is possible to know. But exactly one day before the five boys left to climb Mount Cleveland, a Forest Service landscape architect named Jim Hagemeier was caught in an avalanche in Breckenridge, Colorado. Because he survived, his description of swimming out of the slide, reported in Knox Williams and Betsy Armstrong's *Avalanche Book,* gives a rare glimpse into a successful avalanche escape. "The feeling was like being dunked under water, as the impact took my breath away," Hagemeier said. "For some reason, when I started to move with the slide, I could breathe much easier. I thought about the fact that I didn't have an avalanche cord [a colored rope skiers tie to their waists that they hope will remain on the surface even if they themselves are buried] and that it was up to me to get myself out. My right leg was being bent behind me by the pressure on the ski, which then released. I got a good belt on the shins from one of my skis. The sensation of speed was fantastic. I had put my skis into a schuss on a 30-degree slope and was engulfed immediately. I remember the speed increasing as I went down the slope.

"The ride was very rough, and I was being tossed around quite a bit. It seemed as though I was in a big flume of water, where I was occasionally able to get a breath of air, but most of the time I was overwhelmed by snow. Later, people asked me if I had a sensation of which way was up or down. I can truthfully say that I was unaware of up and down, at least after the initial shock of the slide hitting me. Initially, when the full blast of the slide struck me, I had no idea which way was which. As I moved downhill faster, I was able to orientate myself fairly well with the movement of the snow. I worked myself into a sitting position with my feet downhill and tried to swim as if treading water. This seemed to work, and I instantly started to rise in the snow. I kept doing this as I sped down the hill and increased the swimming motion as the slide began to slow down a little. Actually, it was not a fast decrease, it was just going very fast, then it started to stop slowly. I swam until I could feel the slide coming to a stop. I was still buried at this time. How deep I didn't know, but it seemed deep! I pulled my arms in near to my head; at that second the slide came to a rather abrupt halt, and I found my head and hands sticking out of the snow. The snow was still moving very slightly, and I was able to work my body out to where I was sitting on the surface. As far as injuries go, I was perfectly okay. . . ."

Once caught, the most important thing for the boys to have remembered, if their minds had still allowed for rational thought, would have been to protect their heads and keep their mouths shut, suppressing the desire to swear or shout for help. Since most victims die from suffocation, the first thing they might have done was to try anything to create an airspace in front of their mouths, by throwing an arm or hand up at the last minute to keep snow from plastering around their face. In virtually all cases in which people have survived long burials, air spaces created adequate supplies of oxygen. "As in diplomacy, in the underworld, and in going to the ballet, keeping your mouth shut is helpful," wilderness rescue expert Tim Setnicka writes. In an account reported to Betsy Armstrong and Knox Williams, a survivor named Bill Flanagan tells of the terror of having his mouth packed by snow during an avalanche. "Try as I did, it was absolutely impossible to expel the snow from my mouth," Flanagan reported. "The ball of snow simply packed harder each time I tried to gulp air around it." When Flanagan finally came to a rest, the iceball in his mouth "was so big and hard that I was unable to get it out from behind my teeth. I was able to crush it bit by bit with my front teeth and finally reduced it to a size I could at last spit out."

Should the boys have managed to remain alive—and conscious—by the time the avalanche stopped moving, they might have tried to thrust a hand or foot up through the snow, knowing that three quarters of people buried with a body part protruding have been rescued alive. Of those who were not rescued, some died simply because there was no one there to see their hand sticking out of the snow.

What Jim Kanzler realized, in the moment that Pat Callis saw the backpack, was that his brother and his best friends were buried somewhere on the west face, beneath his feet. Despite all the efforts by the professional rangers, high on the shoulders of Mount Cleveland, brother had discovered brother, friend had discovered friend.

As soon as the west face team reported their find, the search shifted radically. While a half dozen men were left to continue searching Mount Cleveland's north face slide, in case the party had split up and somehow been carried down in separate slides, the rest of the group was immediately helicoptered to the west slope, and intensive probing and scanning the area with a magnetometer began in earnest. Where the arms of the avalanche converged, having followed channels from several sides of the bowl, probers jammed their poles through the snow, expecting at any moment to hit something solid—another pack, a boot, a body. Progress was agonizingly slow. In some places, the avalanched snowpack was so hard that the poles would not even penetrate. Once, the magnetometer sounded, but intensive digging only revealed flecks of metal in a stone.

Finally, a prober broke through and struck something soft. Digging, the team discovered a buried parka, and in its pocket, something even more promising—a camera with film in it and an additional can of black-and-white film. Determining the owner of the parka was especially difficult since the search team still had no idea how many of the boys were actually on the west face—or where on the face they may have been. The pack might have been set down on top of the face and carried down by the avalanche on its own. "There can be little doubt the lost articles came from above on the rocks," said park spokesman Dan Nelson. "We don't know whether a man above set the pack down and it slid down the hill or what."

Hoping that the film would provide some clue as to the boys' final climbing location, their Place Last Seen, searchers gave the film, along with the color film they had found in the tent camp several days earlier, to the Royal Canadian Mounted Police. The black and white was taken to the nearby town of Lethbridge, so that prints could be delivered later that evening. The color film, however, had to be flown all the way to a Kodak plant in Vancouver, where all other production was suspended for one hour while the film was developed. It took an entire day for the rescue team to get the results.

Back in the Flathead Valley, news coverage of the pack discovered by Pat Callis had become frenzied. If hopes of finding the boys alive had diminished to almost nothing, the discovery at least convinced people that the search would bring the agonizing mystery of their disappearance to a close. The *Daily Inter Lake* reported that "climbers were back on the high cliffs today gambling hope, their new clues, and whatever it is that drives men in such a search against old man winter and the threat of new avalanches the predicted snow will bring."

George Ostrom, who along with the rest of the residents of the valley had been watching the Park Service's every subtle move during the progress of the search, suddenly found himself recalling the "incompetence and chaos with which the park administration had faced the several crises of 1967," and decided to take a look himself. A veteran mountain climber, he gathered up his foul weather gear, climbing pack, and snowshoes, examined the maps and photographs he had of Mount Cleveland, and made his way to the mountain. "I had no illusions about a fat and forty-year-old man pulling off any heroic Class 5 climb to rescue anyone on the north face of Cleveland, but I did know I had to do what I could, and see firsthand what was going on," he wrote in a newspaper column a few days later. After convincing himself of the competency of Frauson, Colony, and the rest of the team, Ostrom reassured his readers that the search was in very good hands.

"It is a rare and precious time in anyone's life when he finds 60 or 70 people from all walks of life who momentarily lay selfishness aside and commit themselves wholeheartedly to aiding or comforting all those around them. Some gave of their sleep, their comfort, and their pantries. Others came very close to giving their lives . . . and they all acted as if it was the natural thing to do. One father in his despair wondered if it wouldn't have been better for his son to have died in the jungles of Vietnam and I disagreed. Only those young men who dare to challenge shall ever really accomplish, and I believe the world will be much better off when bold young men can 'find themselves' on a wind-swept mountain instead of in a machine-gun-swept rice paddy. Personal freedom encompasses a choice of where and how to die as well as where and how to live."

As the day came to a close, temperatures continued to drop. The weather bureau predicted the arrival of a severe Pacific front, probably carrying a new load of snow, within six hours. The avalanche risk to rescuers at this point was "considerably dangerous," and park officials debated how long to carry on the mission. Back at the superintendent's office in West Glacier, a telegram arrived on Briggle's desk from a local pastor begging the Park Service not to cancel the search for "our boys."

The film arrived back in Bob Frauson's hands at 5:00 A.M. the next morning. The color film proved to be of little value to the team—it merely chronicled the early stages of the boys' journey, from the boat trip across Waterton Lake to the earliest campsites. The black-and-white photographs, however, seemed more promising. Virtually all of them were taken of the north face, the climbers' original goal. Some of the images were sharp enough to show the upper mountain covered by a heavy blanket of snow when the boys began their trip, indicating that conditions were considerably worse than when rescuers went in. Most of the others were terribly overexposed, probably from the sun's blinding reflection off the snow. Given the number of panoramic shots of the north face, rescuers felt more certain than ever that at least some of the boys had made an attempt on the face after all.

Here, then, the rescue team held in their hands photographs the boys had taken of each other just days, or even hours, before they disappeared. The images were, in their innocence, unbearably poignant, as if apparitions of the boys themselves stood before them, offering clues to their route but little hope for their safe return. Here was a photo of Jerry Kanzler and Clare Pogreba, best of friends, sitting in Alf Baker's boat on the way to the dock, wearing rain slickers and staring off into the middle distance of the park. Clare's arm rests gently on the top of a pack, a leather glove protecting his hand from the cold. Jerry's thin mustache and spotty beard, framing his face beneath a balaclava hat, seems hard-won, as if he hoped they would give his eighteen-year-old visage a touch of maturity, or strength. Here was Ray Martin, on the dock, smiling his goofy smile and standing half again as tall as his companions. There was no posing in these photos, none of the bravado that one might find in records kept by less experienced climbers. The Mount Cleveland team was documenting their journey for future reference, to add to their growing album of brilliant climbs, or to show their route to fellow climbers upon their return. Pat Callis and Jim Kanzler would be proud to see these photos, they figured; maybe they would come along on the next trip. Dr. Levitan would be touched to see photographs of his son, a talented mountaineer as well as a promising scholar, exhibiting the skills the elder Levitan had learned at Camp Hale. Bud Anderson would eat his heart out to see Mount Cleveland in winter, when it took more than a vigorous walk to get to the top.

The boys, in the photos, were so young, so visibly excited about their adventure, it was hard for the rescuers to believe that they weren't still up there on the mountain, cooking breakfast and preparing their gear. Surely the boys, whom all but one or two of the rangers had never met, reminded members of the search team of themselves at a younger age, full of piss and vinegar and determined to test their skills against the park's most challenging peaks. No matter the professional concern the rangers felt at having to perform a search in such trying conditions, they felt more than a little personal attachment to the missing climbers. No one becomes a ranger, after all, who doesn't prefer the silence of wilderness to the busywork of city life, and the bonds between professional backwoodsmen and expert amateurs are strong, if occasionally strained by their position on opposite sides of a federal bureaucracy. Rangers, after all, were young climbers once. They just made their love of the woods a vocation. Bob Frauson and Hal Kanzler knew each other both by reputation and by name; the rangers on the rescue team recognized the boys, whom they had never met, in spirit. Their determination to find them was a determination to save members of their own clan, to save less experienced—and unluckier— versions of themselves.

The pack and the parka, though, had convinced the team that the west face remained the most likely place to find the boys, and with so many men probing a slope that remained vulnerable to avalanches, helicopter flights over the face were discontinued. Rescuers continued to focus on the northwest ridge, think- ing again that perhaps the less experienced Anderson and Levitan had made their way there from the base of the north face, in order to reach the top and offer assistance to the others from above. Dan Nelson said the found articles made it appear that two members of the party had moved from the north face to the northwest slope to help the other three up and over. "They may not have gotten back to the other three on the face," he said. "If they did, the question is where are all five of them?" There was still no evidence that the boys had ever reunited, and despite constant probing, rescuers still had not found any clues at the base of the north face avalanche.

Things were no less frustrating on the west face. "All the climbers were wearing bright-colored clothes and all their equipment was brightly colored," Willie Pfisterer, the alpine rescue specialist from Jasper, told a reporter. "You would think with five sets of every item necessary for the climb we would have found something other than a camera, pack, and parka. Hundreds of feet of rope . . . everything. When climbers fall or are caught in an avalanche, gen- erally they lose many things. They lost nothing we could find. It is almost as if they were swallowed up. This is the first time in all my years I haven't found a body. I just don't understand it. They just seem to have vanished."

One theory circulating among the rangers was that the boys had dug snow caves in the side of the west face and then been buried, along with all their gear. Kurt Seel, the Canadian naturalist who was also a seventeen-year climbing veteran, spent the day combing the entire north and northwest faces. He followed four sets of tracks leading away from the boys' original snow caves at the base of the north face to the rocks above. The tracks eventually disappeared. He followed two sets of tracks along a ridgeline leading to the northwest slope. They also disappeared. Did the boys try a climb of the north face, or did they in fact move along the ridge and over to the west? The tracks were agonizingly short on answers. "Your guess is as good as mine," Seel told a reporter. "The pieces just don't fit together in a logical pattern." Seel conceded that the climbers might have somehow made their way up the north face and across to the northwest face, but that seemed unlikely. "I guess it could be done, but that is a brute of a mountain. Good God, what a trip it would be. I just don't know."

As the probe team moved across the west face, they did their best to figure how the boys might have fallen, and whether in fact they had been carried down the slope by the avalanche. Sleeping bags were laid out on the face to see which way they slid. Probers spray-painted the edges of their route to prevent reworking the same areas twice. By the end of the day, about 10 percent of the most promising places on the west face had been probed and examined with the magnetometer, with no results. Again, the crude instruments were of limited effectiveness. Although the probe poles were 12 feet long, the depth of the snow deposited by the avalanche ran considerably deeper than this; probers jammed into the snow without striking bottom. Likewise, during a test demonstration on the slope, the magnetometer was able to locate a pocket-knife buried six feet under the snowpack, but was unable to turn up a ski pole, a carabiner, or a pack frame. Like most outdoor gear, these things were typically made of aluminum, for lightness and strength, and were thus not magnetic. Still, the rescue team figured, the boys either weren't there, or they were buried too deep to find.

As the exhausting day came to a close, Chuck Trail began shuttling men back to the Waterton ranger station. After so much practice, Trail had managed to cut the length of each trip nearly in half, to six minutes. The added efficiency allowed for one more flight to the top of the mountain to check the climbing register. After Trail touched down on the summit, Ranger Doug Erskine hopped out and looked. He found two logbooks, tucked in metal cannisters, protected from the weather. The last entry in one read August 3; the last in the other read August 24. The boys either never made it to the top, or, in their determination to remain anonymous, had chosen not to announce their achievement. Back at the townsite, one of the rescuers from Butte, Dr. Jack Goebel, an avid climber and the chairman of the math department at Montana Tech, dismissed the empty register as a clue. Goebel knew of the boys' obsession with the north face, and thought it likely that they wouldn't have signed in even if they had made it. "They were just that independent." Erskine took the logbooks with him; they were later placed in the park museum and marked "Register removed due to search for five missing climbers."

With exhausted rangers, diminishing supplies, and a major storm overdue in the area, Superintendent Briggle held a meeting with the parents to discuss ending the search for the winter. "I felt it was my responsibility to discuss all aspects of the situation with them," he told reporters. "You have to be realistic. Their attitude is tremendous. They all express a desire not to endanger the lives of rescue climbers working on the mountain. That makes our job much easier." Briggle approached Dr. Levitan and asked him to join Chuck Trail for a look at the mountain in the helicopter, to see for himself the monumental scale—and the growing futility—of the search mission. Having survived the 10th Mountain Division's brutal training in Colorado, the division's assault on Riva Ridge, and the trial of being taken as a Jewish prisoner of war by German troops, Dr. Levitan had survived enough hardship for ten men. This loss, it seemed, was too much for him. He declined to look at the mountain that had swallowed his boy.

In Dr. Levitan's place, Arthur Martin volunteered, and upon his return told the other families of the obvious dangers for the rescue team high on Mount Cleveland. "Nobody knew how it was going to end up," Arthur's wife, Ruby, said. "I said there was no reason for anyone else to lose their lives—I knew those boys probably weren't going to be coming back. I certainly didn't want to put anyone else's life in jeopardy. I felt at first that maybe they'd dug into an ice cave, but by the end, since they weren't out waving, I knew they probably weren't coming back. It was a harrowing experience as the searchers went out every day. The weather wasn't always good and the possibility of more avalanches was always a threat. The searchers were also in danger, and it was up to us if they should continue the search. I said there was no way we could do the boys any good at this point, and to put other lives in jeopardy was foolish."

Ruby Martin's stoicism seemed the only sustainable response to the boys' disappearance. Their absence was so complete, so unrelenting, that parents could only stand numb in their grief. Like families hoping for the return of missing soldiers, they could not give themselves over fully to mourning, since they were incapable of abandoning even the remotest sense of hope. As they waited, pacing the floors of their makeshift homes or the parking lots outside the rescue headquarters, the families tried to turn their grief into heartbroken offers of reassurance to the rescue team.

Indeed, even as rescuers had gone about their work that day, fracture lines were opening between new and old snow, and rescuers began to worry in earnest about their own vulnerability. "The whole mountain was moving all the time, like a curtain," Kurt Seel said. "Slides were constant. There was hardly a spot that hadn't been hit by sliding snow." During the day, winds had begun to pick up to 40 miles per hour. "I didn't like the idea of going up underneath on the west side," Jerry DeSanto said. "I thought, 'What's the difference? They're dead.' But the feeling was that the parents wanted them out as soon as possible."

The *Daily Inter Lake* reported that the "hope of finding five Montana youths, now eight days overdue in an assault on Mount Cleveland, all but vanished again Wednesday when searchers failed to turn up a single new clue. Although no official word has been received it now appears the search is in its last day unless important new discoveries are made. Climbers are nearing exhaustion. The sky continues to clear in spite of continued threatening weather forecasts but it is bitterly cold on the rocky slopes of the mountain." Readers of the press accounts began writing in to the local papers, expressing their grief. Lessley Perring wrote from Spokane. She had just put down an issue of the *Hungry Horse News,* she wrote, and "quite a few salty tears fell over this paper. It was a terrible thing to have happen, and my heart aches for the families of all those boys." Another letter printed that day, from a Mrs. W. W. Miller of Kalispell, thanked the paper for a recent tribute to the boys. "Thousands of us awaited every word, hoped and prayed with the families that the mission would be successful; wept with them when it failed."

During the day, back at Waterton Townsite, Bob Frauson called a supplier for one more set of equipment: five body bags, to be delivered in unmarked boxes.

On Thursday morning, January 8, with temperatures at the townsite reaching ten below zero, the plumbing in the buildings began to freeze. On the mountain, high winds and blowing snow were also causing problems, with avalanches on the west side falling with such regularity that the probe team was withdrawn to await an airlift out. On the way out, warden Peter Fuhrmann and Pat Callis flew an aerial reconnaissance by helicopter to the north face ridge and the west face, but found no evidence of missing climbers. The magnetometer team worked in comparative calm on the north face, but again found nothing. Later in the day, the winds began to gust up to 50 miles per hour, and brought with them new snow; together, they shut down further helicopter flights. With the end of the search now in sight, the north face team dismantled the boys' tent camp, and returned, along with the rest of the team, to the Waterton ranger station. Some of the team, including Jim Kanzler, Peter Lev, and Pat Callis, were released from the search efforts and taken back to the townsite.

An official release from the Park Service told the story in neutral, bureaucratic language, perhaps the only language appropriate for an event that had so tormented families and professional rescuers alike. "Due to rapidly deteriorating weather conditions and the constant threat of avalanches which are a serious threat to searching parties, the search for the five young men who undertook 14 days ago the climb of Mt. Cleveland in Glacier National Park has been suspended for the winter. The decision to discontinue the ground and air operation conducted jointly by United States and Canadian national park service personnel was made after consultation with the parents and relatives of the missing climbers."

The recovery would now have to wait until spring thaw, which in northern Montana usually meant June or July. The *Daily Inter Lake* reported that the statement, issued jointly by Superintendents Briggle and Ross, "snapped the last thin thread of remaining hope and the secret of the fate of the five youths will have to be unlocked next summer."

On Friday, the major storm that rescuers had been anticipating for days finally blew into Glacier, forcing the last of the team from the mountain. Further search efforts, park officials said, were "out of the question." With snow once again beginning to load up the upper slopes of Mount Cleveland, even the most experienced mountaineers began to think about getting out of Glacier. Kurt Seel said he saw a single avalanche last ten minutes. With winds continuing to blow at 40 miles per hour, the lake frozen, and the helicopter unusable, the remaining rescuers, including the Teton group and what volunteers were left, began to hike the 12 miles from the mountain to the townsite on skis and snowshoes. The Canadians from Banff and Jasper shuttled out six loads of gear using a boxy red Canadian Ski Whiz snowmobile and a pale green

American Ski-Doo, the latter trailing a fiberglass buggy that under other circumstances might have carried a passel of children on a gas-powered sleigh ride.

As the rescuers returned, they were mobbed by a press corps that had grown with every day the search continued. "I wouldn't take that mountain in the winter in any way, shape or form. I wouldn't be caught dead up there in the winter," Kurt Seel told the Associated Press. "That's a brute of a mountain and would be tough enough in the summer. We don't know for certain that any one of them was ever on the west face, but we think so. How else would the parka and pack get there?"

By the next day, January 10, the storm had abated enough to permit several more flights to the ranger station, and the remaining rations, rescue gear, and propane bottles were flown to the townsite. Four of the remaining team also left in the helicopter or by snowmobile, leaving only Jerry DeSanto and Doug Erskine to close the ranger station up for winter. By the time they left three days later, 18 more inches of snow had piled up on the ground, and much more had fallen up high. By January 12, Chuck Trail and his helicopter were safely back in Missoula. The week after the search ended, a foot of new snow fell on Mount Cleveland. Speaking to the press, Bob Frauson expressed his frustration at the failed search. "We won't know what happened until we find them. You could hide an army up there."

Part 3

Runout

Chapter 15

✳

I am of course aware that it is an age which
cares little for the more manly virtues, and
which looks askance at any form of sport that
can, by any stretch of extremest imagination,
be regarded as dangerous: yet since we
cannot all, for most obvious reasons, take our
delight "wallowing in slimy spawn of lucre,"
something may surely be urged in favor of
a sport that teaches, as no other teaches,
endurance and mutual trust, and forces men
occasionally to look death in its grimmest
aspect frankly and squarely in the face.

— Albert F. Mummery,
My Climbs in the Alps
and the Caucasus

Even after the search was called off, the mystery surrounding the mountain and the boys' disappearance continued to grow. In Columbia Falls and Butte, the boys' families and friends were heartbroken but stoic. Reached by the local press at her home on West College Avenue in Bozeman, Jean Kanzler managed to speak through her grief of having lost a husband and a son within the span of two years. "There are regrets, deep ones of course, but no real ones. I couldn't live Jerry's life. This was a spark he caught from his father, Hal, in their climbs to the rim of the world on the Mission Mountains. Call it an eagle's look across the world if you will. But Jerry caught the flame and it absorbed him. This was his way. He knew the risks and the dangers and he had the intensity to want to conquer overall. The regrets span not the eighteen years of Jerry's life but what might have been for him. My son Jim will benefit from this. He will climb some more. He will be more cautious because of this because climbing is a way of life for him, and was for Jerry and for Hal.

My men have learned their way in the sky. How can I deny it? This was their way, something they had to do, and they did it their way. You don't say no to that. You guide and hope they have found their way."

Traditionally bound by mere observation, newspaper reporters began waxing philosophical. The story of boys dying in mountains was too much an epic, too mythic, for reporters to constrain themselves to inverted pyramids. "Why do men climb mountains?" the *Daily Inter Lake* asked. "For some, the spirit of the conqueror runs and is set free in their veins when the top is reached. For others, those of the 'now generation,' this is 'your thing.' Still others climb 'to see where they came from.' Others feel that sense of accomplishment, of having done something worthwhile from their point of view. The list is endless." An accompanying piece reported that compared to the average chute on the mountain, the missing boys "could be likened to the period at the end of this sentence in relation to the size of the [newspaper] page."

Even with the search postponed for the winter, the Glacier community continued to debate the Mount Cleveland incident. A January 9 news story carried a quote from an anonymous "veteran Flathead mountaineer." "There is no such thing as an experienced eighteen-year-old climber. They don't know when to quit. They are nine feet tall, but this is the way you want your boys." The article concluded with a comment in a reporter's voice that showed how much the local media had been taken in by the archetypal saga of men risking their lives in the mountains. "There is realization that young men with the climbing urge aren't going to be climbing mountains that the Girl Scouts hike."

Letters to the editor of the *Hungry Horse News* took all angles, and offered readers the chance to ruminate publicly over the terrible loss and its meaning. With many in the Flathead Valley arguing that the boys should never have been allowed to venture into the park at such a forbidding time of the year, others maintained that any restrictions on adventure would be bad for the soul—both individual and communal. Those who considered the boys' expedition to have been too perilous, aware of the risks of backcountry travel, were perhaps unfamiliar with the joys. Helmuth Matdies, a Whitefish resident, who said he had worked in Austria as a climbing guide and had climbed all through the Austrian Alps, wrote on January 16 to say that criticism of the boys by "sidewalk mountaineers" was in poor taste. "By the age of eighteen I had seen several thousand avalanches because I was raised in the middle of the Tyrolean Alps where avalanches are an everyday thing. How many experiences with avalanches have you people who are criticizing had? All I ask any one of you who has given an opinion on any of the five missing climbers is—are you as qualified as any of those boys? This would only be fair."

Another debate surrounded whether an eighteen-year-old boy possesses the qualities of judgment necessary to attempt such a difficult climb. R. D. Buchanan from Columbia Falls wrote to say that "our country will be doomed when our young people no longer desire to reach new heights, whether they be mountain peaks, scientific discoveries, or philosophical ideals." Bill Lukens, identified as a former resident of the Glacier Park region, asked the Park Service not to let the tragedy turn Glacier into a "sissy park." Rangers over-reacted to the Night of the Grizzlies, he wrote; they should show restraint in response to the boys' disappearance. "Let's not kill the Grizzly. . . . Do not close the park to climbing."

A local priest named Father Best, who knew Anderson and his family, sought in spiritual traditions an apt parallel to the trials his community had been through. All religions look to mountains for inspiration, he wrote, and the Blackfeet and Flathead Indians had spiritual roots right there in Glacier Park. Mountaineers, for their part, seek their own kind of enlightenment experience high in the hills. "Here the spirit of God dwells," Father Best wrote. "And according to the Holy Books the only unforgivable sin is to treat these mountains profanely! The mountaineer can forgive the murderer, the thief, the other bad men of the social world, but like God they see the ultimate sin, the greatest evil, in those who would destroy and blaspheme the mountains. Here the Great Spirit dwells and inspires me to do great things."

The search and rescue operation also made it into the Congressional Record of January 27 in the words of Montana senator Mike Mansfield. "Mr. President, adventure is always an admirable quality in our young people, and each year we hear of new challenges presented by Mother Nature. The lure of mountain climbing is irresistible to many. During the holiday season, five young Montanans attempted to climb Mount Cleveland, the highest and most rugged mountain in Glacier National Park. This is a challenge which has defeated others, and apparently, these five have failed to reach the summit. After two weeks of searching, it was generally determined that the climbers had met an unfortunate fate. This part of Glacier National Park is extremely hazardous because of heavy snowfall and the constant threat of avalanche. The search parties were unable to find any clues as to the possible fate of these young men. It is likely to be spring before the recovery is accomplished.

"This is indeed a tragic occasion, not only the apparent loss of these young men, but the uncertainty which must linger in the hearts of their immediate families. Mrs. Mansfield and I extend our personal bereavement to the mothers and fathers, sisters and brothers of these outstanding young men. This is a very sad story but one which is a tribute to the strength and character of five youthful mountaineers."

Notwithstanding the rhetoric from Montana's politicians, the family members of the boys were inconsolable. Referring to her son as "a searcher who had found his answers," Florence Anderson told a reporter of her appreciation for the work of the search team. "From the bottom of my heart I appreciate the kindness of people and all the efforts to find the boys. It's not just for Jimmy, it's for all of them. So many have asked what they could do to help, and I feel that when the bodies are found, maybe a living memorial—a fountain or something for Canadians as well as for Americans. Because they all helped. I feel that Jimmy went into mountain climbing knowing the dangers. He was prepared for survival or what might happen. He wanted his ashes spread over the park if anything happened. That's how much he loved the park."

If all were distraught, none was more so than Jean Kanzler, who had lost her husband just two years before. "She went to hell in a handbasket after [Hal's] death," George Ostrom said. "All she needed was for this to happen to that boy. She about went up there to dig him up herself."

On January 24, Bud Anderson's wife gave birth to Justin James; Bud had been up there searching for Jim even though his wife, Nina, was eight months pregnant.

The families of the boys, beginning to come to terms with their permanent loss, were also writing more private correspondence. On January 18, a letter from Dr. Levitan came to Bob Frauson. "Dear Bob—I think of you and occasionally would like to talk to you. Right now I have one thought— someone suggested the boys should be buried together in the park near where they died. Before this goes any further I thought I'd check with you. I have not discussed this with relatives."

Ruby Martin sent a handwritten letter to Superintendent Briggle on February 19. Her terrible grief is evident even from the dashes she used, leaving sentences trailing off and incomplete; Emily Dickinson had used the same technique in her poetry to express how sadness never fully resolves. "I'm sorry I have been so slow in writing to you—I have started to write so many times but my emotions usually get the best of me and I end up not accomplishing very much.

"Thank you so very much for your letter of Feb. 13, and for the enclosure of the letter Ray sent to Art Sedlack. It was very thoughtful of you to send it to us. I loved my boy so very much—he was so very special to us—and it just seems like anything of his or anything pertaining to him that we can get just gives us a little more of him to hold on to. The loss has been a great one for all of us—it is so hard to think we have lost these wonderful boys, and to me there just seems to be the feeling of wanting to grasp for any possible thing remaining of him—

"Our home is full of things that were important to him—his rock collection—and so many little things—parts of his climbing equipment—and books and many little things that he just bought for the home or for one of us. It seems like everywhere you look, there is something to remind us of his love and kindness—but still we grasp for more—like this letter and pictures and things that friends have given to us—to me it seems like each little thing brings him a little closer. I also want to take the opportunity at this time to thank you so very much for everything you did for all of us—I know this tragedy affected many lives—many men were put in dangerous situations and it was a hardship on all concerned with the attempted rescue operations. I have great admiration for all of your people—for the efficiency in handling the whole situation and for the kindness and compassion shown to all of us. You will never know how very much we appreciate the way we were treated and the things you were all doing for us. At times it seems as though it surely must be all a bad dream—but the heartache is all too real and we still have to face up to it and to the fact that we still have another ordeal ahead of us yet."

Mrs. Martin closed her letter by hoping that she could consider Bob Frauson and his family "friends rather than just Glacier Park officials," and invited them to stop in if they ever made their way to Butte. "Our home isn't much but there is always room for more friends—so please consider this a personal invitation from Art and myself to the Briggle family—and thank you again—so very much for everything."

Over the two months following the abandoned Mount Cleveland search, Jerry DeSanto and a couple of other rangers hiked and flew the Mount Cleveland area to check on snow conditions and see if any more of the boys' equipment had come to the surface. Weeks went by with little new to report. Superintendent Briggle told reporters that the park would likely wait until the snow cleared sometime in late spring to begin reconnaissance flights over the Mount Cleveland area. "We don't know the date. It could be the middle of May, it could be the middle of June, it depends on what winter deals us. We do know we're going back and continue what winter had forced us to discontinue for now."

One of the rescuers involved from Grand Teton, Richard Reese from Santa Fe, returned his pay to help purchase rescue gear, along with a note: "I suspect that as a result of the publicity which came out of the Mt. Cleveland disaster, mountaineering interest will begin to show a considerable increase in Glacier and the park will probably have to face the problem of mountaineering (winter as well as summer) head on. . . ."

Among the headaches the Park Service faced was the determination of local climbers to head into the mountains to find the boys before it was safe to do so. With so many in the Flathead Valley so wrapped up in the story of the boys' disappearance, rangers feared that a rush of energetic but inexperienced climbers would complicate the work of the professional team. Superintendent Briggle even threatened to close the park around Mount Cleveland to prevent interference. "We recognize there might be well-intentioned people who want to go back to Mount Cleveland to try to find their friends. We intend the National Park Service shall be there first," Briggle told reporters. Even with years of rescue experience and proper equipment, rangers were ambivalent about working in such difficult conditions, Briggle continued. "These men know what they're facing, spring runoff, late season avalanche possibilities, rolling rock, sheer cliffs, mountain climbing to continue along lines of triangulation established last winter. It's going to be a tough mission. We want it to be successful, without further loss of life."

With the snow still too deep to approach the mountain, let alone see what lay beneath the snowpack, there was little for rangers to do. On March 12, Jerry DeSanto ventured on skis to look at the conditions around the mountain, and confirmed the futility of a serious search effort. Rangers and families alike hashed over the possibilities for a summer search, piecing together the few clues that had turned up in January.

If the families of the boys were growing restless for the search to begin again, they had also turned their energies to consideration of the inevitable. In a March 16 letter to Bob Frauson, Dr. Levitan wrote that he had just returned from Bozeman, where he had met with Peter Lev and Jim Kanzler. Kanzler particularly "has been doing a lot of thinking and said he was going to write you," Dr. Levitan wrote. "Some of what he said made so much sense that I'm writing it to you. He was impressed that the NW ridge is not really a ridge but a line where two faces meet. Therefore the boys had to move out on the west face, particularly at the level of the towers. He's convinced they were hit by an avalanche at that level—maybe it's just one that Bud Anderson saw from the plane. How far they were carried is impossible to say. . . .

"Peter Lev said that indirectly and without mentioning names the Parks Dept. did not want any but their own personnel to have anything to do with recovery. I still want to be called immediately when the time comes. I would like Mark to be buried according to Jewish laws without embalming, therefore the body will have to be preserved in ice. Usually we have the funeral within 24 hours. I'm sure you'll level with me."

By mid-April, searchers had begun flights over the west face, but there was still too much snow to see anything. If the search had gone into forced hibernation, the public eye had still not turned from the mountain. Hal Kanzler's former employer, Anaconda, made a $1,000 donation to a memorial for "two Montana Tech students missing and presumed dead since December on a climbing expedition in Glacier National Park." Bob Chebull, president of the Montana Tech climbing club, said the contribution raised the total funds to $2,000; the club planned to use the money to purchase rescue equipment for use around the state.

On May 5, Jerry DeSanto and Gary Bunney, a fire control officer who had been involved in the "Night of the Grizzlies," spent fifty minutes flying over the west face in a small airplane, but they could see nothing but very deep snow. A number of avalanches had recently come down, covering the areas where the boys' gear had been collected in January.

On May 23, DeSanto and Ranger Larry Feser, exploring on foot, made a remarkable discovery on the west slope, one that in an instant answered questions that had plagued northwest Montana since January. There, laying on top of the chunky wet snow, was another camera, flung from its case, its leather strap broken, lens pointed at the sky. The broken strap provided grim evidence of the violence of what must have happened, as did the discovery of the leather camera case some three hundred yards up the west slope. The camera had clearly been wrenched free from its seat around a climber's neck, or from the pocket of a backpack. Somehow, after its descent down the slope and six months in the snow, the camera's lens remained unbroken. A photograph the rangers took of the camera case shows the upper reaches of the west face of Mount Cleveland in the background, looming black and chilling against the blue spring sky.

The case, they discovered, had James Anderson's name on it. This time, the film in Anderson's camera was developed successfully. Although some of the film proved of little value, the last picture in the roll was remarkable: it showed all five boys standing together at about 8,000 feet on the west face. Finally, after months of speculation, rescuers had proof of the boys' progress: after an initial approach up the north side, they had in fact abandoned their route and worked their way up the west side of the mountain. Suddenly, the search was back in full swing.

Two days later, DeSanto and Feser found half of a snapped ice ax at 8,300 feet, sitting atop unusually deep snow. For a moment, as DeSanto reached down to pull it up, he thought he might find an arm attached to it, but no luck. (After the search, DeSanto gave the broken ax handle to Bob Frauson, who kept it on his desk for more than a year. When the second half was found and given to Frauson, the two halves fit together perfectly.) Over the next few weeks several additional pieces of gear were discovered at the toe of the avalanche. A June 1 helicopter-and-foot patrol by DeSanto, Feser, McClelland, and Frauson turned up nothing. Two days later, a handwritten letter arrived at the superintendent's office from Dr. Levitan in Helena. "I've been reading about the resumption of the search," the letter began. "I'm glad that you're making sure that no lives are risked. One of these days I'd like to come up. I just want to get close to where the boy is. If I could go in with one of the rangers to see the general area, I'd appreciate it very much.

"P.S. I repeat I'm not interested in checking on your plans or search operations. That's not my business. I just want to get close to the boy. Sometimes I even hope they don't find him. That it was a rock slide and not an avalanche and that he'll remain forever where it happened." By return post, Briggle wrote to Dr. Levitan. "It is very difficult for me to say to you that it would be better for you not to go into the area; for as a father of a grown son, I can understand your wishes. However, I honestly believe that it would be far better for you to remain away until such time as we locate the boys."

As the snow on the west face began to melt in the warming sunshine, more and more gear began to pop to the surface, like spring buds beginning to sprout from winter hibernation. On June 7, Feser and Ranger Fred Goodsell found a wool knit cap below the ice fall on the main avalanche path, and three days later, a rucksack at the toe of the avalanche. After another week of nothing, Feser, Goodsell, and two Canadian wardens found a plastic bag containing flashlight batteries at the bottom of the slope. On June 18 searchers brought in a helicopter to once again try a magnetometer; two Americans and two Canadians searching all day found only a blue-and-white wool cap. No metal.

On June 21, on foot, Feser and Goodsell turned up a battered canteen at

8,350 feet, the highest find made; when connected schematically with the photos found in Anderson's camera, rangers were able to chart what they thought was the boys' progress up the mountain. How and where they came down, of course, was still a mystery. Four days later, Feser and Goodsell and trail foreman William Huchinson found a shirt and a plastic bag on the lower slopes. With so much snow melted on the upper reaches of the slope, it had become plain that the boys must be buried somewhere along the middle or lower reaches of the bowl, where the original parka and pack had been found and where the snow was still dozens of feet deep.

On June 27, sick of waiting helplessly back in Kalispell, George Ostrom and a ranger decided to climb up the mountain. Perhaps out of a respect for his friend Hal Kanzler, with whom he had hiked so many of Glacier's peaks and with whom he had shown Jerry and Jim the park's backcountry, Ostrom had become obsessed with the search. As poetic as it might have seemed to leave a mountaineer's body where it fell, Ostrom was determined to bring Jerry Kanzler's body home to rest. Like losing a man to the sea, the discomfort of losing a boy to the mountains was inconceivable. "Now, you have to remember that at this point I didn't trust the Park Service at all," Ostrom said. "I felt that the fires in 1967 and the grizzly bear attacks had shown a lack of leadership and an inability to make good decisions. I didn't want to go home and have to tell Jean Kanzler that 'I found the bones of your son, or what was left after the grizzlies got them.' I was going up there whether the Park Service wanted me there or not. I felt like I owed it to the family to get that body back."

After crossing the same scree field that Jim Kanzler, Peter Lev, and Pat Callis had crossed in January, Ostrom came to the waterfall that, frozen over in winter, had now begun to drain the western bowl. Although there was still quite a lot of snow covering the creek above the waterfall—the creek had, in fact, hollowed out a kind of cave underneath the snow—the small plateau above it seemed a natural place to look for the bodies. It was one of a number of breaks in the incline of the west face, a relatively flat space that Terry Kennedy described as a horizontal step in a staircase. But getting to the flat step meant climbing a vertical step that required, especially given the melting snow, more than a little dexterity. Ostrom decided to take a look. With "great trepidation," he stepped up onto the rock wall, and inched his way out toward the fall to see if he could look over the top and then underneath the snow above it. "I thought I'd see bodies or body parts or something, but I was looking at a 35-foot drop into the snow, and there were rocks falling all around me. I figured I have a wife and four kids, I quit."

Perhaps because the west face proved more treacherous than he had imagined, perhaps because he saw the futility of searching the mountain on his own, Ostrom changed his mind about the Park Service and the talents of the professional search team. After discussing his climb with the rangers down at the bottom of the face, Ostrom concluded that they were "competent and experienced. I was then able to relax, because I realized that I didn't have to commit myself to keeping track of Jimmy." He had no idea how close he had come to a devastating discovery.

Although there was only a remote chance that the boys had been hung up on the upper edge of the bowl—perhaps on one of the rock outcroppings above 8,000 feet that were just beginning to become bare—a group of rangers decided to inspect the upper bowl to rule this out. Jack Christiansen and Tremblay, with Feser, DeSanto, and Goodsell, decided to climb back up Mount Cleveland at 5:00 A.M. on June 29 to check the areas that had become clear of snow. At 9:00 A.M., during their ascent in alternating rain and snow, they climbed up the side of the same waterfall Ostrom had approached, leading to the large, flat patch of snow at about 6,800 feet. Above the waterfall, the snow, although solid and deep, had become hollowed out underneath by running meltwater. Thirsty from the climb, Christiansen went down to the creek to get a drink and caught the unmistakable whiff of decomposition.

Gingerly, the rangers walked out along the top of the waterfall. On the slope above them were hundreds of yards of melting snow; below was a 35-foot vertical drop, followed by the runout zone of the west face avalanche. One slip, and a ranger might tumble half a mile and fall 1,500 vertical feet. After carefully approaching the creek, the men shined a flashlight up under the cave that had been hollowed out by the meltwater, and peered into the darkness. The sound of running water, inside the tunnel, was loud; a full-fledged stream course ran right past the wide-eyed men. There, about 30 feet inside the cave, dangling in the meltwater, was a head and a pair of arms hanging down from the six-foot snowpack. It was Ray Martin.

Chapter 16

❄

Had we lived, I should have had a tale to tell of the hardihood, endurance, and courage of my companions which would have stirred the heart of every Englishman. These rough notes and our dead bodies must tell the tale.

— Captain Robert Scott,
quoted in Apsley Cherry-
Garrard, *The Worst Journey
in the World*

When the call came in that the Park Service needed a pilot to finish up the Mount Cleveland search, Jim Kruger was working out of Cut Bank, about 50 miles east of the park. He put on his headset, cranked the engine, and lifted off effortlessly, his Bell G3B floating upward like an oversized dragon-fly. Inside the bubble, Kruger not only felt the trepidation that comes with the recovery of dead bodies, he felt anxiety particular to his own level of experience; this would be his first rescue flight in the high mountains.

Like many bush pilots, Jim Kruger carries himself with something between cool bravado and boyish enthusiasm. Probably this comes from holding a job that less adventurous men would consider to be the apogee of rough masculinity. Who else can say they can look down from their offices and see bald eagles flying beneath them? His twinkling blue eyes are evidence of his wry sense of humor; hanging on an outbuilding next to his home near Flathead Lake is a sign that reads BEWARE OF WIFE. DOG OK. A hangar behind his house shelters not only his helicopter—which he wheels out on a hydraulic lift he built himself and flies from a pad in his backyard—but the vintage cars he restores in his spare time—a 1952 Pontiac Catalina and a 1929 Ford Model A Coupe, among others. Before the Cleveland search, Kruger had spent years flying oil-hunting geologists around places like northern Canada and Greenland, but while he had experience flying in frigid climates, he had never flown among big mountains. When he was called in to remove the bodies, he felt a nervousness he hadn't known above the Arctic Circle. "I was about half scared. The Arctic is pretty barren—there's a lot of rough ground up there, but nothing like this."

Like Willie Colony and other men who have spent considerable time working with mangled or dead climbers, Kruger speaks with a kind of colorful detachment about his line of work. He considers the helicopter to be "the best invention since the female." When speaking of his work as a fire patrol, which any professional bush pilot is asked to do, he says he has lost his enthusiasm. Controlled burns, he says, are controlled "only until they light the match." But Kruger's face becomes more serious when speaking of his longevity in a business that has seen all too many dead bodies. Despite living and working in and above Glacier National Park for more than thirty years, he won't hike in the park. The bears, the brittle rock, the avalanches, all are best left to those limited to walking on the ground. "I've hauled too many people out who have been attacked by grizzlies, and I'm still here talkin'," he says. "The guy with the best judgment lasts the longest. It may seem like you're chicken, but at least you're there to talk about it."

Kruger's assignments over the years have ranged from searching for dead bodies with an infrared light to flying drugged grizzly bears—dangling by a cable—across Glacier's mountain ranges. During a massive flood in 1964, resulting from an enormous snowmelt combined with 11 inches of rain, he was called in to rescue ten people stranded on a road that had washed out near the southern tip of the park, near the Goat Lick Overlook. The 32 drowning victims on the Flathead Reservation, including ten people from a single family, were less fortunate. He's removed the body of a heart attack victim and rescued two men who "pancaked out" in their own private plane but somehow emerged unhurt; Kruger had to make several trips to pick up all the pieces of their tattered plane. Another time he saved a man who had nearly chopped his own leg off with an ax; he picked the man up after midnight, and had to fly home through the mountains in the pitch darkness. "I have a tendency to get a little puckered up flying around up here in the dark," he says. Over the years he has been involved in something close to 100 rescues, and pulled 18 bodies off the slopes, ravines, and valleys of Glacier National Park.

After leaving Cut Bank, Kruger flew over Lake Babb, Billy River, and through Stoney Indian Pass. There, ahead of him, he could see the rescue team leaning into the west face of Mount Cleveland, already digging trenches in the snow. As he began delivering people and equipment to the search site, Kruger found the slope above the waterfall to be so slick and steep that he had a difficult time finding a place to land. Finally, the search team working above the 35-foot waterfall built him a small landing platform out of rocks and snow; even when the landing pad was completed, only half the helicopter could fit on the edge. With the entire tail of the Bell G3B stuck out over the precipice, the rotor, the bubble, and the white fuel tank, with KRUGER stenciled in black letters under an American flag, looked as though the smallest gust of air could knock it off the cliff. Because this was the only landing spot, only one helicopter could be used, and because it was so high up, low clouds at times prevented its being used at all.

Another problem emerged as searchers worked to free Martin's body. Emerging hungry from their winter dens, grizzly bears were beginning to congregate beneath the waterfall below the body, attracted by the smell of decomposing flesh. Although the bodies had been well preserved all winter, the warmer weather was beginning to take its toll, and grizzlies are renowned for their sense of smell. If there was one thing the Park Service didn't need, it was news to leak out that grizzly bears had discovered the boys before the rescuers did.

It took considerable trenching to free Martin's body from the six feet of compacted snow, which had become compressed by the acres and tons that had crashed down from above. Photographs from the search show rangers in shirtsleeves, bending their backs against their shovels under the high-altitude glare of the sun. Once dug down, other rangers were captured with only their helmets and headlamps visible from above, as if they were descending into a mineshaft. This was grim work. Body recovery is not the same as search and rescue, which, regardless of its stresses, always promises at least the chance of finding a buried victim alive. Ray Martin had been buried for six months, and the retrieval of his body, no matter the relief it would bring to his family, was a ranger's darkest task. Subtle taboos have evolved as rescuers have tried to insulate themselves from the horrors they so regularly see. No one, for example, likes to touch the head of a victim, a dynamic also at play in the laboratories of medical schools. It is easier for a medical student to cut open a thigh muscle than it is to look at the face of a corpse; something in a passing glance at the tilt of the head, or the turn of the mouth, brings questions about the human spirit a little too close to the forefront of the mind. Better to deal with bodies, in such moments, than with souls.

"Body recovery bothers a lot of people. Some have bad dreams," Bob Frauson says. "Luckily I never had that problem. I work on the solving of a problem. All my life I've played the 'what if.' I've always had things solved before I had to. With that type of thinking your problems often aren't that bad."

Willie Colony is someone who has nightmares. Long before Mount Cleveland, Colony had become troubled by his role as a body retriever. "At first you become aware of a vague irritation, but by the time I retired I couldn't stand it," he said. "It's like rubbing your arm with sandpaper. You get more sensitive. Pretty soon you can't stand the touch of it. There were days on recovery when I had to quit and go sit somewhere. I couldn't have stayed any longer. You ponder these things. You wonder if the climbers had had a little better knowledge of what they were getting themselves into . . ." There was no heroism in this work. Heroism would have come with a live find, back in January. Then the rescue team would have returned to Columbia Falls or Kalispell or Hungry Horse as triumphant mountain men, escorting their shaken young charges back to their families. This was different. There was no poetry in this ending. Only five dead climbers, all under the age of twenty-two.

When the rescue team finally got down to it, they found Martin's broken body lying facedown, arms extended downhill and legs bent up and over his back. Attached to his body was a red perlon climbing rope extending uphill and to the left of the streambed and disappearing into considerably deeper snow, perhaps 15 to 20 feet. Since the rock of the west face, on its own, was not steep enough to merit the use of a climbing rope for protection, Martin and the others had most likely used the rope to guard against slipping on the snow. The other boys, at least some of them, were almost certainly attached to the other end. All the rescue team had to do was follow the rope to its logical conclusion.

A new rope was attached to Martin's body, the red rope was cut, and the body removed. Once rescuers removed the body from its encasement, the cause of death became grotesquely clear. Martin had not lived long enough to suffocate. He was killed by the fall. The team of climbers, it was estimated, had been carried almost half a mile down the slope and some 1,500 vertical feet. All told, debris from the avalanche had been spread over nearly 3,000 vertical feet—from 8,350 feet to about 5,500 feet—by a vast, tumbling wall of snow. Thirty years later, Ruby Martin would recall that "Ray was six foot six and a half, but when they found him he was six foot thirteen because of a broken back and neck."

After Martin's body had been taken out of the initial hole, rescuers dug a trench following the line of the red rope, and began probing as well. Using flashlights to peer beneath the snow, in the cave in which Martin's body had been found, rangers were able to see the probe poles pushing through. After a time, a ranger saw a pair of boots attached to a second body. Fourteen feet beneath the snow, it was just beyond the reach of the probe pole. James Anderson.

Anderson had come to rest on his back, head uphill, with his legs bent down at the knee. His arms were thrust forward, as though he had died in mid–sit-up. On reaching Anderson, though, the search team was confronted with another mystery: although the red rope from Ray Martin passed just next to Anderson, Anderson was in fact attached to a gold rope, not to the red one. Both ropes were found to be running upslope and slightly to the right, roughly parallel and about a foot apart. Rescuers took pictures of the bodies, but the photographs didn't come out. "It was probably just as well," Frauson said. Rescuers also had to make quick work; the stream was eating away at the integrity of the snowfield, and worries about another slide grew each day. Exhausted from their efforts, the trenching team called it quits for the day.

Once Anderson had been removed, he was bundled along with Martin and tied to the landing gear of Jim Kruger's helicopter. Kruger, wearing khaki from head to toe, pulled back on his stick and gently lifted off, to carry the bodies down to a meadow on the Blackfeet reservation near Lee Creek. They were then shuttled to a mortuary in Browning, to await discovery of their climbing companions.

Predictions of poor weather conditions made the next days of searching seem doubtful. During evening discussions, searchers said they felt sure all the bodies would be discovered simply by following the rope lines; Anderson's position on the end of the gold line matched his position in the last picture in the camera found May 23. From that picture, they deduced, it seemed certain that Levitan would be tied to the middle of the gold line and Pogreba at the other end. Since Martin was at one end of the red line, Kanzler was expected to be at the other end. All the team had to do was dig.

The next day, the search continued despite the deteriorating weather, but conditions inside the trenches were terrible. Because of limited space, only a few men could work at a time, which made progress slow but also limited the number of men exposed to risk. The snow in the pits was wet and heavy in some places and hard-packed and icy in others. Since the trenching team knew the boys' perlon climbing ropes were 150 feet long, not counting any stretching they might have endured during the fall or the ensuing winter months, they were able to estimate to some degree the parameters of their search. Standing at the site where Martin's and Anderson's bodies had been recovered, and peering up the slope's fall line, the team could at least project an uphill "V" that would probably contain the other three bodies. The prospect of digging two 150-foot trenches along the legs of the "V"—to say nothing of the space between the legs, should the initial trenches prove fruitless—was daunting, especially if the two climbing ropes connecting the boys veered apart. More frustrating, only one man at a time could work at the head of the tunnel, and snow had to be moved out as workers progressed. Back on top of the snowpack, rescuers projected the run of the rope and guessed the distance and depth of the other bodies. Probing, trenching, and using sharp-pointed fire shovels and ice chippers proved to be most effective for breaking up the snow, but one of the most effective tools was the Pulaski. A heavy digging tool with an ax on one end of the head and a hoe on the other, the Pulaski was named for a Forest Service firefighter named Edward Pulaski who, in 1910, had helped save the lives of some three dozen men trapped in a mining tunnel during a forest fire.

The Pulaski allowed searchers to hack away at the ice until they could toss it away with their shovels. Initially, diggers tossed excess snow either up and out of the pit or into the stream coursing below the snowpack. Once the trench was deep enough, diggers no longer had the luxury of throwing the snow out of the hole, and as the trench veered away from the stream, that option dried up as well. Down at the bottom of the trench, they were now forced to dig horizontally back out to the surface of the slope so they could more easily remove the snow. Using a fiberglass rescue toboggan known as an *akja,* the diggers— like miners filling a mining car—could now slide the toboggan out rather than having to hoist it vertically. Once, a sled full of snow got away from the team, and began zipping down the slope toward Superintendent Briggle, who was standing near Jim Kruger's helicopter. The boss jumped aside, and the sled flew over the edge and shattered on the rocks below.

With the digging so difficult, Bob Frauson decided to try another approach: rigging up a long hose to a canvas gravity sock hooked up to the waterfall that gushed hundreds of feet uphill from the digging site. The setup, designed for wilderness fire fighting, would use pressurized water to blast the snow away from the remaining bodies. The rig was not easy to lay: the slope between the waterfall and the trenches was steep and still fully under snow; rescuers hooking up the gravity sock had to build kick-steps into the snow to keep from tumbling down the slope, past the trenches, and off the cliff. A photograph taken from the upper waterfall looking down gives perhaps the most terrifying perspective of the slope the boys were carried down during their fatal fall; their descent would have been precipitous, and very fast. Another photo taken from Kruger's helicopter during a final approach to the digging site—a view only he and the rangers he shuttled would have shared—puts the entire drama in a harrowing perspective. The rangers working the slope are barely visible, even against the stark white of the snow, and they are utterly dwarfed by the waterfall and the vertical cliffs just below them. The rock and snow high on the west face bowl, scoured by winds, seem as inhospitable as it is possible to imagine for human activity. To say the face looks dangerous would be missing the point, since the mountain simply looks like a mountain, and nothing more. It is the people on the face that make it look dangerous. Whether it be professional rangers or twenty-year-old boys inching over it, the west face bowl is as it is: a parabolic mirror that fills up with snow and then empties itself out every winter and every spring, year after year after year. It is not the physics or the conditions that make the west face dangerous. It is the presence of people.

Another hazard the rangers faced was falling rock, which kept "zooming down all around us," Jerry DeSanto said. Rangers with silver hard hats climbed gingerly to the top of the slope and hammered pitons into a chunk of exposed rock on either side of the waterfall. Running ropes downhill from both sides, they fixed a large sock at the bottom of the "V." As water poured into the large mouth of the sock, it was then forced through a hose running down the slope to the trenches. By the time the water reached the nozzle at the other end, it was fully pressurized and ready to blast. As with live fire hoses, keeping all that pressure under control was no easy task; a nozzle errantly lifted or flung out of the snow could knock a ranger on his back and send him sliding down the slope.

The next day, with the weather improved, tunneling proceeded slowly, and the search team once again tried jamming the nozzle of the gravity hose into the snow along the rope line. As the water drilled into the snow, searchers looked for signs of the climbing rope; where the rope bent and disappeared into the snow, the trench was dug again until the rope reappeared. After a full day of digging and spraying, the trench had only been extended by 15 feet, with ropes visible along the hose-drilled holes for another ten feet. The trench at this stage was a full ten feet deep, requiring an exhausting amount of shoveling; worse, as the team moved slowly up the slope, the ropes plainly dived deeper and deeper. With two probe poles lashed together, the team figured the next day they would be digging down 18 feet.

On July 2, the weather broke fair, even a bit warm. The team began by splitting up and simultaneously digging the trench, installing a second gravity sock, and cutting a tunnel to the right of the trench, in order to intersect again with the streambed as a way of helping remove the snow. When the tunnel finally broke into the streambed, a full 25 feet below the surface, searchers again saw the red rope that had been attached to Ray Martin. Following it 40 feet up the stream, step by step, toward a conclusion they knew would be another dead boy, they finally discovered Jerry Kanzler's head protruding from the cavern roof. Kanzler had landed facing downhill, his head down in the snow and his arms thrust up and over his head. He had come to rest in midsomersault.

A few minutes later, by crawling further into the cavern, the team found Clare Pogreba suspended ten feet beyond Kanzler. Pogreba, tied to the gold rope that had been attached to James Anderson, had come to rest completely upside down, his arms extended over his head, like he had just completed a dive into the snow, and his lower half bent uphill at the waist. Shortly thereafter, between Pogreba and Kanzler, Mark Levitan's arm was discovered protruding down from the snow into the cavern near Kanzler's boot. Levitan, also tied to the gold rope, looked like he was swimming freestyle downhill.

Two possibilities now existed for the removal of the three bodies. Hoses could be forced through the snow (now about 25 feet deep) into the cavern above the streambed and the bodies could be removed from the snow with water pressure, put in body bags, and slid downstream through the tunnel opening in which Jerry DeSanto had first discovered Martin. In this scenario, the men would be working deep beneath the surface, and in terribly cramped quarters, especially when the time came to put the bodies into the bags. The official report later called the conditions in the trench "extremely unpleasant." Handling corpses in a dark hole 25 feet below the surface gave even the most hardened ranger pause. Beyond the grim prospect of retrieving bodies that after six months in the snow were beginning to decompose in the summer melt, the team also had to worry about the trench caving in on top of them.

The second choice would be to trench down to the bodies from above. This would be much more time-consuming, given the depth of the snow, but it presented far lower risk from collapsing walls. Given the open air and sunlight, it would also be considerably less stressful for the rescuers. The only difficulty lay in figuring out where the bodies were from above: since they had only been seen from beneath the snow, digging down from the surface would be guesswork.

By running lines along the snow about three feet apart in the approximate positions of the bodies, the trenching area was laid out on the surface. While one ranger crawled along the underwater stream, following the line of the climbing rope, rescuers above the surface used the hoses to drill down from the slope. If the drill hole was off to the right or left, the crawling ranger would shout directions from inside the cave. Using the high-pressure hose like a giant probe pole, the team proceeded slowly and laboriously, trenching down along the path of the rope. Several men could now dig at once; with more elbow room, snow removal was also far easier. Excavation began at 12:30 P.M., and after seven hours of shoveling, the team had removed two thirds of the snow, but no more bodies. Exhausted, they decided to quit for the day and head back to their quarters at the Goat Haunt ranger station.

On July 3, Superintendents Briggle and Ross were taken to the trench site to await the removal of the bodies.

At about 11:45, after intensive digging, the search team above the far end of the trench broke through exactly above Clare Pogreba. After forty-five minutes of chipping with shovels, the body was removed. As the team hauled Pogreba's body back to the surface, they noticed a boot protruding from the snow; digging it out, they discovered it was attached to Mark Levitan's foot. By working back toward the entrance to the tunnel, rescuers were able to remove Levitan's body by 2:00 P.M. Jerry Kanzler, still wearing a red sweater and a blue jacket, was found to be under the deepest snow, and was removed an hour later. Even though the bodies had been on the mountain for more than six months, they had only just recently been exposed to air and running water; their encasement in snow had left them well preserved. George Ostrom had a close look at the bodies once they were down, and said there was no doubt that the boys had died from traumatic injuries rather than suffocation. "They were banged off the rocks. These guys were all tangled up together like beads tied to a necklace. It was like they had died an hour ago; they had just begun bleeding from their wounds." Jerry DeSanto, who did most of the work hauling the bodies out of the snow, noted that a couple of the boys were bare-handed;

while it's possible that their gloves had been ripped off during the fall, it is also possible that the day they had been climbing had been warmer than rescuers had figured.

The way the boys had landed—Ray Martin flat against the ground and covered with six feet of snow, the others buried in deeper and deeper snow the further uphill they landed, with Clare Pogreba found beneath a full 25 feet—made sense, now that they had been found. There had been little snow down low, as rangers and the Callis team alike had noticed back in January. But the cumulative amount of snow that had released out of the west face bowl had been enormous. Had the rescue team been able to dig a single three-foot-wide trench long and deep enough to reveal all five climbers, they would have had to remove—in just that one thin line alone—some 4,000 cubic feet of snow.

Nowhere, among all the scattered gear, in any of the boys' clothing, in all the snow, did the rescue team discover a pistol. They did, however, find a watch that had stopped on December 29. Hal Kanzler's birthday.

As workers gathered up their equipment, which after five days of digging was spread all over the slope, Jim Kruger shuttled the bodies down to the meadow at Chief Mountain, where they too were taken to the Browning mortuary. After six months of burial, the boys were finally pronounced dead.

Once all rescue operations had been concluded, the west face of Mount Cleveland was again opened to the public—seven months after the boys were killed. The cost of the rescue was estimated at $25,000 to the Americans and $10,000 to the Canadians. In a report dated July 11, 1970, Frauson wrote that the accident might have been prevented if the boys "had considered the extreme avalanche conditions and turned back from their climb." For the record, Frauson suggested "more mountaineering and avalanche training for people who venture into high places, to be able to *judge* when to turn back or not to venture on a mountain under these conditions."

The American and Canadian rescue teams were honored with an "excellence of service award" given by Rogers C. Morton, U.S. Secretary of the Interior. Individual rangers had their own ways of summing up the experience. For Willie Colony, "Cleveland had more people and was more intense than anything I've been involved with, before or since."

With the boys finally off the mountain, their families and friends began to arrive to take them home. George Ostrom, who had waited for seven years for his younger brother's body to be returned from the Korean War, tried to convince Jean Kanzler, who was then living in Hawaii, not to come home to visit the scene, but to entrust the identification and burial of her son to him. "I knew that bodies were nothing for a mother to see," Ostrom said. "Mamas always want to open up the coffins." Ostrom was determined to make sure Mrs. Kanzler's last impression of her son would not be as troubling as his had been. He took the pine box that she had had made, and, without her present, put a climbing rope in with the body, placed Jerry's favorite "hippie" vest around his shoulders and a peace-symbol necklace around his neck, and closed the coffin. He then put the box in his pickup truck and drove it to the nearby ranger station, where he used glue and three-inch screws to seal the coffin shut. "I told Jean that his body had been badly battered and that he had died instantly, and she understood," Ostrom said. "In my belief this was the right thing to do."

He then drove the body to a cemetery in Kalispell, and unloaded it near the grave site. A small crowd had gathered, and Jean Kanzler delivered the eulogy in the form of a poem just as the sun was setting.

> I watched Jer grow up, go up
> To the joys of mountains, high nights.
> There to juxtapose himself,
> Frailty amidst their might.
> Having shown, I bade him stay
> He had learned, as was his right.
> I gave him to the jagged sky
> Since I could never scale those heights.

Several years later, Ostrom would dedicate an entire section of his newspaper to his friend Hal Kanzler and his family. Under a photograph of Jerry, age ten, asleep, openmouthed, atop Mount Jackson, Ostrom wrote: "Three years after Hal's death, his youngest son, Jerry, was buried by a December avalanche on Mt. Cleveland. After the snow melted in July, I placed Jer in a plain pine coffin on a sunlit meadow, and brought him back to Kalispell. I felt he had died almost like his father . . . reaching for the stars." Thirty years later, Ostrom's voice still trails off when remembering the final days of the Mount Cleveland disaster, and the memory of Jean Kanzler particularly. "I had a hell of a time to keep from crying. The courage of that woman was unbelievable."

For the next twenty years, Jean Kanzler would visit her son's grave and leave him a bouquet of lilacs. Jerry had always loved Rod McKuen, she said, and used to sing one of his songs to her. "If I die before you, cover my grave with lilacs and smell up the old world for me."

In Butte, Ray Martin's funeral was held in the drawing room of Sayatovic White's Funeral Home, the memorial service conducted by Bishop Baldur Schindler. He was buried in the Mountain View Cemetery, as was Clare Pogreba. The Martins were devastated by the loss. "The Mount Cleveland tragedy really took its toll on us. It was really almost more than any of us could handle," Ruby Martin would recall. "I don't think anything hits you harder than having one of your kids die. I guess you have to have faith that it was meant to be. It's hard to believe that these things happen in life."

A memorial service for Clare Pogreba was conducted by the Reverend Thomas Smatla at the First Presbyterian Church. Pogreba's family asked that memorials be sent to the church or the Montana Tech climbing club.

James Anderson's body was cremated, and a memorial mass celebrated by Father D. A. Okorn was held at St. Catherine's Catholic Church in Big Fork. "That experience bonded us pretty good up there," said Don Anderson, a soft-spoken man who was sixteen at the time of his brother's death. "Our dad was in his mellow years, and it was real emotional for him. This was also tough on me. Jim and I were very, very close. I looked to him an awful lot. You can't imagine someone with so much vitality and enthusiasm and such a good mind just not being there." Thirty years after the accident, Don still has Jim's climbing gear. After the cremation, Bud flew his plane back over the same mountain where he had looked fruitlessly for his brother six months before, and sprinkled the ashes over Mount Cleveland.

Morton Levitan built a plain pine box for his son. Mark was buried in a cemetery in Helena, with both a minister from his mother's Protestant church and his grandfather officiating.

As he spoke with the families, Bob Frauson did his best to mark the epic nature of their grief. "Anyway, they're climbers," Frauson told them. "What better tombstone could you have than Mount Cleveland?"

On July 28, Ruby Martin wrote to William Briggle, asking for names of men involved in the recovery, so she could thank them personally. "There aren't words enough to express to you and all the others how very much we appreciate the great kindness and consideration shown to all of us this last 6 months at the loss of our loved ones on Mt. Cleveland," she wrote. "Thank God for men like you and Bob Frauson and all the others who gave of your time and energy and even took a chance on your own lives to help others. You will never know how much it has all meant to us."

Back at park headquarters, Superintendent Briggle felt obliged to address the concerns of climbers worried about the way the tragedy would effect their own plans. "It's their park and their mountain, waiting there to be climbed, to challenge that inner urge some have to climb a mountain because it is there. If they insist, there's nothing we can do about it. They have the right to make the attempt. But we'll try to guide them in making their decisions. And we'll tell them the story of five young men and 188 days. But there's not much else you can do if they're determined to make the climb. Mount Cleveland can speak louder than we can. It's still there, alive, big against the sky."

Soon after the bodies had been laid to rest, Jim Anderson's father built a stone monument to the five boys near the shore of Flathead Lake's Yellow Bay State Park, next to a small footbridge he also built over a creek pouring into the lake. The plaque reads: IN MEMORY OF JAMES ANDERSON, CLARE POGREBA, MARK LEVITAN, RAY MARTIN, JERRY KANZLER. THESE MEN DIED WHILE SCALING MOUNT CLEVELAND, GLACIER NATIONAL PARK, DEC. 29, 1969.

Beneath this statement is a passage from the Bhagavad Gita:

NEVER THE SPIRIT WAS BORN:
THE SPIRIT SHALL CEASE TO BE NEVER:
NEVER WAS TIME WHEN IT WAS NOT; END
AND BEGINNINGS ARE DREAMS!
BIRTHLESS AND DEATHLESS AND CHANGELESS REMAINETH
THE SPIRIT FOR EVER. DEATH HATH NOT TOUCHED IT AT
ALL. DEAD THOUGH THE HOUSE OF IT SEEMS!

Epilogue

❄

The North Face, 1976

In memories we were rich.
We had pierced the veneer of outside things . . .
We had seen God in His splendours, heard
the text that Nature renders. We had reached
the naked soul of man.

— Sir Ernest Shackleton, *South*

Thirty years later, the Mount Cleveland disaster remains among the deadliest avalanches in American mountaineering history. Involving virtually the entire climbing community in Montana and some of the period's best winter rescue personnel in both the United States and Canada, the tragedy left an indelible mark on an entire generation of outdoorsmen. Equally ominous, however, has been the event's benchmark place in the ever-expanding tradition of winter adventure sports, an expansion that seems to pick up speed with the passing of every season. In 1975, five people died on Forsyth Glacier on the north slope of Oregon's Mount St. Helens. Six years later, in what avalanche historians called "a moment of extraordinary bad timing," 11 out of 22 people climbing near Mount Rainier's Ingraham Glacier were crushed by a huge chunk of ice that had broken free above their heads—still the deadliest American mountaineering avalanche.

The last five years have seen more people die in American avalanches than any five-year period since record keeping began in 1950. Since midcentury, there have been nearly 400 documented fatal avalanche accidents, claiming almost 600 lives. Of those who died, 80 percent were sports enthusiasts; climbers, backcountry skiers, out-of-bounds downhill skiers, and snowmobilers head the list. Europe has also seen its share of tragedy. In France, in 1998, nine French schoolchildren and their teacher were killed by a slide as they hiked in the Alps. Their professional guide, who took the group into the mountains despite highly dangerous avalanche conditions, was arrested, police said, mostly to protect him from the fury of the children's friends and families.

In the winter of 1998–99 the most dangerous places seemed to be not high on the alpine slopes but inside chalets in resort towns, which have been steadily creeping their way higher and higher into known avalanche zones. In the space of just two weeks, more than four dozen people were killed in avalanches in the French, Swiss, and Austrian Alps that destroyed chalets built in high-risk areas. Military helicopters airlifted thousands of tourists out of snowed-in resorts and dropped tons of food for thousands more. The resort town of Davos, Switzerland, home of the Federal Institute for Avalanche Research and host just days before to some of the planet's most powerful people at the World Economic Forum, was inaccessible by road or rail; undeterred by the deadly slides, *The New York Times* reported, ski resorts boasted of "fantastic ski conditions and most are clearly expecting a new infusion of guests as soon as the roads reopen." A headline in a British newspaper called the Alps a DANGEROUS PLAYGROUND; another reported that despite the deaths, HOLIDAY FIRMS TELL THOUSANDS IT'S SAFE TO SKI IN THE ALPS. One skier, waiting for snow reports before leaving for Kitzbuhel, said the avalanche deaths had left him undeterred; he had paid for his ski vacation, and he was going to go, avalanches or no. "At the end of the day, you have to go for it, otherwise you lose the cash."

Although the American West has yet to experience the kind of residential disasters that have struck the more populated slopes of Europe for centuries, many experts think it is just a matter of time. Ski areas have become the golf resorts for the winter set, full of exclusive condominium communities, high-end restaurants, and overpriced boutiques. Even as high-speed chairlifts have made the mountains accessible to a large number of people, they have also eliminated much of the rigor once associated with mountain travel. Ask an out-of-shape tourist why he prefers downhill skiing to cross-country skiing, and likely as not he will answer that cross-country skiing requires too much work, or is not sufficiently exciting, or social. As with golf, which some claim to be a great way to get "outdoors," downhill skiing by its very nature also requires the absolute control of the natural environment. Slopes must be denuded of trees and smoothed over by bulldozers. They are sprayed with pesticides to prevent them from becoming overgrown with unwanted trees and shrubs. If there is not enough snow, they must be covered with man-made snow. There are currently some 1,200 snow-making systems in use worldwide; every major ski resort in the United States has one. In 1991, 73 percent of eastern ski slopes and 26 percent of western slopes were covered in synthetic snow. Because man-made snow is two to five times as wet and dense as natural snow, resorts must draw enormous quantities of water from the local watersheds to cover their slopes. At 150,000 gallons of water for every foot-deep acre of snow, the impact on local water systems is profound. A study conducted in New Mexico estimated that the removal of such vast quantities of water had cut in half the number of organisms able to live in the Rio Hondo, from which water sprayed on the slopes of the Taos resort is taken. Downstream agriculture, dependent on the water for irrigation, was also threatened.

If there is too much snow, ski slopes must be groomed, or, more dramatically, blown up. Look out at a slope on a western American mountain in the early morning and you will see and hear things that will make you wonder about the nature—in both senses of the word—of downhill skiing. There, crawling through the early morning darkness, will be dozens of Sno-Cats, looking like giant cuttlefish scuttling across the silent slopes, their flood lamps illuminating the snow in eerie light as they make the runs safe for intermediate skiers. In the distance, you will hear the bombs exploding, as ski patrollers toss hand charges off ridgelines to take out overhanging cornices, or launch artillery shells from howitzers mounted to metal stands alongside the upper slopes. This is, of course, nothing new; as early as 1956, Monty Atwater reports, artillery shells and bombs fired from avalaunchers were exploding all over the western United States. Since then, days on which patrollers drop bombs have been called "control" days. There is something troubling in this, as there must be any time bombs are dropped; ask a Native American what he thinks about using explosives to carve a giant Crazy Horse out of the mountains of South Dakota and you will see the point. What does it mean to require a full-scale bombing so skiers can experience the outdoors? Controlling nature in order to enjoy it seems counterintuitive at best.

Although the number of skier visits are beginning to level off throughout the country (Colorado's Steamboat Springs still had 1.1 million visits in

1997), many ski resorts are still expanding rapidly, turning themselves into expensive time-share real estate and attracting business conventions as well as tourists. The American Skiing Company, which owns and operates resorts in New England and the Rockies, has poured $18 million into an expansion of its Utah development called The Canyons, in preparation for the 2002 Olympics. The area has 1,300 acres of "skiable terrain," complete with hotels and condominiums to support it. Colorado's Breckenridge recently unveiled plans to build 853 ski-in, ski-out condominiums; a few peaks to the east, Keystone Resort plans to build another 1,700 single-family homes and condominiums over the next five years. Copper Mountain recently sold $53 million worth of real estate in seven hours. As elsewhere in the Rockies, all of this construction, all these new roads and homes, means, eventually, more avalanche trouble. No matter the money poured into bombing slopes or building snow fences, avalanches will continue to build up and release, as they always have, and anything built downhill is sure to pay the price. "We don't have the narrow, heavily inhabited valleys of the Alps," Knox Williams told *The New York Times* last year, "but if there is enough of this condo-mania, enough of this expansion of home sites, we will start to see this problem in this country."

In and above mountain villages, deforestation—especially the clear-cutting that developers use to create downhill ski slopes—remains one of the most predictable antecedents for major avalanche disasters. A healthy forest prevents avalanches by anchoring the snow cover and preventing snow from drifting into massive piles. For the last five hundred years, Europeans have been cutting down forests in the Alps and other mountain regions to make way for settlements, highways, and resorts, thus removing one of the most effective deterrents to massive snowslides. The United States appears to be following suit. With only recently restricted housing development in mountain basins—often in the very places where avalanches empty out—avalanche disasters have increased with the number of people entering the mountains. "It's easy to blame a real estate agent for peddling such murderous ground. But I blame the buyers too," Monty Atwater wrote in 1968, at a fairly early stage of the American mountain-building boom. "If you come to the mountains you should know something about the perils as well as the joys."

In 1982, in what is still considered the worst avalanche ever at an American ski resort, a slab of snow ten feet deep and 3,000 feet wide broke loose above the Alpine Meadows area near Lake Tahoe and came tearing down the mountain at 80 miles per hour. Within seconds, the wall of snow had grown to 30 feet high, and began smashing into ski lifts, buildings, and people. In something under fifteen seconds, a mountain of snow estimated at 65,000 tons had killed seven people and caused some $2 million in property damage. Although the ski resort was not held liable for the deaths, an appeal and two additional negligence suits were settled out of court. The slope on which the avalanche released had been fired upon with a 75-mm howitzer and a recoilless rifle without giving way; six hours after the shooting stopped, it finally came down, apparently in its own good time. This case and others like it— pointing to the lengths to which people will go to live and play in avalanche zones—have forced mountain enthusiasts to reconsider everything from zoning regulations and natural disaster liability law to building design. Like stubborn hill-dwelling home owners in southern California, who build swimming pools uphill of their houses to protect against regular, predictable mud slides, these strategies are both ingenious and somehow crazy; why not take a cue from prevailing forces and live beyond the reach of danger?

Transportation corridors have long presented serious avalanche hazards, as the Wellington train disaster amply demonstrated. Today, it is the state and federal highway system that attracts the most attention, and the most avalanche prevention funding. Nearly 450 inches of snow fall each winter on Snoqualmie Pass, in the Cascade Mountains outside Seattle, but this doesn't stop 12,400 cars and trucks—more than a million during holiday weekends— from traveling over the pass every day. In 1971, a motorist was trapped in a snowshed by a slide on the pass. Soon after a tow truck pulled him out alive a short time later, the motorist and his car were buried under ten feet of snow by a second slide. After an hour of digging by the highway crew, the man was found dead. A year later, at the same spot, three schoolteachers were buried in a slide that smashed their front and rear windshields but somehow left them room to breathe. Ninety minutes later, the driver saw a rescuer's probe pole poking through the snow, and grabbed it. All three survived.

With mountain passes serving as the only arteries to growing alpine communities, contemporary avalanche rangers have been given an unmistakable mandate to keep roads safe and clear. They bomb the slopes with 25-pound packages of ammonium nitrate, tied together like two loaves of bread and hooked to a wire hanging from a tree; or they use compressed-air avalaunchers or 105-mm recoilless rifles to fire explosives across unstable slopes. Most often this goes well; there hasn't been a driver killed in an avalanche in Colorado since 1963. Sometimes it goes less well. Utah highway officials consider the winter of 1998 one of the worst avalanche seasons in years because of a weak snowfall at the beginning of the season, followed by heavy storms that deposited snow too heavy for the lower layers to support. In an effort to ward off a potentially disastrous spontaneous avalanche in Provo Canyon, about two miles west of the Sundance Resort turnoff—in full swing during the Sundance Film Festival—road crews dropped explosives from helicopters onto the snowy slopes. They got more than they bargained for. The first bomb caused 15 feet of powder to cascade onto a 400-foot stretch of U.S. Highway 189. The snow and debris released in Provo Canyon from the first of 75 blasts generated winds estimated at 80 miles per hour as the mass roared down onto the road. One transportation official reported breathlessly that a guardrail had been "pushed like a ribbon in front of the snow." No one was trapped in the slide because officials had closed the road about ten minutes before the snow let loose.

Once an avalanche has started, there is little that men have made that will withstand a direct hit, so the engineering objective has been to direct the snow around, or above, human activity. Snowsheds are ubiquitous along the mountain roads of the western United States; appearing like concrete tunnels over the highway, they are built to allow avalanches to flow over moving traffic. Some villages in Europe have traditionally left a wedge of trees—pointing uphill—above their homes, in an effort to deflect the course of avalanches. Other towns have built equivalent "splitting wedges" out of masonry. A church in Oberwald in the Valais has a wedge twenty-five feet high and five feet thick; another in Villa, Tessin, has a wedge the full height of its steeple; a third, protecting the village of Pequerel, west of Turin, has branches six feet thick, sixteen feet high, and one hundred yards long. Absent trees, engineers have built steel cable "nets" and aluminum or steel "bridges" and "rakes" uphill of towns and train tracks; rather than stopping an avalanche already in progress, these rather fragile structures are built to try to hold the snow in place. Switzerland alone has installed some 250 miles of steel and stone fences for this purpose, but winds up to 150 miles per hour along high passes have sent snow flying over, and in some cases right through, these barriers. At a recent International Snow Science Workshop, a researcher from Iceland reported that his country spent $100 million on avalanche defense structures—to protect $340 million worth of property. In Iceland in January 1995, a snow-and-ice slide fell upon the middle of the northwestern town of Sudavik, killing 14 people, most of them children. The avalanche hit the town with a force so great that houses broke into small pieces, trapping 30 people. Six were rescued immediately and four more were later also found alive. Following the disaster, the entire village was placed within an official avalanche danger zone, and construction began on a new village center farther down the coastline. A news report put the tragedy in context: "Casualties and fatalities would seem small in contrast to disasters like earthquakes and hurricanes in the U.S. or Japan. However, in a country with a population as small as Iceland's, it's catastrophic. It is almost certain that most of the citizens of Iceland have friends or relatives there that are affected by this tragedy." Between 20,000 and 30,000 people took part in a torchlight procession through the center of Reykjavik to commemorate the victims. Ten months later, in the Icelandic town of Flateyri, another avalanche, this one carrying some 250,000 tons of snow, killed 20 more people. Flateyri had relied on computer-generated maps of known avalanche slopes to help predict dangerous slides, but this one came down a path that had never before been run. Rather than move the town, residents decided to turn 20 million cubic feet of earth into a 60-foot-high deflecting wall—large enough to deter an avalanche twice the size of the one that had caused so much destruction—and continued living there.

Beyond its prominent place in the history of fatal avalanches, the Mount Cleveland tragedy can also be seen as a kind of watershed moment for American mountaineering, between a period when most climbing was done by relatively few, highly skilled outdoorsmen, and the current period, in which many more people with inadequate training are heading into the hills. It is still true that the vast majority of visitors to our national parks never leave their cars; walk ninety minutes into the Great Smoky Mountains or Yellowstone or Glacier and you will be amazed how few people will join you. Yet with both skiing and climbing coming of age in the 1960s and 1970s and blossoming into the hugely popular sports they are today, entire industries—fashion, outdoor gear, even carmakers pushing their ubiquitous "sport utility vehicles"—are convincing people to move beyond the safety of summer hikes or groomed mountain ski slopes and get into "the wilderness." Many contemporary "outdoorsmen" may live fifty weeks a year without knowing what stage the moon is in. Upmarket outdoor magazines tempt image-conscious city dwellers with photographs of outrageous—and outrageously expensive—adventures in dangerous terrain. A recent piece in *Outside* magazine, promoting "100 Ideas Toward a Larger Life," showed a photograph of a skier navigating "a nasty elevator shaft, funnel-shaped with a 48-degree pitch." The caption urges the reader to forget about the safety of groomed trails and head off into the uncharted ravines of the backcountry: "Inflate Your Ego. Bomb the Couloir Extreme."

The glut of money that has accompanied the bull market of the last ten years has also contributed to making mountains and wilderness a fashionable place to be. The new ski and golf resort called the Yellowstone Club, outside Bozeman, Montana, requires a $250,000 membership fee, $16,000 annual dues, and up to $5 million for a piece of land. The median household income of people visiting the Colorado Rockies has climbed 57 percent in the last five years to $87,200; the number of those earning more than $200,000 has tripled, and now accounts for close to one fifth of all skiers. If socialites with little mountaineering experience can pay an outfitter $65,000 for the chance to climb Mount Everest, those with equivalent means but less ambition can still buy themselves the latest gear and pay a helicopter pilot to drop them on a gorgeous slope in the Canadian Bugaboos. Heliskiing is currently the height of fashion for wealthy skiers; although most are given some cursory avalanche training before they go out, the fact that they are in utterly remote winter backcountry in the first place raises uncomfortable questions. What does the threat of an avalanche mean to someone who starts their trip from the *top* of a mountain? And who wouldn't think they were invulnerable if, with a few thousand dollars, they can be effortlessly deposited on the top of otherwise unapproachable peaks? Some, of course, find out the hard way. In 1991, an avalanche broke above a party of 12 heliskiers and their guide and carried them down a 2,000-foot slope. Nine of them died.

New technology, from cold weather sleeping bags to Gore-Tex clothing to computerized search devices for avalanche victims, has allowed climbers, backcountry skiers, and snowmobilers alike to greatly expand their reach; a recent *National Geographic* showed photographs of the "camp" of three climbers—including the legendary American Alex Lowe—midway up the blank wall of Baffin Island's Great Sail Peak. Their three nylon bivouacs, dangling on the wall by ropes clipped to bolts drilled into the rock face, look like the work of tent caterpillars. If anyone had stepped out in the middle of the night for a cup of water, the first step would have been 1,000 feet down. Technological advances have given wilderness enthusiasts unprecedented access to formerly unreachable terrain, and allowed them to put miles, days, and thousands of vertical feet between themselves and rescue help. Better equipment, in other words, has allowed people to get to places their lack of training, experience, or skill would not previously have allowed. Where eager, inexperienced hikers might once have shuddered at the thought of venturing into the winter wilds of Glacier or Yellowstone or Yosemite, now their equipment, if not their wisdom, allows them to do so. (A bumper sticker in Jackson, Wyoming, offers this wry comment on late-twentieth-century mountaineering: WE STILL REMEMBER WHEN SEX WAS SAFE AND CLIMBING WAS DANGEROUS.) Unlike their predecessors of even ten years ago, snowmobiles can now operate beautifully in deep powder, allowing riders to "high-point" up steeper and steeper slopes. Just last winter, six snowmobilers high-pointing near Turnagain Pass in Alaska's Chugach National Forest were buried by an avalanche that reached an estimated 150 miles per hour.

To be sure, some of this technology has saved lives. Avalanche experts recommend, and sometimes require, that backcountry skiers and climbers carry electronic transceivers—handheld direction finders worn around the neck like futuristic compasses—to help searchers locate them in the snow should they become buried. Transceivers have become the most relied-upon advance in backcountry safety, and have managed to instill a rather naive sense of confidence in those who use them. But transceivers don't always help. Climbers forget to turn them on. Batteries die. Skiers panic, and forget how to use them in the moment of crisis. It's not as simple as turning on a beacon and following its signal to the victim; searchers have to track in a complicated grid pattern, walking in a series of tightening right angle turns near the debris site until they are standing directly above the point of burial. And since transceivers can either send or receive electronic signals, but not both, they must be switched to the proper configuration or they won't work; if someone is buried with their transceiver accidentally still switched to "receive," no signal will be sent to the search party. And for transceivers to work, they must be worn by every member of a team; there have been cases where the only person killed in an avalanche was the one not wearing a transceiver. Of course, having a transceiver and knowing how to use it is only part of the answer; people have died because their companions, having located the buried bodies, have stood in helpless despair because they left their shovels at home. Technology has widened the gap between what a climber needs to know and what a mountain has to offer. In the field, relying on technology not only gives inexperienced skiers and backpackers a false sense of security, since even the latest technology can fail, it further separates the person in the wilderness from the wilderness itself. Using a transceiver rather than training (or informed respect) as avalanche precaution is like using a digital watch to see what time it is; not only can't the LED crystals teach you how to tell time, they remove you one step further from looking at the sun.

———

Jerry DeSanto, now in his seventies, still roams the Glacier back-country and knows the northern Rockies as intimately as any man alive. He has also accumulated enough wilderness experience for an entire crew of rangers. A few years ago, DeSanto received a call from his brother, who in his late sixties had decided he wanted to climb the highest peaks in all 50 states. He had already made his way up California's Mount Whitney, Nevada's Boundary Peak, Idaho's Borah Peak, and Texas's Guadeloupe—all comparatively gentle mountains—but when he came to Montana, he asked Jerry along for the trip. Part of the Beartooth Range just north of the Wyoming border, Granite Peak, at 12,799 feet, is nearly a third higher than Mount Cleveland and a challenging climb, particularly for someone in their seventh decade. "We got there, four of us, and my brother was getting pretty steamed up, thought he was a big-time mountaineer," DeSanto says. When the group came to a large snowfield, DeSanto's brother blanched at the prospect of confronting the mysteries of hidden crevasses and lurking avalanches, and turned around. Jerry decided to finish the ascent with one of the others on the climb, but felt grateful, when he got back down, still to have a brother.

Robert Madsen, who decided not to join the five boys on the Mount Cleveland expedition, is another man lucky to still have a brother. Over the years, Madsen has become an accomplished technical climber: he made first winter ascents on Mount McDonald and Mount Harding in Montana's Mission Mountains, and has made challenging climbs in the Tetons, including Mount Moran, Mount Owen, and the north face of the Grand Teton. For his bachelor party in 1997, at the age of fifty, he climbed the "nose" of Yosemite's El Capitan. But while conducting a climb on Symmetry Spire in the Tetons in the 1970s, Madsen saw his brother Eric free-fall 70 feet and land flat on his back on a rock. The fall crushed Eric's helmet and "split his legs open like tomatoes." In a brilliant stroke of inventive first aid, Madsen cut strips from a roll of tape to make more than a hundred makeshift butterfly bandages to stanch the river of blood flowing out of his brother's legs. Robert was able to help him off the mountain and onto a Jenny Lake tourist boat heading toward town. When the group of sightseers laid eyes on Eric, they "practically threw up." Miraculously, Eric had broken no bones; the fall so caught the attention of the media that Johnny Carson joked about it on *The Tonight Show.*

In 1985, while about to climb a wall in Washington State called Private Idaho, Madsen watched as another man fell 50 feet to his death just two feet from where he stood. "His head hit a tree stump and he was dead, dead, dead.

When I blew into his mouth we had to keep our hands over his ears to keep the air in his head. I was covered in blood clear up to my armpits, but after I got cleaned up, I was there climbing again the next day."

Virtually every serious mountaineer, that is, anyone who has spent considerable time either on vertical rock faces or climbing at high altitude or in winter weather, has had close contact with serious injury and death. Indeed, in addition to the foolish who ski out of bounds in spite of warning signs, and the reckless who climb mountains beyond their skill level, the greatest number of people who die in avalanches are experienced, skilled climbers. Only the highly competent, after all, can successfully navigate the winter high country long enough to get beyond the reach of reasonably quick rescue help, and this very competency often leads to tragedy. On April 12, 1964, a group of Olympic skiers were making a film at St. Moritz when an avalanche buried the American Bud Werner and the German Barbi Henniberger. Anatoli Boukreev, a Russian climber who had managed to survive the May 1996 tragedy that killed 12 climbers on Mount Everest, died two years later on the 26,700-foot Annapurna, when a falling cornice triggered an avalanche that also killed a photographer. An Italian climber named Simone Moro was carried 800 feet down the slope but somehow managed to stay atop the slide, and survived.

In October 1999, Alex Lowe, whose exploits on Baffin Island had been chronicled in *National Geographic,* was killed by an avalanche during an attempt on Shishapangma, a Himalayan peak that at 26,291 feet is the fourteenth highest in the world. When the avalanche hit Lowe and David Bridges, a cameraman who was also killed, it was reportedly moving at 100 miles per hour. The list goes on and on.

In an odd way, the deaths of accomplished climbers, and the deaths of those pretending to be accomplished, have become an emblem of the sport, the price to pay. Ask a climber about danger and he will give you a tart answer about the beauty of risk, about the need, in this time of office work and litigation and clean, safely lit suburbs, for situations that force people to rely on their innate, physical capacities, those that snap a person to wakefulness. They will tell you that mountains are places where they can test themselves, push themselves, even scare themselves, and that this is good for the soul. All of this is true. It is especially true, of course, for those with enough money to get themselves from these selfsame suburbs into the mountains in the first place. One does not read about people in the inner city or slaving away in industrial jobs looking to add more risk to their lives. But then these are not the people driving the machine of outdoor gear, ski resorts, and adventure travel. In this, death in the outdoors can be seen as another symptom of our time, a time in which a significant number of Americans are both flush with cash and wondering why their professional struggles have left them spiritually bereft. Risk, in any real sense of the word, has been squeezed out of their lives. They have all the food and shelter they could possibly want, and then some; the greatest threat to life has become a speeding automobile, a stressful corporate job, or a diet consisting of too much butter. How, then, to live a "larger life"? The answer for many seems proportional to their degree of disaffection. The rise of "extreme" sports—climbing 3,000-foot walls, buying a place on a Himalayan expedition, skiing "the couloir extreme"—can be read as a reflection of distress staring Americans back in the face. It's as if people, sheltered from danger for too long, try to take on a lifetime's worth of trouble in a single journey.

If a certain amount of risk is inherent in any backcountry travel, the breathless daring of contemporary skiers and climbers—moving precariously like Icarus toward the sun—gives pause to veteran climbers and old-school park rangers alike. Pat Callis, who by any measure has long been one of the country's premier climbers, has in recent years considered—even in his sixties—a major climb up Yosemite's El Capitan. But the thought of meeting one of the new breed of climbers, some of whom jump *off* the top of a cliff tied only to a bungee cord or a length of climbing rope, leaves him chilled. "I don't know if I can stand having the base jumpers falling past me during the bivouacs, making snide remarks to the climbers before their chutes open," he says. Recently, he reports with incredulity, some people *skied* the north face of Canada's Mount Robson, a climb that in the mid-1960s marked Callis and his partner Dan Davis as two of the finest mountaineers on the continent.

When he began at Colorado's Longs Peak in the 1960s, Willie Colony would see about a thousand visitors a year, and would try to talk to each one about their climbing plans and the risks involved. "If it sounded like they were biting off more than they could chew, we'd try to talk them out of it," Colony says. "Now there are a thousand visitors a day, and there's no way to talk to all of them. A lot of people are slipping through that shouldn't be getting up there. A lot of people are doing it on guts rather than on training. I find it difficult to relate to these so-called edge climbers. I've always been conservative, and I can't understand these people getting up there and hanging by their fingernails."

Bob Frauson, despite his two hip replacements and seventy-six years, still skis regularly and can ride his mountain bike for 17 miles near his home in Columbia Falls. He no longer climbs the way he once did, but he maintains close contact with other 10th Mountain Division veterans, and uses the refined silversmithing skills he picked up after the war to make pins with the division's trademark, crossed skis circled by a climbing rope. To him, the climbing craze has gotten out of hand, and reminds him of a time when mountaineers in another country were also pursuing their craft for unnerving reasons. "It's almost like it was during the Hitler Youth movement—kids out there 'climbing for the Fuhrer,' " he says.

Frauson and Colony know all too well the dangers that wilderness search and rescue missions have on those called in to provide assistance. Bob Schellinger, the highly decorated helicopter pilot who worked on the Mount Cleveland rescue and countless others afterward, attempted in 1981 to haul a couple of surveyors off a steep slope in Montana's Cabinet Mountains. Hovering down low while the men tried to get themselves and their gear aboard, his chopper was suddenly knocked off balance; its rear rotor struck a rock and spun wildly out of control. Rather than drive the bubble into the hillside and risk killing the surveyors, Schellinger somehow managed to roll the helicopter away and down a 200-foot ravine, where it burst into flames, killing him. By the time he died, Schellinger had logged some 12,000 hours as a pilot, many of them performing some of the most daring rescues his profession has seen.

Peter Lev has witnessed more than his share of death in the mountains as well. A tall, graceful man now in his sixties, Lev for more than two decades has been part owner of the Glenn Exum climbing school in Jackson, Wyoming. Just seven years after the Mount Cleveland tragedy, Lev joined Willi Unsoeld—one of the first Americans atop Everest—and several other world-class climbers on an expedition on the 25,645-foot Himalayan peak Nanda Devi. Unsoeld considered the mountain so beautiful that he had named his daughter for it, and, on this trip, had brought her along. During the expedition, now legendary in climbing circles, Nanda Devi died at 24,000 feet of an abdominal illness, exacerbated by the altitude, on the very mountain for which she had been named. "We agreed that it would be most fitting for Devi's body to be committed to the snows of the mountain for which she had come to feel such a deep attachment," Unsoeld, the theology professor, would write. "Andy, Peter and I knelt in a circle in the snow and grasped hands while each chanted a broken farewell to the comrade who had so recently filled such a vivid place in our lives. My final prayer was one of thanksgiving for a world filled with the sublimity of high places, for the sheer beauty of the mountains and for the surpassing miracle that we should be so formed as to respond with ecstasy to such beauty, and for the constant element of danger without which the mountain experience would not exercise such a grip on our sensibilities." Two years after this, Unsoeld himself was climbing with a group of students on Washington's Mount Rainier. The trip was to be Unsoeld's last on the mountain, since his chronic arthritis had made such rigorous climbing untenable. After two days of stormy weather, several of the students were in danger of hypothermia and frostbite. Unsoeld decided to try descending a risky chute called Cadaver Gap, and got caught in an avalanche. Unsoeld and a twenty-one-year-old student named Janie Diepenbrock were buried for a mere fifteen minutes. Both died nonetheless.

Despite being directly involved in both the Mount Cleveland and Nanda Devi tragedies, and losing more than a few intimate friends in the high mountains, Peter Lev maintains the quiet, even dignified detachment that marks many professional climbers. "In adventure climbing, every generation takes off from the generation before, and people have died in all eras," Lev says.

Asked about the heartbreak that seems inherent in making a living in the mountains, Peter Lev answers with a smile, both proud and resigned, that is common among both climbers and rangers.

"Climbing keeps you from dying in other ways."

In the middle of autumn 1976, six years after the events on Mount Cleveland reached their terrible resolution, Terry Kennedy decided to see if Jim Kanzler was ready to try the mountain's still-unclimbed north face. A longtime friend of the Kanzler boys and an accomplished climber with a number of difficult first ascents already to his credit, Kennedy had been haunted by the disaster from the moment he'd heard about it. Six years younger than Jim Kanzler, he had bought his first pair of climbing boots while the boys' bodies were still on the mountain, and on the day they were found, he was climbing Mount Gould with a boy who had grown up across the fence from the Kanzlers. As the search and rescue teams finally brought back the five bodies, Kennedy decided that the only way to conclude the tragedy would be to help write another chapter.

"I knew at fifteen that I was going to climb Mount Cleveland," Kennedy says. "Not a day went by that I didn't think about the north face. Hal Kanzler was this mysterious guy that did things that no one would ever consider doing. He was legendary. Then he killed himself. Lo and behold two and a half years later his son got killed, and for a long time no one knew how. It crushed that community when Hal killed himself and it crushed them again when Jerry was killed."

After Hal's death, many of the slides and photographs he had taken over the years were given to a friend of the family, who happened to be the coach of Kennedy's high school wrestling team. The coach had boxes of slides that Hal had taken of Glacier peaks, and Kennedy spent hours looking them over. One night, Kennedy's parents invited another old friend of Hal Kanzler's over for dinner, and Terry started asking him about the Cleveland boys and their intention to climb the north face. "Yeah, those guys were good climbers. They coulda climbed it," he told Kanzler's friend. "He looked at me and said, 'I'm sorry. There is no such thing as an experienced eighteen-year-old.' That just about killed me."

The question of whether the five boys were foolish or simply unlucky remained with many in the Glacier community for years, and in part depended on the observer's age and point of view. Kennedy clearly had made up his mind. As the years went by, he trained hard in preparation for a climb of the north face of Mount Cleveland. In 1973, when he was nineteen, he climbed the north route of the Grand Teton; the next year he pioneered a new route up the west face of Glacier's Mount St. Nicholas. All the while, he continued to research the Cleveland climb, and continued to try to convince Jim Kanzler to give it a try as well. Jim had always refused. He was often off climbing elsewhere, but even when he was in the area Mount Cleveland still seemed shrouded by too much grief. The last hours Jim had spent on the mountain had been that terrible night on the west face with Peter Lev and Pat Callis, when they were locked down by winter darkness. The following day, Callis found the backpack, and the mystery of the boys' disappearance had essentially been solved.

Not that he had given up climbing. If anything, Kanzler's experience on Mount Cleveland had only redoubled his interest in mountaineering, and, like many others who have seen death in the hills, Kanzler began taking on even greater challenges, even greater risks. For several summers, Jim and Pat Callis had been trying an epic climb in the Canadian Rockies—the Emperor Face of Mount Robson, one of the most dangerous big-wall climbs in North America—and had had some very close calls with bad weather and near precipitous falls. But one way or another, Jim had decided not to tempt the mountain that had killed his brother.

Although the north face had been tried in 1971 by a group of five climbers from Minnesota, the team had traversed off some 800 feet below the summit and climbed the rest of the way up the northwest ridge. By avoiding the massive pyramid at the top, the team had sidestepped the most challenging part of the climb, and thus failed to earn credit for a true first ascent. Five years after this, in August 1976, Kennedy called Barry Frost, a local climber who had been an avalanche lookout during the 1969 search, and the pair "gave it a very nervous go," but, with the weather deteriorating, turned around partway up. Although the face "looked intimidating as hell," Kennedy left a cache of gear at the base, committing himself to another try. A month later, Kennedy recruited another hotshot local climber named Steve Jackson, with whom he had made the climb of Mount St. Nick. He also called Jim Kanzler again, but Kanzler was once more off exploring in Canada. As luck would have it, however, Kanzler returned home at precisely the time Kennedy and Jackson were preparing the assault on Cleveland. Kennedy arrived home one day and found a message waiting for him. "Jim Kanzler called. In Waterton. Face looks good. Will meet you in three days."

Kennedy was ecstatic. "I was so relieved because I figured if we get into trouble at least we have Jim on the sharp end of the rope," he said. "But then I thought, here we go. We were repeating history. Everyone in Glacier Park was on edge. The park rangers were going, 'Oh, shit.' "

For Jim Kanzler, the pull of the north face had finally proved too much. In addition to his desire to honor his brother and his closest friends, Jim had always been haunted by the fate of the revolver his father had used to kill himself. Sometime after the avalanche, Jim had asked Ray Martin's father about the gun, but Arthur Martin said he did not know what had happened to it. Perhaps it was still somewhere on the mountain.

Kennedy, Jackson, and Kanzler repeated the boys' approach to Mount Cleveland almost precisely. They took a boat to Goat Haunt on the next to last day that the commercial service would be in operation, and walked to the base of the mountain the next day. The weather did not look promising: overcast skies had occluded the entire upper half of the mountain, which included by far the toughest section of the climb—the last 800 feet. They had a decision to make: should they start the climb, which they anticipated would take two days, and hope the clouds blew off the upper reaches of the mountain? Or should they abandon the trip, which would mean another year at least before they could give it another try?

Kennedy looked at the others and said, "What would Pat Callis do?" Kanzler said, "Callis would not go up there with conditions like this." The boys collapsed. They cursed the bad weather that plagues northern Montana, and decided there and then that what they needed was a road trip to the deserts of the Southwest, where the sun always shines and the climbing is terrific. As they made their way back to the dock, they heard the tourist boat honk its horn for the last time of the season. If the boys missed the boat, they would have to walk the ten miles back to Waterton. The three friends decided to stay the night.

By the next morning, the weather had broken. The climbers stamped around swearing that they could have climbed the face after all, and now they had eaten most of the food they had planned to eat during the ascent. Just for kicks, they decided to make a call from the ranger station and check in with the local airport to see what the weather forecast held for the next several days, and were told it would be clear and calm. The next morning, at 6:00 A.M., they began the climb.

They climbed all day. A thousand feet higher than the legendary face of Yosemite's El Capitan, the north face offered challenges that the granite walls of the Sierra didn't: a choppy, irregular surface that at several points made seeing above impossible; and slabby sedimentary rock that routinely sent rocks whizzing past the climbers. Coming upon two separate gullies, they had to strap on crampons and make their way over ice. Nevertheless, by early evening they had made it to within about 500 feet of the summit. As night fell, the three friends tied themselves onto a narrow lip of rock, and made camp. When an empty tin of sardines pitched over the side, the team could hear it clank its way down to the apron of scree 3,500 feet below. With the ledge too narrow for them to bed down even two abreast, and too uneven for them to find a level place to lie down flat, the team gathered some loose rock and created makeshift nests and lay their sleeping bags out head-to-toe. To keep themselves from hurtling off into the darkness during the night, they clipped themselves into place with their ropes and carabiners, leaving just enough slack in the rope to lie down. They slept in their wool sweaters and down parkas and put their feet in their empty packs to stay warm. Laying flat on the lip, three quarters of a mile up a rock face, they sang some Bob Dylan songs. Later, cold, thrilled, and terrified, they slept.

At some point during the night, Kanzler and Kennedy were woken by the sound of something heavy jarring loose from the lip, falling into the abyss, and shattering on a ledge below. To their relief, it was not Jackson that had gone over, but a large stone he had kicked loose from under his sleeping platform.

The next day, Jim Kanzler led the final assault. As he neared the top, Kanzler's remarkable climbing skills both impressed and scared his climbing companions. It seemed, close to the top, that he was pushing even his own limits, relying less on hammering pitons into the rock for protection and more on his own intuitive sense of the rock. "It was steeper than an elevator shaft, and loose, and a very long runout from his last piton protection," Kennedy said. "Every time he had to brush a loose rock from a handhold Steve and I had to sit there and listen to it bound 4,000 feet. I was scared shitless. I couldn't decide if I was more scared of going down if Jim couldn't make it, or following up his lead if he did. I just remember him clenching his teeth and grunting, 'God damn it, we're not going back now. This is *it.*' "

After eighteen total hours of climbing, the three friends became the first climbers ever to scale the north face of Cleveland. When they checked the logbook at the top of the mountain, they found an entry written by the Minnesota team, who five years previously had scrambled out before reaching the top. "We tried it and didn't make it. Good luck Kanzler or whoever."

If reaching the top of the north face initially felt "like winning a gold medal in the Olympics," the climbers were otherwise reticent about what they had just accomplished. They decided to make their way down the west face, which was significantly less dangerous than the route they had just climbed. For Jim Kanzler especially, the west face was harrowing in its own right. Approaching the spot where the five boys had been found, the power of the moment became too much for him. Even today, thirty years after the rescue effort, he cannot find the words to talk about the return to his brother's burial spot, relying on Kennedy's memory instead.

"I knew exactly where the avalanche path was, even though I'd never been there," Kennedy remembers. "I kept waiting for Jim to initiate something. I was going to stop and have a ceremony up there, but Jim was ahead of us, and it looked like the moment was gonna get away. I said, 'Let's stop and rest a minute.' Jim stopped 50 feet ahead of me. He walked up to me and said, 'This is where my brother and my friends were killed.' I said, 'Yeah, I know.' We emptied out our water bottles and filled them up with water from the stream and drank a toast to them. Jim said, 'Yep. This is the place. This is the place.' "

At the bottom of the west face, Kanzler, Kennedy, and Jackson came to a spot where the water came tumbling off the mountain. The three climbers stripped naked and took a shower in the waterfall, rinsing themselves in the mountain's runoff.

Although he never did find the missing gun, returning to the spot where his brother died did bring back memories of the night Jim had spent on the west face, looking for bodies, or gear, or anything in the piles of avalanche debris spread out over the slope. "With the knowledge I have now I would have figured it out sooner," he said three decades after the boys died. "That's the trick—seeing things that are not apparent to untrained eyes. Even Dr. Montagne's training couldn't totally impart everything we needed to know about avalanches. It took me throwing explosives as a ski patroller to realize the quickness of the release of slabs. That's the advantage that these guys didn't have. I ask myself, if I had been there with them, would I be dead? I probably would be. Now I know it's stupid to walk up into a slab. It's like walking into the mouth of a dragon."

Over the last thirty years, Jim Kanzler has become one of the top mountain guides at the Glenn Exum climbing school, working for Peter Lev. His considerable physical strength still apparent at the age of fifty, Kanzler now wears his graying brown hair long and carries an unmistakable shadow under his round glasses, evidence of his struggle to navigate a life that would have broken many others. His memories of the Mount Cleveland tragedy are spotty, perhaps mercifully. What he does remember he recounts in a quiet, very controlled voice, which breaks only when he discusses the deaths of his father and brother. He prefers to talk about his role as a mentor to younger climbers; certainly, few other mountaineers have such poignant lessons to impart. As an Exum guide, Kanzler has long considered his work to be an extension of everything his father taught him about wilderness.

"I work a lot with younger kids, seventeen-year-olds who come out here from the urban concrete areas and get to see nature," he says. "To see these kids, I wonder. They're so isolated from nature. Their environment is so alien to the earth. But you watch them on a rock, you see them come alive. It's such a simple thing. You turn kids loose, you see them expand. I get a great deal of gratification from seeing these kids light up. These are the things my father introduced to me. Now I understand what he was saying."

Part of what Hal Kanzler was saying, what Jerry Kanzler was seeking, and what Jim Kanzler is teaching, is the way that mountains have of reflecting our own desires. Mountains are indeed the lair of dragons, capable of inspiring great heroism and great terror. Because they are unconquerable, and impassive, mountains remind us of our vulnerability in ways that civilization cannot; mountains still offer us a good way to die. There is beauty in this, and mystery, something beyond our reach. There is in danger the increasingly rare chance to confront the limits of our own physical powers. There is in the mountains the chance to encounter immanence, the presence of God; they offer the chance to get reacquainted with the nonhuman world, a world uninterested in stories of human achievement. Like primitive people, like mythical people, we enter the mountains knowing the dangers, knowing that true honor can only exist when it is accompanied by great respect. Like other elements that exist and proceed beyond man's control, mountains and avalanches are mirrors in which we can examine our own perceptions of heroism and folly. No matter how we have defined our relationship to mountains, avalanches have always fatally foiled our best efforts to move through, inhabit, or climb them. No matter the technology, no matter the potential profits, no matter the attendant celebrity, avalanches have always found their way down the slope, and have always refused to accommodate the vagaries of human desire. In a way, avalanches have forced us to tell different stories about ourselves, and about the haunting wilderness that surrounds us. Stories not of heroism, but of humility.

Selected Reading

❄

Allen, E. John B. *From Skisport to Skiing: One Hundred Years of an American Sport.* Amherst: University of Massachusetts Press, 1993.

Armstrong, Betsy, and Knox Williams. *The Avalanche Book.* Golden, CO: Fulcrum, Inc., 1986, 1992.

Atwater, Monty. *The Avalanche Hunters.* Philadelphia: MacRae Smith Co., 1968.

Bentley, W. A., and W. J. Humphreys. *Snow Crystals.* New York: Dover Publications, 1962.

Bernbaum, Edwin. *Sacred Mountains of the World.* Berkeley: University of California Press, 1997.

Bolin, Ronald L., trans. "Immanuel Kant's Physical Geography," master's thesis, Department of Geography, Indiana University, 1968.

Bonington, Chris. *Heroic Climbs.* Seattle: The Mountaineers, 1994.

Brower, David. *Manual of Ski Mountaineering.* San Francisco: Sierra Club Books, 1962.

Craighead, Charlie, ed. *Glenn Exum: Never a Bad Word or a Twisted Rope.* Moose, WY: Grand Teton National Historical Association, 1998.

Daffern, Tony. *Avalanche Safety for Skiers and Climbers.* Calgary: Cloudcap Press, 1983.

Dudley, Charles M. *60 Centuries of Skiing.* Brattleboro, VT: Stephen Daye Press, 1935.

Dusenbery, Harris. *Ski the High Trail: World War II Ski Troopers in the High Colorado Rockies.* Portland, OR: Binford and Mort, 1991.

Edwards, J. Gordon. *A Climber's Guide to Glacier National Park.* Helena, MT: Falcon Press, 1995.

El Hult, Ruby. *Northwest Disaster: Avalanche and Fire.* Portland, OR: Binford and Mort, 1960.

Ellis, Robert B. *See Naples and Die: A World War II Memoir.* Jefferson, NC: McFarland & Co., 1996.

Espy, James P. *The Philosophy of Storms.* Boston: Charles Little and James Brown, 1841.

Farabee, Charles R. *Death, Daring, and Disaster: Search and Rescue in the National Parks.* Boulder, CO: Roberts Rinehart, 1998.

Firestone, Clarke B. *The Coasts of Illusion: A Study of Travel Tales.* New York: Harper and Brothers, 1924.

Fraser, Colin. *Avalanches and Snow Safety.* London: John Murray Ltd., 1978.

Fredston, Jill and Doug Fesler. *Snow Sense: A Guide to Evaluating Snow Avalanche Hazard.* Anchorage: Alaska Mountain Safety Center, 1994.

Gray, D. M. and D. H. Male. *Handbook of Snow: Principles, Processes and Use.* Toronto: Pergamon Press, 1981.

Govinda, Lama Anagarika. *The Way of the White Clouds.* Berkeley: Shambhala, 1970.

Green, Randall. *The Rock Climber's Guide to Montana.* Helena, MT: Falcon Publishing Co., 1995.

Harding, Warren. *Downward Bound: A Mad! Guide to Rock Climbing.* Birmingham, AL: Menasha Ridge Press, 1975.

Harper, Frank. *Military Ski Manual.* Harrisburg, PA: The Military Service Publishing Company, 1943.

Jamieson, Bruce. *Avalanche Safety for Snowmobilers.* Calgary: Snowline Technical Services, 1994.

Jerome, John. *On Mountains.* New York: Harcourt Brace Jovanovich, 1978.

Jones, Chris. *Climbing in North America.* Berkeley: University of California Press, 1976.

Krakauer, Jon. *Eiger Dreams.* New York: Anchor Books, 1990.

————. *Into the Wild.* New York: Villard, 1996.

————. *Into Thin Air.* New York: Anchor Books, 1997.

LaChapelle, Dolores. *Deep Powder: 40 Year of Ecstatic Skiing, Avalanches, and Earth Wisdom.* Durango, CO: Kivaki Press, 1993.

LaChapelle, Ed. *The ABC of Avalanche Safety.* Seattle: The Mountaineers, 1985.

Logan, Nick, and Dale Atkins. *The Snowy Torrents: Avalanche Accidents in the United States, 1980–86.* Denver: Colorado Geological Survey, 1996.

Loomis, Elias. *A Treatise on Meteorology.* New York: Harper and Brothers, 1885.

Maclean, Norman. *Young Men and Fire.* Chicago: University of Chicago Press, 1992.

Matthiessen, Peter. *The Snow Leopard.* New York: Penguin Books, 1978.

McCrae, W. C. and Judy Jewell. *Montana Handbook.* Chico, CA: Moon Publications, 1996.

Mergen, Bernard. *Snow in America.* Washington: The Smithsonian Institution, 1997.

Nash, Roderick. *Wilderness and the American Mind.* New Haven: Yale University Press, 1967.

National Research Council. *Snow Avalanches and Mitigation in the United States.* Washington: National Academy Press, 1990.

Nicolson, Marjorie Hope. *Mountain Gloom and Mountain Glory: The Development of the Aesthetic of the Infinite.* Ithaca: Cornell University Press, 1959.

O'Connell, Nicholas, ed. *Beyond Risk: Conversations with Climbers.* Seattle: The Mountaineers, 1993.

Olson, Jack. *Night of the Grizzlies.* Moose, WY: Homestead Press, 1969.

Ostrom, George. *Glacier's Secrets: Beyond the Roads and Above the Clouds.* Helena, MT: American and World Geographic Publishing, 1997.

Peacock, Doug. *Grizzly Years.* New York: Henry Holt, 1990.

Peters, Ed, ed. *Mountaineering: The Freedom of the Hills.* Seattle: The Mountaineers, 1982.

Reuther, David, and John Thorn, eds. *The Armchair Mountaineer.* Birmingham, AL: Menasha Ridge Press, 1989.

Ringholz, Raye C. *On Belay! The Life of Legendary Mountaineer Paul Petzoldt.* Seattle: The Mountaineers, 1997.

Rockwell, David. *Glacier National Park.* Boston: Houghton Mifflin, 1995.

Schneider, Bill. *Hiking Montana.* Helena, MT: Falcon Press, 1994.

Seligman, Gerald. *Snow Structure and Ski Fields.* Brussels: Joseph Adams, 1962.

Setnicka, Tim J. *Wilderness Search and Rescue.* Boston: Appalachian Mountain Club, 1980.

Suzuki, Daisetz T. *Zen and Japanese Culture.* Princeton: Princeton University Press, 1959.

Thurman, Robert, and Tad Wise. *Circling the Sacred Mountain: A Spiritual Adventure Through the Himalayas.* New York: Bantam, 1999.

United States Forest Service. *Avalanche Protection in Switzerland.* Fort Collins, CO: U.S. Department of Agriculture, 1975.

Vitaliano, Dorothy B. *Legends of the Earth.* Bloomington: University of Indiana Press, 1973.

Ward, Geoffrey. *The West: An Illustrated History.* Boston: Little, Brown, 1996.

Waterman, Jonathan, ed. *Cloud Dancers: Portraits of North American Mountaineers.* Golden, CO: American Alpine Club Press, 1993.

Williams, Knox. *The Snowy Torrents: Avalanche Accidents in the United States, 1967–71.* Denver: Colorado Geological Survey, 1975.

Index

❄

About the Author

McKay Jenkins has backpacked, paddled, bicycled, and skied in wilderness all over the world. He has written for *Outside, Outdoor Explorer,* and *Orion,* among many other publications, and is also the author of *The South in Black and White,* a book about race and literature in the 1940s, and the editor of *The Peter Matthiessen Reader.* He has a master's degree in journalism from Columbia and a Ph.D. in English from Princeton. A former staff writer for *The Atlanta Constitution,* he currently teaches literature and nonfiction writing at the University of Delaware. He lives in Philadelphia with his wife and two dogs.

About the Type

This book was set in Times New Roman, designed by Stanley Morrison specifically for *The Times* of London. The typeface was introduced in the newspaper in 1932. Times New Roman has had its greatest success in the United States as a book and commercial typeface rather than one used in newspapers.